UFOs of the
FIRST WORLD WAR

T0346962

UFOs of the FIRST WORLD WAR

Phantom Airships, Balloons, Aircraft and Other Mysterious Aerial Phenomema

NIGEL WATSON

For Granville Oldroyd

First published 2015

The History Press
The Mill, Brimscombe Port
Stroud, Gloucestershire, GL5 2QG
www.thehistorypress.co.uk

© Nigel Watson, 2015

The right of Nigel Watson to be identified as the Author
of this work has been asserted in accordance with the
Copyright, Designs and Patents Act 1988.

All rights reserved. No part of this book may be reprinted
or reproduced or utilised in any form or by any electronic,
mechanical or other means, now known or hereafter invented,
including photocopying and recording, or in any information
storage or retrieval system, without the permission in writing
from the Publishers.

British Library Cataloguing in Publication Data.
A catalogue record for this book is available from the British Library.

ISBN 978 0 7509 5914 8

Typesetting and origination by The History Press
Printed and bound by TJ Books Limited, Padstow, Cornwall.

CONTENTS

ACKNOWLEDGEMENTS

Researchers throughout the world have helped to collect a vast body of information about the phantoms of the sky seen prior to, and during, the First World War. I'd like to thank all of them who have made this book possible.

A vast majority of research into British reports of this period was collected by the late Granville Oldroyd, to whom this work is dedicated.

I would also like to thank David Clarke, whose outstanding work has helped bring the subject out of the shadows of ufology.

Carl Grove and Roger Sandell for their work on researching and appraising British cases.

Thomas Bullard and Robert Bartholomew for their extensive contributions to this topic.

Mr X for information about the Canadian aviation scare.

Brett Holman for information about Australian reports and his collection of information and views on the early airship scares.

Thanks also to the following for their comments about the Angel of Mons visions: Philip Mantle, Nigel Wright, Albert S. Rosales, Robert Moore, Kevin Goodman, Cas Lake, Andrew Hennessey, Paul Bennett, John Rimmer.

And, special mentions to: Peter Rogerson, Chris Aubeck, Kevin McClure, Hilary Evans, Martin Kottmeyer, Mark Pilkington, Robert Rickard, Kay Massingill, Ole Jonny Brænne, Chuck Flood, Gerry Connelly, Ken Gerhard, John Hind, Jerome Clark, Dirk van der Werff,

Dr Joaquim Fernandes, John Harney, Jean Sider, Rudy de Groote, Mack Maloney, Thierry Pinvidic, Bill Chalker, Mervyn Wyn Hopkins, David Rees, Lucius Farish, Andy Roberts, Dwight Whalen, Donald Johnson, Harry Wood, Mike Dash, Rob Waugh, Ulrich Magin, Paul Screeton.

To contact Nigel Watson, please email: nigelwatson1@gmail.com, or via the UFOs of the First World War, Facebook page at: www.facebook.com/UFOScares.

INTRODUCTION

'In the future the nation which will count the most will be the one which has command of the air.'

Sheffield Telegraph, 25 February 1913.

Strange objects in the sky have baffled humanity since the dawn of time. Today they are called flying saucers or unidentified flying objects (UFOs). In the past, unusual lights in the sky were regarded as chariots of fire, angels, will o' the wisps, demonic processions, dragons, witches riding to their Sabbath rituals, dancing fairies, spirits and many other types of threatening supernatural or religious visitations. Most sightings from the 1850s to the 1920s were regarded as 'phantom airships', then there were 'mystery aircraft', followed by 'foo fighters' in the Second World War, and then 'ghost rockets' before we arrived at 'flying saucers' in 1947.

The use of different terminology, and the associated frames of reference, helps determine how these sightings were perceived, reported, interpreted and explained. From the above we can see that initially sightings were of things of a fantastic, supernatural or religious nature, and then with the phantom airship sightings they were seen as being secular, man-made, mechanical constructions.

The frames of reference are conditioned by many different social, political and cultural factors. For example, the phantom airships seen in the USA in 1896–7, and worldwide during the early years of the

French and German airship commanders decide to make a little trip to England in 1907, underlining *England's Worry* about the threat presented by foreign airships in Simplicissimus, the German satirical weekly magazine.

twentieth century, can be compared with the airships described in the fiction of the period. The question is, did the reports inspire the fiction or did the fiction inspire the reports?

As Ron Miller notes in his excellent article 'Jules Verne and the Great Airship Scare', the phantom airship sightings in America during 1896 to 1897:

> … could be either imaginative interpretations of anomalous and amorphous phenomena, simple bandwagoning, or even outright hoaxes. In other words, nothing that we haven't seen taking place in so many modern UFO reports. Those of a century ago are different only in using 19th-century visual references.[1]

Hilary Evans similarly saw that historical encounters and today's alien abduction stories are shaped by our expectations and subconscious:

> What varies is the form and the circumstances. From the distant past, the material survives as myth, with fairies, angels or demons as the agents. SF writers regurgitate it in the form of adventure stories; in the 1920s, they tended to attribute responsibility to 'mad science' seeking to dominate the world. We, if we are subjected to hypnosis or drugs in a lab, regurgitate the material of the form of an imaginary encounter, now with extraterrestrial humanoids playing the leading parts.[2]

Some of the American sightings could have been caused by secret inventors, and in the early twentieth century it was even more likely that they could be triggered by real airships or aeroplanes. In the American case, there was a wholehearted delight in the thought that a secret inventor had perfected a flying machine.

Elsewhere, new aerial contraptions were regarded as a severe threat to national security. The art of aerial navigation became increasingly possible with the use of lighter-than-air dirigibles. Ever since his first flight over Lake Constance on 2 July 1909, Count Zeppelin's name was continually associated with the huge dirigible airship. These craft could travel great distances and carry passengers along with a heavy cargo.

Unfortunately, they proved to be very unwieldy at take-off and landing, when they could easily be destroyed by strong winds or bad handling by the ground crew. They were kept aloft by hydrogen gas, which is highly flammable and this factor helped bring about the demise of the airship in the 1930s. In the lead-up to the First World War, these problems were eclipsed by the prestige and power they gave to Germany.

Aeroplanes, on the other hand, were much smaller and had a limited range. They were more highly favoured by the British Government, although it preferred to let private or foreign pioneers do all the research work on the grounds that it would save money and it was not keen on perfecting new forms of transport that would help upset the balance of power.

The Zeppelin and the ever-growing new aeronautical inventions were potentially powerful new weapons that made every country vulnerable to attack. The prophets of doom worried that these craft could easily spy out the land in advance of naval and ground attacks, and they could rain down bombs to devastate cities and towns. They literally put everyone on the frontline, making civilians as vulnerable as combat troops.

For those who possessed the secret of aerial navigation, the promise of a great technological utopia was just around the corner. For this reason, the Americans showed a great enthusiasm for any type of aeronautical invention during their 1896–7 and 1909–10 'airship scares'. in contrast, if the enemy was seen to possess this invention, fear of the new and the unpredictable horrors it might unleash took the upper hand. In Britain, this was certainly the case and even in the USA, the wonders of technology soured during the First World War, as is evident from the reports of mystery aeroplanes and associated activities of spies and saboteurs.

The press was largely responsible for helping create, sustain and then deflate most of these airship scares. Indeed, the British 1909 phantom airship scare took on such a life of its own that even the hawkish newspaper baron, Lord Northcliffe (who owned the *Daily Express* and *Evening News*), had to put a brake on it to stop the nation looking foolish in the eyes of the world. A fellow scaremonger, Leo Maxse, welcomed this action, because:

People were making pretty considerable asses of themselves over these imaginary airships and they required sitting upon as you have done. The real thing is so serious, it is maddening to have people going off at tangents.[3]

In contrast, the newspapers that wanted to see more expenditure on social reforms and welfare were more cautious and sceptical about these sightings from the very beginning.

Whether you regard UFOs as a manifestation of psychological and sociological factors, or 'real' exotic craft or phenomena, the accounts in this book serve to provide plenty of stimulating food for thought.

References

1. Miller, Ron, 'Jules Verne and the Great Airship Scare', *International UFO Reporter*, Vol. 12, No. 3, May–June 1987.
2. Evans, Hilary, 'Abducted by an Archetype', *Fortean Times*, No. 33, Autumn 1980, pp. 6–10.
3. Quoted in Morris, A.J.A., *The Scaremongers* (London: Routledge & Kegan Paul, 1984), p. 159.

ONE

EARLY AIRSHIP SCARES

Phantom airship, mystery aircraft, flying saucer and UFO sightings generally occur during relatively short periods of time in just one town, county, state or country. These clusters are known as 'flaps'. If many sightings are also reported in other countries at the same time, this phenomenon is known as a 'wave'. These two words are often interchangeable, and there are no hard and fast definitions of them. The words scare, panic, rumour, sensation or mass delusion can be applied to these clusters.

Originally, UFO researchers tended to think in terms of historical UFO flaps or waves, but as more studies have been carried out it seems that you can find plenty of individual sightings scattered throughout the world in any year. In addition, flaps of sightings are still being discovered as newspaper and other archives are being digitised and made easier to access via the World Wide Web.

Although the view that mysterious aerial objects represent man-made craft came to dominate, this did not entirely stop the perception of them as religious or supernatural phenomenon in certain circumstances. Even today ambiguous objects in the sky can be interpreted as angels, phantom (Black Operations) helicopters, or extraterrestrial UFOs. These sightings are usually shaped by the prevailing social/cultural/religious context of the observers, so in wartime they are more likely to be viewed in terms of supernatural saviours or enemy aircraft.

UFOs were not seen out of the blue during the First World War. They were conditioned and shaped in much the same way as the pre-war waves. Waves of sightings that were related to enemy activities began in 1908 and continued in many parts of the world right up to the beginning of the First World War.

USA 1908 sightings

This was an active year for US sightings. On the night of 23 January, a bright light was seen at Kent, Washington, and it returned for several evenings at the beginning of February.

There was speculation in the newspapers, in a tongue-in-cheek fashion, that the red glowing light was a Japanese airship, spying on the land.

Further sightings at Tacoma, of a searchlight beam on 12 February and a swaying light at Mud Bay on 27 February, led to speculation that an airship was in the area. An alternative explanation was that these were lights attached to kites that smugglers were using to signal to each other.

Venus, the stars and other planets were also called in as explanations. At that time there was a good deal of fear about Japanese spies in the area, so it was quite easy for witnesses to interpret anything unusual as due to their activities. Similar fears (of Germans instead of Japanese) helped fuel the later British airship scares.[1]

New England became the focus of airship activity later in the year. On 25 July, at 6.00 p.m., a large airship was sighted at Forestville. As it went westwards, towards Wolcott Mountain, some witnesses thought they could see a man on board it. Later, a resident in east Bristol claimed this was a paper balloon launched at his daughter's birthday party.

On 31 July, at 3.00 a.m., an airship with a circular row of lights was seen hovering over Springfield, and a mystery balloon made an appearance at Pittsfield, Massachusetts, in September.

In October citizens to the north of Rochester saw a large balloon carrying a passenger sailing high in the sky at noon on the 11th.

Even weirder, on the 24th, Mr W.E. Foster at the Ware railway power-house was asked by a voice from the sky: 'What place is this?' As he answered he could see a flashlight about 150 to 200 feet above him.

On 31 October a balloon was seen at 4.00 a.m. at Bridgewater, Massachusetts. Two witnesses, both undertakers, saw a searchlight moving rapidly before it neared the Earth and played its light on the ground.

Pittsfield again hosted a mystery light in the early hours of 10 December. The next day, a balloon was seen at Lowell, going south-eastwards towards Boston.

Most of the sightings were reported because the witnesses thought they had seen the flights of aeronauts who had received publicity in the press. However, they occurred at times or places when real aircraft were not in the vicinity.[2]

Danish 1908 Wave

A dark object projecting two beams of light, one upwards, one downwards, was seen by several witnesses to the north of Gammel Skagen on 27 June 1908. More sightings were made on the night of 29 June at Hjorring, Nibe, Norhalne and Robling between 9.00 and 11.00 p.m. One witness said the lights looked like lanterns on an airship; another said they looked like fireworks, but they were much higher up and lasted longer for that explanation to be plausible. The 2 July edition of the *Aalborg Amtstidende* newspaper published this testimony from Mr Wibroe:

> At 22.25 hrs I was sitting looking out of my window. Over Oland, between Hojskoven and Osterby, I saw a large object about the size of an eagle. Through my binoculars I could see two wings, but in about ten minutes it disappeared from view over Jammer Bay. Three other members of my family also saw the airship.

The next night, at Hasseris, a long object was seen through binoculars by Mr Bye-Jorgensen at 10.50 p.m. At first it looked like an unusually large bird, at an elevation of 30 degrees and about 99 feet away. The accountant watched it for 30 minutes and noticed that it seemed to have a motor or steering gear protruding from it. After briefly passing behind a cloud it went away in a north-westerly direction.

On either 26 June or 3 July, at Odense, what looked like a burning balloon was spotted by hundreds of people.

The majority of the reports came from northern Denmark, and it was suspected that the British Navy was responsible as it was carrying out a major exercise in the North Sea at that time. However, it seems unlikely that any British warships were carrying out experiments with balloons or aircraft at that time and location.

Willy Wagner, who unearthed these reports, noted:

1. Many independent witnesses saw something, which they described as an airship, in the sky over the Vendayasel area of Northern Denmark in June 1908.
2. There were no officially notified flights in that period.
3. It is established that there was no possibility of it being a British airship, as was generally supposed at the time.
4. An examination of the flight characteristics and known movements of other airships of that period make it very unlikely that a French or German vessel could have flown in secret to this part of Denmark.[3]

Sweden 1909

At 7.00 a.m. on 23 September, an airship was seen to fly over Grason. It was heading towards the south-west at an altitude of about 100 metres. The next morning, an aircraft was seen heading westwards at Osthammar, flying at a similar altitude. At 6.00 p.m. a huge elliptical object with wings was visible near Gothenburg. From Olskroken, in Gothenburg, a fast-moving lighted balloon was seen in the west heading out to sea. A few minutes before it went out of sight, a rocket was shot from the balloon in the direction of Redburgs Park. That incident occurred on 2 December at about 8.30 p.m.

Earlier, on 24 August, an unidentified airship circled over Tallinn, the capital of Estonia, before heading towards Finland. This worried the local population so much that they demanded a 'defensive air-fleet' to prevent further aerial intruders.[4]

References

1. Bullard, Thomas, *The Airship File* (Bloomington, Indiana: Privately published, 1982), p.257, p.259 and p.372; Keel, John, *Operation Trojan Horse* (London: Abacus, 1976), p.109.
2. Bullard, Thomas, pp.259–260; Fort, Charles, *The Complete Books of Charles Fort* (New York: Dover, 1974), pp.507–508.
3. Wagner, Willy, 'The Danish "Airship" of 1908', *Magonia*, new series, No. 9, Winter 1977–78, pp.11–12. At: magonia.haaan.com/2009/danish-airship/
4. Bullard, Thomas, p.270; Keel, ibid., p.110; Keel, John A., 'Mystery Aeroplanes of the 1930s', *Flying Saucer Review*, Vol. 16, No. 3, May 1970.

TWO

BRITAIN 1909

The 1909 scare began in March and lasted until the end of May. Many reports came from the east of England, South Wales and some from as as far away as Ireland.

One of the earliest sightings occurred on 23 March in the town of Peterborough. Police Constable Kettle was on patrol when, at 5.15 a.m., he saw a powerful light and heard the sound of a high-powered engine. He described it as travelling at a rapid speed, at a height of 1,200 feet. The light was carried by a narrow oblong-shaped dark-coloured craft.[1]

Two nights after PC Kettle's sighting, Arthur Banyard, an engine driver at March Station, near Peterborough, saw with his fellow workers an airship with powerful lights attached to it. It came into view at 11.00 p.m. from the direction of Peterborough and was moving at a good pace even though it looked to be fighting a heavy wind.[2]

PC Kettle's sighting, and by implication others made in and around Peterborough, was explained as a 'fine kite' that had been launched regularly on the times in question with a Chinese lantern attached to it. The motor sound was explained as a motor at the Co-operative bakery in Cobden Street.[3] Though it does not explain why anyone would be flying such a thing at 5.15 in the morning.

By early May there were so many sightings of lights and the whirring sound of a large, fast-moving airship in East Anglia that the national newspapers took as much interest in the sightings as the local media. A *Daily Express* reporter toured the roads around Peterborough in search of the craft and its base, and found many other motorists taking to the roads at night on the same mission. He also interviewed Mr C.W. Allen who said that on 5 May, when driving through the village of Kelmarsh with two friends, they heard the 'tock-tock-tock' of a motor engine. He said:

It was an oblong airship, with lights in front and behind, flying swiftly through the air … it passed out of sight in a northeasterly direction towards Peterborough.[4]

The airship was viewed at 9.45 p.m. by Mr Egerton Free on 7 May. From his home on a cliff edge near Clacton-on-Sea, Essex, he saw two bright lights attached to a long, torpedo-shaped object. It travelled swiftly and after a few minutes it went out of sight.[5] An odd twist to this story is that the next morning Mr Free found a 3-foot-long, hard grey rubber object like a flattened football, with a 5-foot-long steel bar running through it. It had the words 'Muller Fabrik Bremen' on the side of the ball, and it was thought it had dropped off the airship the previous night.[6] The War Office removed the object and explained it was a 'reindeer buoy' used for target practice and had nothing to do with airships.[7] In the meantime, two 'foreign' looking men were seen hanging around Mr Free's house and where the object was found for five hours on the afternoon of 16 May. When their young servant girl left for church, the men spoke to her in a strange language that frightened her so much that she ran back to the house.[8] Two days later, a 'foreigner' came to the house who was most eager to see the object, but Mrs Free sent him away. A local photographer later confessed that he had gone there to take a picture of the object, and was obviously mistaken for a foreigner.[9]

In the garrison town of Colchester, only a few miles north-west of Clacton, on 18 May, it was reported that two foreigners who spoke with a guttural accent were seen on the East Bridge. They seemed interested in getting details about the East Mills, owned by Messrs. Marriage and Sons. It was also alleged that a foreigner with a fractured skull was found in the district, and it was wondered if he had fallen out of a German airship. Police and other authorities had recently noticed the presence of several foreigners taking notes about the crossroads and buildings in the area.[10]

An even more startling story came from Mr C. Verney Grahame and Mr W. Bond, who were crossing Ham Common, London, at 11.10 p.m. on the night of 13 May, when they saw a 250 foot-long airship land in front of them:

> There were two men on the aeroplane. The first man, who was near the forepart seemed to be in a sort of steel wire cage and had a row of handles in front of him, like the handles of a beer-engine, only thinner.
>
> The moment they saw us this first man, who was clean shaven and looked like a Yankee, turned the searchlight right round on us, and there he was doing this over and over again, blinding us with the glare, evidently so that we could not see too much of the shape of the airship.
>
> The second man, who stood in the middle of the airship, looked like a German, and was smoking a calabash pipe.[11]

On the same night, 10 minutes earlier, Mr Alfred Moreton saw a large airship that had a cage suspended below it containing two men. It carried a faint light and travelled at a speed of up to 40mph over Nuneaton, near Coventry.[12] A torpedo-shaped airship was seen over Tottenham, north-east London, at 3.30 a.m. the following morning.[13]

The Ham Common encounter sounds more like a tongue-in-cheek joke, with the reference to beer-engine handles. The craft was described as being built of aluminium with steel landing legs to prevent the three propellers, located at its stern, from hitting the ground. Rather than a balloon, Mr Grahame said it was 'a pure aeroplane'.

A more credible close encounter with an airship occurred on 18 May, at 11.00 p.m., near the summit of Caerphilly Mountain, South Wales. The witness was Mr C. Lethbridge, a Punch and Judy showman, who was described as 'an elderly man, of quiet demeanour, and did not strike one as given to romancing'.[14]

He had performed a show at Senghenydd, and as he was walking home with his spring cart loaded with props, he was surprised to see a long tube-shaped object near the summit of the mountain. The sound of his cart surprised two men near the object, who did not seem pleased to see him. They loudly jabbered at each other in a strange language and gathered something up from the ground. The men, who were wearing heavy fur coats and close-fitting fur caps, jumped inside a carriage suspended from the cigar-shaped tube, that had slowly risen into the air.

The next morning, he told reporters at the *Western Mail* newspaper offices in Cardiff, that:

> Gradually the whole affair and the men rose into the air in a zigzag fashion. When they cleared the telegraph wires that pass over the mountain two lights, like electric lamps, shone out and the thing went higher into the air and sailed away towards Cardiff ...
>
> When the thing went into the air I distinctly saw what looked like a couple of wheels on the bottom of a little carriage, and at the tail end of it was a fan whirring away as you hear a motorcar do sometimes.[15]

The reporters took Mr Lethbridge back to where he had seen the airship, where they found a 54-foot-long gouge in the hard ground and recently trampled grass. An assortment of news clippings relating to aircraft and warfare, thick blue pieces of paper with figures and strange letters on them, the lid of a polish tin and a pin linked by a small chain to a red label, were found in the area. The pin might have belonged to a gas cylinder used for inflating car tyres or a fire extinguisher. These items could have been coincidental, or, if it was a hoax, planted there by the perpetrators.

To add credence to Mr Lethbridge's story, the residents of Salisbury Road, Cathays, Cardiff, said that they saw the airship on the same night between 10.40 and 10.50 p.m.[16] On the following day, at 1.15 a.m., workers at the Queen Alexandra Dock, Cardiff, saw a cigar-shaped 'boat' in the sky, travelling at high speed. It carried two lights and flew from the north-east, curved over Cardiff and went away to the south-west over the Bristol Channel.[17]

Although these sightings seem to independently confirm Lethbridge's sighting, it is noteworthy that he worked on the docks during the winter months. So it could have been a hoax organised by Lethbridge and his fellow dock workers.

Another explanation was that Paul Brodtman, the managing director of the Continental Tyre Company, had launched a model airship and towed it with a motor car to experiment with the art of aerial advertisement. Shortly after this revelation, Mr Brodtman vigorously denied any connection with the airship sightings and claimed he was totally misrepresented.[18]

May 29th, 1909.

THE NORTHAMPTON INDEPENDENT.

THE AIRSHIP SCARE.

WHAT NORTHAMPTONIANS SAID THEY SAW, OR THOUGHT THEY SAW.

WHAT IT REALLY WAS!

The above amusing cartoons are sent to us by a reader who was prompted to draw them after reading the account in last week's *Independent* of the airship hoax at Northampton.

The British 1909 airship sightings were ridiculed by the *Northampton Independent* newspaper. (Author's collection)

PUNCH, OR THE LONDON CHARIVARI.—June 9, 1909.

THE NEW PEGASUS.

AERONAUT *(clearing all the jumps in one).* "TALK ABOUT HORSEFLESH! GIVE ME ALUMINIUM AND GOLD-BEATER'S SKIN!"

'The new Pegasus', *Punch*, June 1909.

Percival Spencer, a well-known aeronaut and airship constructor, revealed that he had sold several 25-foot-long model airships. These used a small lamp to generate heat to keep them aloft, which might explain why people always saw a 'searchlight' coming from the airship. He had also sold five large man-carrying airships, though none of them were attributed to Lethbridge's sighting.

The idea of a secret inventor was also discussed. A Dr M.B. Boyd even came forward to say that he had spent eight years perfecting an airship that was 120 feet long and capable of travelling 1,000 miles non-stop. It carried two wings, had a three-crew cabin integrated into the envelope and three sets of wheels that enabled it to be used like a motor car on the ground. The craft was kept in a secret shed only an hour's drive from London. He said his craft was responsible for Lethbridge's sighting and for the sightings in Ireland. Needless to say, no more was ever heard of this unlikely aircraft.[19]

On 16 May, the same day that foreigners were seen by Mr Free near Clacton, a stockbroker's clerk saw five foreigners on Caerphilly Mountain. They rode from spot to spot in two traps (carriages), photographing and surveying the area. They finished their work at midday, and one of the traps went on the road to Llanishen while the other one took the road to Cardiff.[20] The question is left open as to whether they were surveying the area in preparation for an airship visitation or had nothing to do with spying and/or airships.

On the east coast, at Grimsby and surrounding areas, numerous spy rumours went into circulation. The town's Member of Parliament, Sir George Doughty, asked Mr McKenna, the First Lord of the Admiralty, in the House of Commons, if he knew anything about the story that the German Army had suddenly commandeered two steamers at Hamburg. They had reportedly loaded them with soldiers before crossing the North Sea, then steamed up the Humber with them before returning to Hamburg. Mr McKenna replied that he had no information about this war exercise, and that he would be pleased to have any further information about the episode.[21]

The next day, 15 May, a rumour was spread that two foreign spies had stolen codebooks from the Admiralty wireless station in Humberstone Avenue, and three German businessmen were regarded as spies when they took photographs of Grimsby docks and attempted to visit Immingham deep-water dock.[22] Another story told how workmen at Killingholm, near Immingham, had encountered motorists who wanted to know if there had been any local airship sightings, and whether the Humber between Immingham and Spurn had been mined. But, as a newspaper columnist reported, 'this story, however, ends rather tamely with the intimation that the motorists finished by enquiring the way to the nearest refreshment house'.[23]

That evening, airship sightings spread to Ireland. A light high in the sky was seen over Colin Mountain, in the districts of Balmoral and Malone, Belfast.[24] A more detailed sighting came from Captain Egenes who skippered the *St Olaf* steamer. On the night of 14 May, the *St Olaf* was just a few miles off the coast of Blyth, Northumberland, when:

> ... a large airship carrying five searchlights suddenly appeared, and hovered directly above the vessel, directed all its lights onto the steamer's bridge ... suddenly the airship swung off after another steamer a mile or so away, on which also the searchlights were directed. The airship afterwards made off at a sharp rate towards the south.[25]

There were other sightings of an airship in the North Sea, including one by fishermen returning to Ostend, Belgium, after working in the Icelandic fishing grounds. This was on the night of 18 May, and they described it as a 'dirigible balloon' manoeuvring about.[26]

The end of this scare came when Lord Northcliffe, the owner of the *Daily Mail*, which had given prominent coverage to these sightings, declared that it was causing harm. He warned that the real danger was the German Navy building programme and her alliance with Italy and Austria-Hungary. These 'imaginary' Zeppelins he noted, had caused the Germans 'to believe that England is becoming the home of mere nervous degenerates.'[27]

THE INVASION OF 1910.

WITH A FULL ACCOUNT OF THE SIEGE OF LONDON.

WHAT LORD ROBERTS SAYS TO YOU:

Speaking in the House of Lords on the 10th July, 1905, I said: "It is to the people of the country I appeal to take up the question of the Army in a sensible, practical manner. For the sake of all they hold dear, let them bring home to themselves what would be the condition of Great Britain if it were to lose far wealth, its power, its position."

The catastrophe that may happen if we still remain in our present state of unpreparedness is vividly and forcibly illustrated in Mr. Le Queux's new book, which I recommend to the perusal of everyone who has the welfare of the British Empire at heart—ROBERTS, F.M.

Keep this Map for Reference.

It will be Valuable.

Keep this Map for Reference.

It will be Valuable.

This Intensely Interesting Narrative by Mr. Wm. Le Queux begins in the
LONDON "DAILY MAIL" TO-MORROW.

ORDER THE "DAILY MAIL" TO-DAY.   *ORDER THE "DAILY MAIL" TO-DAY.*

Left: 'The catastrophe that may happen if we still remain in our current state of unpreparedness …' (Lord Roberts)

Below: The crash of LZ-4 at Echterdingen on 5 August 1908 prompted the German public to contribute 6 million marks to build a new Zeppelin. The outpouring of national pride became known as the 'Miracle at Echterdingen'.

Aufstieg bei Manzell 4. August 08 morgens.

Im Fluge.

Auffahrt, Flug u. Ende des Zeppelin'schen Luftschiffes Modell 4.

Katastrophe bei Echterdingen 5. Aug. 08.

References

1. *Peterborough Advertiser*, 25 March 1909; Anon, 'What Did PC Kettle See?', *Flying Saucer Review*, Vol. 6, No. 4, July/August 1960, pp. 11–12.
2. *Evening Star* (London), 11 May 1909; *Weekly Dispatch* (London), 16 May 1909.
3. *Peterborough Express*, 19 May 1909; *Northampton Independent*, 15 May 1909.
4. *Daily Express*, 12 May 1909.
5. *Daily Express*, 18 May 1909; *East Coast Illustrated News* (Clacton), 22 May 1909.
6. *Daily Express*, 18 May 1909.
7. *Evening News* (London), 18 May 1909; *Daily Express*, 20 and 21 May 1909.
8. *East Anglian Daily Times*, 18 May 1909.
9. *East Anglian Daily Times*, 18 May 1909.
10. *Birmingham Gazette and Express*, 20 May 1909.
11. *Evening Star* (London), 15 May 1909.
12. *Midland Counties Tribune* (Nuneaton, Warwickshire), 15 May 1909.
13. *Evening News* (London), 20 May 1909; *East Anglian Daily Times*, 21 May 1909.
14. *South Wales Daily News*, 20 May 1909.
15. *Cardiff Evening Express*, 19 May 1909; *Daily Express, South Wales Daily News, Western Mail*, 20 May 1909.
16. *South Wales Daily News*, 20 May 1909.
17. *South Wales Echo*, 19 May 1909.
18. *Evening Standard*, 21 May 1909.
19. *Daily News* (London), 6 July 1909; *The Aero*, 13 July 1909.
20. *South Wales Daily News*, 21 May 1909.
21. *Retford, Worksop, Isle of Axholme and Gainsborough News*, 14 May 1909.
22. *Grimsby News*, 14 and 21 May 1909; *Sheffield Daily Telegraph*, 15 May 1909; *The Times*, 20 May 1909; *Sheffield Daily Telegraph*, 19 May 1909.
23. *Louth and North Lincolnshire Advertiser*, 22 May 1909.
24. *Belfast Telegraph*, 18 May 1909.
25. *East Anglian Daily Times*, 19 May 1909.
26. *Daily Mail*, 20 May 1909.
27. *Daily Mail*, 21 May 1909.

THREE

NEW ZEALAND AND AUSTRALIA 1909

In contrast to the British scare of 1909, the New Zealand sightings mainly occurred during daytime and were concentrated in the south-east region of the South Island. One of the first, and best, reports came from the town of Kelso. At noon on 23 July, Mrs James Russell and several schoolchildren saw an object flying towards them from the direction of the Blue Mountains. They said it was broad at the middle and pointed at each end, so that it looked like a boat. Reinforcing its boat-like appearance was a 'pontoon-shaped part' and a small mast at its centre. A man was visible inside the craft as it flew over Kelso school. It flew at an indeterminate height as it performed a u-turn over the school and returned in the direction of the Blue Mountains.

When a reporter visited the witnesses a few days later, Mrs Russell claimed the black craft frightened her so much that she thought the end of the world had arrived. One boy said it had a big wheel spinning at its rear, and another said it also had wings on either side of its body.[1]

Although only Mrs Russell described the airship as boat-like, this impression of its shape was repeated by later witnesses to the craft's gyrations. Indeed, on 27 July, at 10 a.m., Mr Allan Mitchell and Mr

AERIAL NAVIGATION

THE KELSO AIRSHIP

The following figures are those drawn independently before our reporter by those persons who saw the airship at Kelso on Friday and Saturday:—

Drawn by Agnes Falconer, school girl.

Drawn by Thomas Jenkins. The bottom view of vessel is also drawn by this boy.

Drawn by Thomas M'Donald, who saw the propellor whirling.

This is the drawing of George M'Duff, who saw it at 5 p.m. on Saturday.

This shape was indicated by Mrs Russell, who saw it very briefly, and was very much upset, as she had just had an illness. Allowance must therefore be made, but even so, a distinct resemblance can be seen to bottom view following.

This is the bottom view drawn by Thomas Jenkins.

These figures were all drawn independently before our reporter, and with no assistance from anyone. Only two children were in the room at the same time, and these were entirely separated. In every case save one these drawings were the first attempted by scholars. In the one case, young M'Duff, who saw it on Saturday, had already drawn one to convince his father, but this was not by him when he

Alex Riach saw such a craft with a mast on top of it. Near the mouth of the Pomahaka River, they observed it high over Pukepeto, heading for the Blue Mountains. As it travelled it kept dipping and rising with a gentle motion as if under intelligent control.[2]

On the same night, a man said that he was riding his horse when it was disturbed by a grey-coloured, torpedo-shaped object passing overhead. It was carrying three men, and one of them shouted at him in a foreign language. After that it displayed two bright lights and went away, apparently under perfect control.[3]

A 'great black thing with a searchlight attached' was seen at 2.00 a.m., on 28 July, by John McNeill at Northeast Valley.[4] The next day there were four more sightings. Mr H.D. Baily saw a boat-like craft with a flat top pass over his yard at Kauroo Hill, which disturbed his horses.[5] That afternoon twenty-three children at North Invercargill school saw a long cigar-shaped craft.[6] In the evening the lights of a presumed airship were seen in the vicinity of Geraldine.[7]

Drawings of the airship seen by children at Kelso, New Zealand, in 1909. (Author's collection)

To the north of Gore, in Waikaka Valley, two dredge hands saw a narrow boat-shaped craft at 5 a.m. on 30 July. At both ends it carried a light and they could plainly see two figures inside it. For several minutes it rose and fell like a bird and circled close to their dredge boat before shooting off, leaving a yellow haze behind it.[8]

Mr and Mrs Brand, on Saturday night, 31 July, watched a bright light moving like a boat over the Blue Mountains. It seemed to have two large fans on either side of it. Mrs Brand saw it again at 1 a.m. and 3 a.m.[9]

By now the boat-like shape and movement of the craft was well established. This is reminiscent of when Kenneth Arnold reported his sighting of 'flying saucers' over Mount Rainier, USA, on 24 June 1947. He described the objects as moving like saucers would if skipped across water rather than saucer-shaped, but the image of a spinning round disc stuck in the popular imagination.

In New Zealand, a large boat-shaped craft containing two figures appeared over Oamaru, near Sumpter's Hill. It was seen at 3.00 a.m., on 2 August, by a baker called Mr Thomas Robertson.[10] A couple of hours later, Mr Edward Nicholls, in Grosvenor Street, Dunedin, heard a sound like a threshing mill in the sky. On going outside, he saw an object with tapering ends, carrying 'a monster acetylene lamp' at the front.[11]

A correspondent to a local newspaper claimed he saw a large airship heading towards Castlecliff on 4 August. It had two large wings that made a hissing sound, and he calculated it was travelling at a height of 200 feet at a speed of 90mph.[12] Two days later, an airship with two occupants was seen over the district of Waihi for a period of three hours.[13]

As the interest in the reports began to die down, Charlie Baker reported seeing an airship fly up from Maxwelltown early on the morning of 11 August. It was silent, very large, shaped like an egg and carried a sail. As it flew around for a few minutes he distinctly heard voices coming from it before it darted away.[14]

These stories had at least some credit and authenticity, but as interest in the subject took hold, rumours and fantastic stories soon came into circulation. In early August, a man claimed that as he was cruising along Marlborough Sounds an airship flew overhead. The occupants threw down missiles that missed his launch and fizzled when they hit the water.[15]

In an isolated part of the Black Hills, a farmer found two petrol cans, which he thought were abandoned by a visiting airship. Another farmer found some screw wrenches in a field near Otama, making him think the airship had stopped there to carry out repairs. More tools were found at Wooden Hill and at the Blue Mountains near Kelso, leading to similar conclusions.[16]

One rumour spread on the afternoon of 30 July was that an airship had crashed at Waikaka and that its crew of three Germans had been killed. There was also a belief that a special train had been arranged to collect the wreckage. This inspired hundreds of people to rush to the local newspaper office to see if it was true.[17]

That evening, a well-respected man told the Milton Farmers Club that an airship had crashed on the roof of his stables.[18] Another equally 'honest' person said he saw the airship land at Port Molyneux, Clutha, and he had a conversation with the crew, who were Japanese. UFO researcher Patrick Gross regards this as a hoax, though he is wrong in thinking that people at that time had 'no notion of space-ships and extraterrestrial visitors'.[19]

A resident of Waharoa was even more outrageous. He said that an airship containing the German Emperor flew 2 feet above his head, and he could plainly hear him talking about the native land question. When the Emperor saw the man, he put his mailed thumb on his nose and extended his four other digits in a rude gesture before heading off in the direction of Berlin.[20]

Nonetheless, there was a serious concern that a German ship off the coast of New Zealand was being used to launch the airship. Some identified the German cruiser *Condor* or the German Government yacht *Seestern* as the culprits.[21]

There were fears that foreigners were using the airship to spy out the land or that it was even being used to bring in illegal immigrants.[22]

Since the Kelso sighting by schoolchildren on 23 July sparked off this airship scare, the newspapers went back to them to see if they could find any clues as to the origins of this craft. One explanation was that they saw a flock of black swans, though it was noted that such creatures do not carry propellers.[23]

A more serious suggestion was that the children had been influenced by magazines that often carried pictures of airships. The *Windsor Magazine* had only recently published such a picture, and the children's magazine *Chums* had just finished publishing an airship story titled 'The Peril of the Motherland'.[24]

Australia

August and September 1909

As sightings in New Zealand started to fade away, Australia became the target for the phantom airship. Beginning on the night of 5 August and for five nights afterwards, residents at Goulburn, New South Wales, saw a bright, moving light like a 'motor car lamp'.[25]

At Eltham, near Melbourne, the Rev. B. Cozens saw, with four other people, two lights revolving over Dandenong Ranges on Saturday 7 August, between 10.00 p.m. and midnight. They dipped up and down, and changed their colours from white to red, then to blue. Other witnesses at North Malvern, saw similar lights on the nights of 6 and 7 August.[26]

Two nights later, at Moss Vale, south-west of Sydney, a light with a large body attached to it was seen moving in the south-east, and was viewed by witnesses who gathered in the main street. Passengers on the Melbourne Express saw a light in the east on the same night of 9 August.[27]

On Tuesday 10 August, two lights only a few feet apart, which were thought to be attached to an airship, flew rapidly over Pingelly, a town located to the east of Perth. A telegram was sent to the Government Astronomer about this sighting, which occurred at 7.30 p.m. Later that night, mysterious lights were seen in the Victoria Park suburb of Perth. About the same time on Thursday 12 August, a red and blue light was seen over Victoria Park, but the many witnesses who gathered to watch it concluded it was a star. As the newspapermen and police at the scene lost interest, Mr and Mrs

McIntyre said that they had seen boat-shaped lights dipping close to the ground the previous night, and lights were again seen over Victoria Park on Friday night. The Perth Observatory trained its telescope at the locality on Friday but saw nothing unusual.[28]

Also on 10 August, at 6.50 p.m., Mr C. Bruce Nicoll, who was a passenger on a train leaving Picton Station, saw two orange lights high in the sky. They were going in a northerly direction and he thought they were probably fire balloons.

Two lights were seen moving against the wind at Zeehan, Tasmania at 7.00 p.m. on 12 August, heading towards Australia. The following night, between 7.00 and 8.00 p.m., lights were seen in the suburbs of Sydney.[29] The next night at Glen Innes, several residents saw an 'object like a balloon' at 11.00 p.m. It drifted northwards 'and as the body revolved a light like a small flashlight kept turning on the land beneath.'

Just when reports became less frequent, an unusual aircraft carrying flashing head and tail lights, which looked at first torpedo-shaped and then assumed the shape of an umbrella, was seen at Colebrook, Tasmania, on 21 August 1909.[30]

Perth again attracted the attention of the airship on 26 August. W.A. Fearn at East Fremantle saw it going towards Perth at a speed of 160mph.[31]

One of the last sightings of this mini-wave occurred at noon on 1 September. It carried three wings and passed over Dorrigo, New South Wales, flying westwards. At one point it hovered, as if about to descend, and then it continued its course.[32]

On the same day, a cigar-shaped airship with a car attached made a return visit to New Zealand. Two Gore residents saw it drift over the Tapanui Hills at 4.30 p.m., before disappearing towards Kelso. A few days later, to the east of Otaraia, a party of golfers and some children saw a cigar-shaped craft. It sailed backwards and forwards at great speed between 5.45 and 6.15 p.m.[33]

Australia 1910

Another visit to Australia was made at 5.30 p.m., on 25 October 1910 (some sources mistakenly say 1909). Several people at Minderoo

Station, 22 miles from Onslow, Western Australia, saw a revolving object like a compact dirigible that 'appeared to be squarer and more like an aeroplane'. It reflected bright flashes of light from the sun off its metallic surface.[34]

References

1. *Otago Daily Times*, 26 and 27 July 1909; *Clutha Leader*, 27 July 1909; *Bay of Plenty Times*, 28 July 1909; *Bay of Plenty Herald*, 30 July 1909; *Auckland Star*, 27 July 1909.
2. *New Zealand Times*, 2 August 1909; *Otago Daily Times*, 31 July 1909; *Poverty Bay Herald*, 4 August 1909.
3. *Auckland Star*, 5 August 1909; *New Zealand Herald*, 6 August 1909; *Otago Daily Times*, 6 August 1909.
4. *Poverty Bay Herald*, 29 July 1909; *Southland Times*, 29 July 1909; *Otago Daily Times*, 29 July 1909.
5. *Geraldine Guardian*, 31 July 1909; *New Zealand Herald*, 30 July 1909; *Poverty Bay Herald*, 30 July 1909; *Temuka Leader*, 31 July 1909.
6. *Southland Daily News*, 30 July 1909; *Manawatu Evening Standard*, 31 July 1909; *The Dominion*, 31 July 1909.
7. *Geraldine Guardian*, 31 July 1909; *Temuka Leader*, 31 July 1909; *Southland Times*, 31 July 1909; *Southland Daily News*, 31 July 1909.
8. *The Dominion*, 31 July 1909; *New Zealand Herald*, 31 July 1909; *Southland Times*, 31 July 1909; *Otago Daily Times*, 31 July 1909; *Southland Daily News*, 31 July 1909.
9. *Southland Daily News*, 2 August 1909; *Otago Daily Times*, 3 August 1909; *Manawatu Evening Standard*, 3 August 1909.
10. *North Otago Times*, 4 August 1909.
11. *Southland Daily News*, 3 August 1909.
12. *Wanganui Chronicle*, 5 August 1909.
13. *Otago Daily Times*, 11 August 1909; *Geraldine Guardian*, 12 August 1909; *New Zealand Herald*, 13 November 1963.
14. *Wanganui Chronicle*, 13 August 1909.
15. *Marlborough Express*, 7 August 1909.
16. *Wanganui Chronicle*, 17 August 1909; *Otago Daily Times*, day and month unknown, 1966; *Otago Daily Times*, 13 July 1968.
17. *Southland Times*, 31 July 1909; *Southland Daily News*, 31 July 1909; *The Dominion*, 31 July 1909.
18. *Otago Daily Times*, 3 August 1909.
19. *Bruce Herald*, 2 August 1909; URECAT (UFO Related Entities Catalog) website, at: ufologie.patrickgross.org/ce3/1909-07-25-nzealand-portmolyneux.htm.
20. *New Zealand Herald*, 13 November 1963.
21. *Otago Daily Times*, 3 August 1909; *Southland Daily News*, 28 and 31 July 1909; *Otago Daily Times*, 31 July 1909.

22. *Southland Times*, 2 August 1909; *Geraldine Guardian*, 5 August 1909; *Southland Daily News*, 31 July 1909.

23. *Otago Daily Times*, 29 July 1909.

24. *Otago Daily Times*, 27 and 31 July 1909; Ibid., 3 August 1909.

25. *Sydney Morning Herald*, 10 August and 11 Aaugust 1909; *Daily Telegraph* (Sydney), 11 August 1909.

26. *Sydney Morning Herald*, 9 August 1909. *Argus* (Melbourne), 9 August 1909.

27. *Sydney Morning Herald*, 10 August 1909.

28. *West Australian* (Perth), 14 August 1909.

29. *Sydney Morning Herald*, 14 August 1909.

30. *The Mercury* (Hobart, Tasmania), 25 August 1909, p.4.

31. *West Australian*, 1 September 1909, p.8.

32. *The Advertiser* (Adelaide), 3 September 1909, p.7.

33. Chalker, Bill, 'Early Australian Historical Encounters', Project 1947 website, at: www.project1947.com/forum/bcausenc.htm
Holman, Brett, 'Scareships Over Australia - II', Airminded blog, 23 October 2010, at: airminded.org/2010/10/23/scareships-over-australia-ii/.

34. *Sydney Morning Herald*, 5 December 1910; Holman, Brett, 'Scareships Over Australia - IV', Airminded blog, 27 October 2010, at: airminded.org/2010/10/27/scareships-over-australia-iv/.

FOUR

THE TILLINGHAST AIRSHIP?

'An amusing befuddlement.'

Charles Fort.[1]

The afternoon editions of the *Pittsburg Press* told its readers that the Japanese had attacked and invaded America. Her fleet had blown San Francisco 'off the map', sunk US naval vessels and landed troops that were devastating the country. Gigantic aerial craft supported this operation by hurling bombs to the ground as they crossed the Rockies. An angry mob gathered in the city centre to find out more news of this attack and was quickly reminded of the date, 1 April. It was all a newspaper hoax.[2]

There were a few isolated phantom airship sightings in the USA during 1909, but, like the Pittsburg incident, we must wonder how much hoaxing was involved with these stories.

One ripple of aircraft activity occurred on 1 June, when an object that looked like a basket with two wings attached was seen hovering over the Salton Sea, California. The next night, a similar object appeared. Sceptics explained that the sightings were caused by mirages while others thought a secret aircraft inventor was carrying out night-time experiments.[3]

These sightings were nothing compared to the claims of Wallace Elmer Tillinghast. On 12 December, he told a reporter that he had flown from his secret base in Worcester, Massachusetts to New York and back. This 200-mile round trip was said to have occurred on 8 September. He claimed that:

> With two mechanics, I left the shop where the machine is stored, which is within 60 miles of Worcester and 14 miles from a railroad station, and set out in the machine for New York, which we reached, coming close to the Statue of Liberty, went to Boston and then back again to the starting point without alighting. When near Fire Island one of the cylinders ran irregularly, so the motors were stopped and the two mechanics took plenty of time in repairing it and doing a little work of precautionary nature with other parts of the machinery. Before stopping the motor we rose to an altitude of 4000 feet and [sailed] during the 46 minutes taken in repairing the cylinder and looking over the other machinery. When the motor was started we were so near land that the headlight and general outline of the aeroplane with the men in it were seen by a member of the life saving crew patrolling the beach and notice of this discovery appeared in a brief dispatch in a Boston paper a day or so after the trip. This is the longest trip I have ever made, but it is sufficient to make me believe that the machine surpasses anything that has yet appeared.[4]

This account is backed up by William Leach, who said that one night, at 7.15 p.m., he was at the Fire Island lifesaving station when he heard the rattle and hum of a motor flying overhead going towards the New Jersey shore. Unfortunately, due to the cloudy conditions, he could not see anything in the sky.[5] Mr E.B. Hanna of Windham, Connecticut also came forward to say he saw a searchlight at 7.30 p.m. one day in September. It swayed back and forth in the sky for about an hour before heading for Lebanon. Now Mr Hanna believed he had seen Tillinghast on his epic voyage.[6]

Apparently, Tillinghast was the vice-president of the Seal Manufacturing Company, and had spent the last seven years perfecting his aircraft. Over this period he constructed four flying machines and had made 100 trial flights, eighteen of them in his perfected monoplane that took him and his crew to New York. This aeroplane weighed 1,550 pounds and had a wingspan of 72 feet. Its 120-horse-power engine could propel it at a speed of 120mph over a distance of 300 miles without refuelling. So as not to give too much away to his rivals, he refused to say what maximum speed or altitude it could reach when stretched to its limits. For the sake of navigation at night, it produced its own acetylene gas to power the headlights mounted on the front of the craft. Another novel feature was that the pilot and passengers sat on the body of the craft rather than within the framework.

Dr Arthur G. Webster, an aeronautical expert at Clark University, declared that Tillinghast's aircraft went against all the rules of aeronautical science. Wilbur Wright was equally sceptical and gave the opinion, 'Well, it might have been possible for Tillinghast.'[7]

A thousand miles away at Mabelvale, near Little Rock, Arkansas, Mr A.W. Norris saw the searchlight of an airship pass at a height of 300 feet over his home on 13 December, at 10 p.m.[8] A shaft of light, considered to be from an airship, was seen again in the vicinity of Little Rock just before midnight on 19 December, although some explained it as a lunar halo.[9]

A policeman saw a fast-moving airship or meteor streak across the sky at 4 a.m. on 19 December at Worcester.[10] The next morning at 1.15 a.m., immigration inspector Arthur W. Hoe saw a light attached to a framework over Boston Harbor.[11]

These were as nothing to the flood of airship sightings starting on the night of Wednesday 22 December at Worcester. A squad of policemen leaving their Waldo Street station at 6.40 p.m. saw a searchlight attached to a dimly visible dark mass. In Main Street, the staff and patrons of the Pitman and Thurston restaurant came out to watch two red lights and a black form behind them. Some even saw one or two figures piloting the craft. It made four great circles above the hundred or more witnesses before it went in a westerly direction.

Only 16 miles away at Marlboro, the craft was seen between 5.20 and 6 p.m. followed by hundreds more sightings at 7.30 p.m. People said it had been regularly seen there since 14 December and it always went away in the direction of Worcester.[12]

As many as 2,000 people saw a light hover over the State Mutual Life building, Worcester. A policeman described seeing a great expanse of wings behind the light, while others heard the sound of its engines. It circled overhead, illuminating trees and buildings, before heading eastwards.[13]

Wildly different times and descriptions were given by the newspapers, although they all did point the finger at Tillinghast. When they tracked him down he would only say that, 'Where I have my machine is a personal matter and you men of the press will have one fine time finding it.'[14]

Sceptics suggested that a hydrogen balloon launched by hoaxers at Marlboro had created the sightings.[15] Another explanation was that it was a North Carolina white owl with a lantern attached to it, which was sent aloft by a Worcester resident at 6 p.m.[16]

Whatever the merits of the various explanations, the night of Thursday 23 December brought more sighting reports from Worcester, Boston and the surrounding townships. In Worcester, 50,000 people crowded into the streets to watch some lights in the sky that were either caused by hot air balloons launched by hoaxers or Venus. Tillinghast was kept under surveillance so it couldn't have been him.[17]

Thousands of Christmas shoppers in Boston saw what they thought was Tillinghast's machine over Boston Common, and a squad of policemen was ordered to follow the light in case it landed.

Passengers on the Boston and Worcester railway viewed an erratic moving light that came as low as 150 feet. Its powerful light seemed to be attached to a long monoplane of the Bleriot or Latham type. It carried had a red rear light and carried two men.[18]

The craft also invaded the skies of Connecticut, centring its activities on Willimantic. Here hundreds watched a searchlight come from the south-east, circle around and then go away eastwards. Some said it was Venus or a star. At nearby Baltic, P.D. Donahue saw a flying machine with two men inside it pass overhead.[19]

At Rhode Island, two fast-moving lights were seen at Pawtucket, and at Providence a reddish-coloured searchlight was seen moving eastwards.[20]

Even on Christmas Eve, the sky ship did not rest. Like previous nights, it was seen over Massachusetts, Rhode Island, Connecticut and Vermont. Crowds packed the streets of New York, Worcester and Boston to watch lights in the sky and word quickly passed around that it was Tillinghast on one of his flights. Sceptics dismissed the lights as the misperception of stars or the planet Venus. Hoaxers also had a field day launching fire balloons. In Worcester, one of these balloons set fire to the two-storey wooden Franklin Square Garage. Fortunately, it was spotted in time and was put out by the fire department before it reached thirty cars and a large store of petrol. When the crowds of Christmas shoppers heard about this, there was a great deal of hostility felt towards the hoaxers.[21]

One eyewitness in Providence was H.P. Lovecraft, the horror writer who became the unsung pioneer of 'weird fantasy'. Though he thought the sightings were caused by Venus rather than by creatures from another time or outer space.[22]

On Christmas Day, there were sightings at New Haven, Connecticut and Willimantic, and on Boxing Day there were no sightings at all. After that there were a scattering of sightings until 30 December.

On 1 January, handbills signed by 'Tillinghast' fluttered down from an airship on to the streets of Worcester. They read, 'January 1, 1910, on my way to New York.' The initial excitement quickly died away when it was leaked that this was a New Year prank organised by Warden Edwin Hitchcock. He had launched a large fire balloon bought from a local store, and got his friends to throw the handbills down from the top of nearby buildings.[23]

Mr R.W. Tyler viewed the airship through a telescope at 7.30 p.m. on 6 January, from his home in East Poultney, Rutland, Vermont. He said he could plainly see a curious machine of some kind. The local newspaper wondered:

Is it possible that some aerial traveller is braving these brisk zero temperatures for the purpose of trying-out an airship? Is

Tillinghast actually demonstrating his epoch-making flyer in the first weeks of 1910, as he promised, or is the extraordinary brilliancy of Venus, assisted by a prefixed impression of the mind, misleading all those good people?[24]

John H. Cray, the manager of the Loomer Opera House, Willimantic, and PC John Manley both saw at 1 a.m. on 7 January 1910 a series of lights that were linked by a chain of fire. They estimated it was 50 feet long and speculated that it was either a comet or an airship 'stopped for repairs' over Main Street. After 10 minutes it was no longer visible.[25]

On Sunday 16 January 1910, an astronomer was crossing the Quinnipiac River when he came across a crowd of people watching bobbing lights in the direction of Lake Saltonstall. He quickly saw that what they thought was the airship, was nothing more than the Dog Star, Sirius, and other stars in the vicinity.[26]

Another airship report was made by a large number of people at Pittsfield, Massachusetts, on 23 January 1910. There was speculation that it was Tillinghast's craft, but this time it was explained as the arrival of comet Innes and that the airship's searchlight was its bright tail.[27]

Much later in the year, there was a mini-wave in New England from August to October. On the night of 22 September, the police were informed that a cigar-shaped object with a basket beneath it was flying over Point Gratiot, Lake Erie. A young man admitted he was flying a box-kite there at the time, which seems to explain that incident. There were further sightings of mystery aircraft in New York City in August and September 1910.[28]

The *Springfield Republican* neatly summed up the reasons for this scare:

What taxes the human mind today is not an ignorant supernaturalism, but such rapidity in achievements for the industry of the powers of the earth and all as to make the natural appear as fairly supernatural in its possibilities. The past year's developments in air navigation, attended also by the sudden extension of human knowledge to embrace conditions obtaining at the northern pole of the earth, have no doubt brought the popular mind under no little strain and made it more susceptible than common to seeing phantoms in the air if not ghosts on the earth.[29]

References

1. Fort, Charles, *The Complete Books of Charles Fort* (New York: Dover, 1974), pp. 512–516.
2. *Fairbanks Daily News-Miner*, 12 May 1909; Holman, Brett, 'An Awful Day in History', Airminded, at: airminded.org/2012/10/29/an-awful-day-in-history/.
3. *Los Angeles Times*, 4 June 1909; *Imperial Valley Press*, 5 June 1909; *San Francisco Call*, 5 June 1909.
4. *Boston Herald*, 13 December 1909; *Berkshire Evening Eagle*, 14 December 1909. Keel, John, *Operation Trojan Horse*, (London: Abacus, 1973), p. 112.
5. Keel, p. 112; *Boston Herald*, 13 December 1909.
6. *Willimantic Chronicle*, 14 December 1909; *Hartford Courant*, 15 December 1909.
7. *Wheeling Register*, 26 December 1909; *Evening Gazette*, 23 December 1909; *Berkshire Evening Eagle*, 14 December 1909.
8. *Arkansas Gazette*, 15 December 1909.
9. *Arkansas Gazette*, 20 December and 21 December 1909.
10. Cohen, Daniel, *The Great Airship Mystery* (New York: Dodd, Mead & Co., 1981), pp. 174–175.
11. *Daily Herald*, 23 December 1909.
12. *Boston Herald*, 23 December 1909; *Hartford Courant*, 23 December 1909; *Boston Globe*, 23 December 1909.
13. *Boston Herald*, 23 December 1909; *Boston Globe*, 23 December 1909; *Hartford Courant*, 23 December 1909; *New York Tribune*, 23 December 1909; *Boston Journal*, 23 December, 1909.
14. *Boston Journal*, 24 December 1909; *Daily Eastern Argus*, 24 December 1909; *Wheeling Register*, 26 December 1909.
15. *Boston Herald*, 24 December 1909.
16. *Boston Sunday Herald*, 26 December 1909; *Worcester Telegram*, 25 December 1909.
17. *Boston Herald*, 24 December 1909; *Boston Globe*, 24 December 1909; *New York Tribune*, 25 December 1909; *Evening Gazette*, 24 December 1909; *Wheeling Register*, 26 December.
18. *Boston Herald*, 24 December 1909.
19. *Hartford Courant*, 23 December 1909; *Hartford Daily Times*, 24 December 1909; *Willimantic Daily Chronicle*, 24 December 1909.
20. *Providence Journal*, 25 December 1909; *Boston Sunday Herald*, 26 December 1909.
21. *Boston Herald*, 25 December 1909; *Wheeling Register*, 26 December 1909.
22. *Providence Sunday Journal*, 26 December 1909.
23. *Hartford Daily Courant*, 1 January 1910, p. 14.
24. *Rutland Daily Herald*, 10 January 1910, p. 4.

25. *Willimantic Daily Chronicle*, 7 January 1909; *Hartford Courant*, 8 January 1909, p.1.

26. *Hartford Daily Times*, 19 January 1910, p.9.

27. *Berkshire Evening Eagle*, 24 January 1910, p.2.

28. Bullard, Thomas, *The Airship File* (Bloomington, Indiana; privately published, 1982), pp.291–293 and pp.372–373; Keel, pp.120–121; Keel, John A., 'Mystery Aeroplanes of the 1930s – Pt. 1', *Flying Saucer Review*, Vol. 16, No. 3, May/June 1970, p.11.

29. *Springfield Republican*, 2 January 1910, p.6.

FIVE

INCIDENT AT SHEERNESS

On the night of 14 October 1912, it was rumoured that a German Zeppelin flew over Sheerness, Kent, at 8 p.m. When Mr Joynson-Hicks, the MP for Brentford, asked about this rumour in the House of Commons on 18 November 1912, the First Lord of the Admiralty, Winston Churchill, supplied this written reply:

> I have caused inquires to be made and have ascertained that an unknown aircraft was heard over Sheerness about 7.00 p.m. on the evening of 14 October. Flares were lighted at Eastchurch, but the aircraft did not make a landing. There is nothing in the evidence to indicate the nationality of the aircraft.[1]

Newspaper reporters quickly went to Sheerness and Eastchurch to track down any witnesses. The *Daily Mirror* got this story from an unnamed naval officer:

> I believe the noise of the engines was first heard at Eastchurch. When the noise was first heard it was recognised as emanating from a dirigible and not from an aeroplane, and then, I am told, the officers saw hovering in the distance a dark object in the sky, which was admittedly an airship. Believing that it was a British airship that had lost its way in the night and was trying to land, the officers of the Royal Flying Corps lit large flares on the flying

ground at Eastchurch as a guide to the airmen. Nothing more, however, happened. The black form of the airship gradually disappeared, the noise of the engine died away, and we heard no more of its identity.[2]

The Public Record Office (PRO) files contain several reports about this incident. The Admiralty Air Department learnt about the visitation from Charles R. Samson, the commander of the Naval Flying School at Eastchurch and in response instructed Captain Charles D. Johnson, the commander of the Royal Navy torpedo school HMS *Actaeon*, to investigate the matter.

The main evidence was collected from Lieutenant Fitzmaurice who, in a report dated 28 October 1912, told his superiors that between 6.30 and 7.00 p.m., he heard a noise overhead as he walked from Sheerness Post Office to his lodgings. He thought the noise came from an aeroplane and it made him wonder how it would land in the dark. The matter was dismissed from his mind until the next morning when many people at Eastchurch were talking about the airship visitation. It was then that he realised that he had heard the motors of an airship and not those of an aeroplane.

Some other reports were attached to Fitzmaurice's account. A Miss Walker, who was working in the High Street, Sheerness, was attracted outside by the curious behaviour of several people who were looking skywards. On going outside, she saw a bright light moving at a fairly fast speed, heading eastwards. She could not estimate its height, but she could hear its engines. The light seemed to illuminate a large dark object, which was presumably the main body of the craft. She was in the company of Mr Herbert R. Hounsell, who owned an ironmonger shop in the High Street. He said the light in the sky was reddish coloured, but he was unable to see the body of the craft.

As a result of this report, which was sent to the Air Department on 9 November, attempts were made to discover if one of the German Zeppelin airships was responsible for it. The prime suspects were the *Viktoria Luise* (LZ11), *Hansa* (LZ13) and *L.1.* (LZ14).[3]

Most attention was focused on the *L.1.*, which was the first Zeppelin built for the German Navy. It carried wireless equipment to enable it to communicate with ground bases and for navigation. To protect it from aerial attack a machine gun was positioned on the top of the Zeppelin's envelope.

At 8.35 a.m. on 13 October, *L.1.* set off from Friedrichshafen to carry out a long-distance endurance flight that ended in Berlin at 3.43 p.m. on 14 October.[4] As the aviation magazine, *Flight*, noted:

> If the German version of the dates on which the voyage took place is to be relied upon, then it is manifestly impossible that the mysterious craft which is said to have passed over Sheerness on the evening of the 14th could have been the Zeppelin.[5]

The *Daily Mail*'s coverage of the story was so extensive that it prompted Count von Zeppelin to send this telegram to its editor:

> None of my airships approached the English coast on the night of 14 October.[6]

Having eliminated *L.1.* as the culprit, Mr C.G. Grey, the editor of *The Aeroplane*, put forward the view that *Hansa* caused the mystery. He told the *Daily Dispatch*:

> The foreign airship came over at the time that one was reported to have been seen over Eastchurch in October.
>
> The aircraft was hired from a private company … and it must be remembered in this connection that Count Zeppelin's and the German official denials at the time did not refer to anything but official or military visits – and at the time an east wind was blowing.[7]

He went on to state:

> It was in all respects a friendly visit – for it was really intended as a sort of social international call by means of the most up-to-date method of long distance travelling – but it supplies the evidence that such a visit is just as possible with unfriendly motives.

The German airship contained besides its crew, Prince Henry of Pless and ten German officers, whose intention it was to pay a call on a certain nobleman; but, owing to the force of the wind making a landing difficult, the airship returned without a landing being attempted.

The popular idea of a German Zeppelin loaded down with photo-reconnaissance equipment, bombs and German officers intent on surveying Britain with an eye to a future war seemed fanciful enough, but to say the Sheerness visit was no more than a party of friendly Germans making a social visit is even more bizarre.

A sub-committee of the Committee of Imperial Defence prepared a report in November 1912 that considered what the Government should do about the menace from the air. This not only mentions the incident at Sheerness but includes references to several uninvited flights by German airships over Switzerland, Sweden and Denmark. In particular, it mentions that the Viktoria Luise Zeppelin flew at a height of 300 feet over Dutch defence works on 18 June 1912.

As a consequence of this report, the Aerial Navigation Act 1911 was quickly amended to give the Secretary of State the power to prohibit aerial navigation over strategic areas of Britain, and powers to control the movement of aircraft. Anyone caught conducting aerial espionage was liable to seven years' imprisonment.[8]

References

1. Hansard, Vol. 44 H.C. DEB 5s. Proceedings for 18 November 1912, p.14. Oral Answers; Hansard, Vol. 44 H.C. DEB 5s. Proceedings for 21 November 1912, p.504. Written Answers.
2. *Daily Mirror* (London), 16 November 1912.
3. Public Record Office (PRO): Air 1/2456. This was referred to the First Sea Lord.
4. *Manchester Guardian*, 20 November 1912.
5. 'German Airships and British Fortresses', *Flight*, 23 November 1912, No. 204, pp.1069–1070.
6. *Daily Mail* (London), 21 November 1912.
7. *Daily Dispatch*, 3 March 1913; PRO: Air 2/196.
8. 'Control of Aircraft', *Report and Proceedings of a Sub-Committee of the Committee of Imperial Defence*, dated 11 November 1912, printed May 1913. PRO: Cab 16/22; *Recent Legislation Regarding the control of Aircraft*. PRO: Cabinet 38/24, No. 21, p.19.

SIX

THE BRITISH 1913 SCARE

> It is now established beyond all question that the airships of some foreign Power, presumably Germany, are making regular and systematic flights over this country ... The first essential, of course, is to avoid any impression of scare. The facts are here, and they must be faced – that is all.[1]

A notable side effect of the Sheerness incident was a new wave of phantom airship sightings throughout Britain. They came to a peak on the nights of 17 January and 5 February, centring on South Wales. Then Yorkshire and Lancashire became the main locations on 21, 25 and 27 February, when thousands of people in villages and city centres saw the phantoms in the sky.

Intriguingly, there was a flurry of strange lights seen in Ireland during December 1912 and January 1913. Lights moving around the ruins on Church Island, Lough Beg, County Derry, were shot at. An old lady said she smelt sulphur and brimstone when a light passed close to her, and others said the light burnt their faces and singed their hair when they got too close to it. Rather than being associated with the activities of German aircraft, they were explained as, 'firebugs; phosphorescent gases emanating from the surrounding bogs; or some form of radiant matter possessing some state of potential force, power or energy.'[2] Failing that, the stories were dismissed as the rantings of superstitious rural folk who didn't know any better.

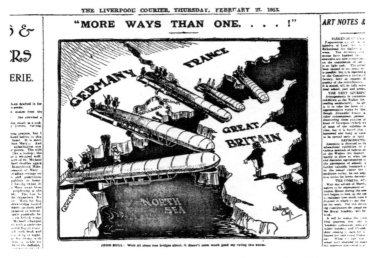

THE LIVERPOOL COURIER, THURSDAY, FEBRUARY 27, 1913.

Foreign airships were a threat to the power of the Royal Navy and its ability to protect Britain. (*Liverpool Courier*, 27 February 1913)

By January 1913, Ireland succumbed to the airship craze. On 8 January, a light with a halo surrounding it became visible over the sea by a crowd of onlookers in Newport, County Mayo. Some thought they could hear the propellers of the craft and the word 'Germans' was passed around. It was at an altitude of between 500 and 1,000 feet and seemed to be struggling against the wind, but after about an hour it disappeared from view at 7.40 p.m.[3]

On the same evening, a brilliant light was seen travelling between Caher Island and Inishturk Island. A local pilot viewed it through a powerful telescope and claimed he saw two men seated in the machine before it landed on Inishturk Island. The following day, the curious witnesses on Clare Island were eager to visit Inishturk Island to find out if the craft was still there, but the weather conditions prevented them making that journey.[4] Given the conditions and locality, it seems highly unlikely this was any man-made craft.

The earliest sighting in England was at Dover on 4 January. John Hobbs, a Corporation employee, was inspecting the roads when he heard the sound of aircraft engines. Mr Langley, a local tradesman, and

Police Constable Pierce also heard it, though John was the only one to see a fast-moving light come from the sea and pass over Dover. This was possibly a sighting of a meteor and the aircraft noises could have been a coincidence.[5]

It was on the night of 17 January that a series of sightings triggered a full-scale scare that did not subside until March. The best report was made by Captain Lionel Lindsay, the Chief Constable of Glamorganshire. He saw a fast-moving object trailing a great column of smoke as it headed away from Cardiff in a north-westerly direction.[6]

Only 45 minutes into the next day, two policemen on patrol in Long Street, Wotton-under-Edge, saw a large airship coming from the direction of Wales. It occasionally flashed a powerful searchlight towards the ground, as if the crew were trying to 'ascertain its exact whereabouts'.[7]

In the evening, several people in Swansea saw a reddish-coloured light moving west to east at a rapid speed. An hour later, at 8.30 p.m., Master Harold Gibbs and his brother heard a hooting noise fly over Swansea.[8] Mr Jenkins of Uplands House, Swansea, claimed he released a fire balloon that night, though what the brothers heard sounds like it was caused by a flock of geese.[9]

The concentration of sightings in South Wales and the nearby English counties over this period led to speculation that there was a secret airbase in Devon or Somerset. The *South Wales Daily Post* noted:

> The wilder portion of Exmoor possesses many places in which those desirous of making experiments with airships would be able to carry on their experiments in quietness and without attracting public notice.[10]

The number of sightings soared in the first week of February. Another characteristic of the week was that people in Lancashire, Yorkshire and along the east coast, also began seeing the airship. On the night of 5 February, hundreds of people throughout South Wales saw an unusual light, and at Manchester a 'phenomenally large star' was seen.[11]

At Newport, Chas. H. Bailet, a radio operator, looked at the light through a powerful telescope. He was able to see a huge cigar moving westwards. He even tried to communicate with the craft with a Morse signal lamp, but got no response from it.[12]

Sightings dwindled until 21 February when Yorkshire became the centre of airship activity, with incidents in Selby, Riccall, Beningborough, Bridlington, Bubwith Highfield, York, Whitby, Scarborough, Church Fenton, Escrick, Cliffe, Stillingfleet and Barlby. There were also sightings in Exhall and Longford in Warwickshire, Ipswich, Suffolk and Old Hunstanton, Norfolk.

Despite the extent of the sightings, the majority were of lights in the sky. The exception was a report by Mr Daniels, a grocer, in the village of Riccall, 5 miles north of Selby. He and some friends observed a long cigar-shaped craft after being attracted outside by the noise of its engines. It flashed a searchlight downwards and carried a small rear light.[13]

At 9 p.m., roughly the same time as the Riccall sighting, Mr John Riply and Mr T. Clarke onboard the sand barge *Star of York*, saw a light going round and round, as if surveying the area. Anchored at Beningborough, on the River Ouse, they saw it for a total of 90 minutes. They described it as having a wheel on either side of its cigar-shaped body, with another wheel at the rear. The craft seemed to have a central bulge and the searchlight was positioned on its left side. The crew compartment seemed to be boxed in.[14]

There were thirty-two separate sightings on the night of 21 February, and this overshadows the fourteen separate sightings on 17 and 18 January, and 5 February. On 22 February, the number of sightings dropped to thirteen and most were in Yorkshire.

One of the better reports for 22 February came from the captain of the *City of Leeds* steamer. His ship was just 1.5 miles from Grimsby, on a voyage to Hamburg, when the aerial object came into view at 9.15 p.m. On arriving at Hamburg, Captain Lundie immediately reported his sighting to his superiors in England:

It was coming over the narrow strip of land forming Spurn Point direct towards Grimsby. Second Officer Williams was on the bridge with me. He saw the ship at the same time and got it under observation with the bridge binoculars. The moon shone brightly for a time, and we saw the hull with perfect distinctness, with its wing attachments, for fully two minutes. There were no lights visible on the airship at any time, and there could be no suggestion that we were deceived or misled.[15]

It stayed at a high altitude and after 5 minutes it disappeared over Grimsby. A few days later, it was discovered that a box-kite carrying two lights had been regularly flown near Grimsby, and was probably the cause of the *City of Leeds* sighting.[16]

Sightings of a light in the sky were made further north at Scarborough, though these were explained as being caused by a fire balloon launched by a gamekeeper on the Houghton Hall Estate, near Market Weighton.[17]

Most of the best reports took place between 23 and 28 February, when this particular scare hit its peak. Sightings spread as far north as Sanday Island, part of the Orkney Islands, where an airship was seen in broad daylight, moving rapidly southwards on 24 February. At one time witnesses thought it was making an approach to land.[18] Further south at Deerness, Ronaldsay Island, an airship was seen, but was later dismissed as a flock of geese.[19] Lights were also seen at Aberdovey, Wales and throughout England at such widespread locations as York, Ipswich, Portsmouth, Withernsea, Ipswich and the Humber Estuary.[20]

During February John Joseph Collins was on his yacht docked at Killary Harbour, Galway, Ireland, when he saw a 'foreign aircraft' land nearby:

I ran to shore thinking they might want help or information, as it might be a breakdown. I saw it was of the bi-plane type. The occupants were three in number, and one apparently a mechanic whom I could not see, was tinkering at the engines. The other two were foreigners, pretty stout, with florid complexions, and very intelligent foreheads, apparently Germans – from my travels on the continent I thought so. I saluted them in German, asking if there was anything wrong. One of them answered me in French, saying he didn't understand. I repeated my question in French, and he curtly told me I could go, as they could help themselves. I went away and although I was in the bay for several hours afterwards, I saw no sign of them returning, but saw a steamer standing on the horizon, so the machine must have been a hydroplane and the steamer a war vessel waiting for it. Where were the British cruisers?[21]

It is not surprising that nobody else saw this or that he did not immediately inform the authorities about its presence. It could be possible that he encountered a real aircraft and that it was not a figment of his imagination. For example, the Breguet III was a biplane capable of carrying a pilot and two crew. In 1912 the French Army ordered thirty-two of these machines, though we still have to wonder why they were flying along the west coast of Ireland.

There were thirteen sightings on 22 February and fourteen on the 24th, but strangely enough there was only one sighting on the 23 February. That was probably due to unfavourable weather conditions. In contrast, the largest number of reports was on 25 February when there were thirty-seven separate sightings, most of which took place between 8.00 and 10 p.m. Thousands saw something at York, Manchester, Leeds, Doncaster, Whitby, Hornsea, Hull, Grimsby, Withernsea and Sheffield. Sightings also occurred in the counties of Suffolk, Kent, Devon and Leicestershire. After the initial excitement generated by local and national newspapers they were soon downplayed as misidentifications of planets, stars or balloons sent up by hoaxers.

Ten sightings occurred on Wednesday 26 February and there were twenty-nine incidents on 27 February. After that there was a serious decline in sightings. One of the most impressive was made by the crew of the *Othello*. A powerful searchlight was seen at 8.00 p.m. on 28 February, just as the ship was sailing 170 miles north-east of Spurn Point. Skipper H. Parker and his Chief Engineer were on the bridge when they saw a powerful searchlight coming towards them:

Long before it was overhead, the whirr of the propellers could be heard. The skipper was admittedly alarmed by the oncoming

Skipper Parker, of the trawler "Othello," and his crew, state that, when 120 miles from the English coast, and double that distance from the nearest point on the German coast, on Friday, they were alarmed by an airship, with a powerful searchlight, which came so near that they feared it would strike the trawler's masts. The whole of the ship's crew have deposited written statements with their owners testifying to their extraordinary experience, which is implicitly believed.

The *Othello* trawler was bathed by light from a phantom airship in 1913. (*Whitby Gazette*, 7 March 1913)

visitor, and gave an unaccustomed blow on his whistle which brought all the crew on deck to ascertain the cause of the alarm. By that time the airship was very low down, and the light from the airship lit the trawler from stern to stern ... The light was so powerful that the men assert that it was possible to read by it.[22]

The craft carried two other lights, which were about 5 feet apart and 14 feet behind the searchlight. It circled over the vessel twice, keeping its searchlight fixed on the ship as it did so. When it flew away westwards the skipper blew another blast from his siren and in return the airship flashed its searchlight.[23]

On 7 March, hundreds of people viewed a bright light travelling from the north-west to the south-west over St Paul's Cathedral, central London. Some put it down to a hoax started by a Smithfield Market meat porter, others to the flight of the *Delta*, a British military airship.[24]

After that, there was a scattering of a few sightings in April, June and August. There were several sightings of a cigar-shaped craft flying over the island of Stronsay on the night of 12 April, and a light was seen in early June at Flotta and Stromness in the Orkney Islands.[25] At the end of August lights were seen at Scarborough and Whitby, Yorkshire. These were explained as being caused by balloons and astronomical phenomena.[26]

Finally, on 23 September, three visitors thought they saw a seaplane crash into the sea at Filey, Yorkshire. Moments later, it rose out of the sea and flew away. Coastguards thought the witnesses had misidentified a flock of seabirds seen through haze. At the same time navy seaplanes where conducting flying experiments in the area, so it is quite reasonable that they might have caused the sighting.[27]

A dirigible takes centre stage in *Sealed Orders*, performed at the Drury Lane Theatre in September 1913. (Author's collection)

Underlying this scare was the fear of Germany's ever-growing fleet of Zeppelins and aeroplanes. Britain still ruled the waves with its massive naval fleet and powerful Dreadnought battleships, but would they be enough to protect this island from the new dangers from the air? What new horrors could the airships unleash whilst Britain remained defenceless and impotent against them? No doubt these fears and questions were a big factor that caused so many people 'see' these airships over Britain in 1913 and rumours of them to be spread throughout the land.[28]

References

1. *Evening News* (London), 24 February 1913.
2. Clarke, David and Oldroyd, Granville, *Spooklights: A British Survey* (Sheffield: Privately published, 1986), pp.4–6.
3. *The Irish Times*, 11 January 1913.
4. *Mayo News*, 25 January 1913.
5. *The Times* (London), 6 January 1913.
6. *Western Mail*, 21 January 1913.
7. *Dursley, Berkeley and Sharpness Gazette*, 25 January 1913.
8. *South Wales Daily News*, 23 January 1913; *Cumbria Daily Leader* (Swansea), 23 January 1913.
9. *South Wales Daily Post* (Swansea), 22 January 1913.
10. *South Wales Daily Post*, 3 February 1913.
11. *Manchester Evening Chronicle*, 6 February 1913.
12. *South Wales Argus* (Newport), 6 February 1913.
13. *The Standard* (London), 26 February 1913.
14. *Yorkshire Evening Press*, 24 February 1913.
15. *Grimsby News*, 4 March 1913.
16. *Sheffield Daily Telegraph*, 6 March 1913.
17. *Daily Telegraph* (London), 28 February 1913.
18. *The Orkney Herald*, 5 March 1913.
19. *The Orkney Herald*, 5 March 1913.
20. *Daily Mirror* (London), 27 February 1913.
21. *Northern Daily Mail*, 25 February 1913.
22. *Northern Daily Mail*, 5 March 1913.
23. *Daily Telegraph*, 6 March 1913.
24. *Liverpool Echo*, 8 March 1913; *Daily Chronicle* (London), 8 March 1913; *Western Mail*, 8 March 1913.
25. *The Orcadian* (Kirkwall), 26 April 1913 and 14 June 1913.
26. *Scarborough Evening News*, 23 August 1913 and 25 August 1913; *Manchester*

Guardian, 25 August 1913; *Whitby Gazette*, 29 August 1913; *Scarborough Evening News*, 25 August 1913.

27. *The Orcadian*, 27 September 1913.

28. Holman, Brett, *The airship panic of 1913: the birth of aerial theatre and the British fear of Germany on the eve of the Great War*, unpublished at time of going to press.

SEVEN

PRE-WAR SCARES AND SIGHTINGS

At the end of 1912 two aircraft were seen to come from Austria, and fly over Kamenetz-Prodosk, Russia. It was feared that the Austrians were using aircraft to spy on Russian territory, including Russian Poland (again).

Russian aircraft with powerful searchlights flew over military sites in Jaroslaw (Galicia), Austria, on 18 January and the following nights, leading to the Austro-Hungarian authorities allowing them to be shot at. One Russian aircraft crashed after it was shot at by sentries at Jaroslaw, and when the body of the dead pilot was recovered he was identified as a member of the Russian General Staff. Another aircraft was accused of flying over Jassy, Romania, on 30 January 1913. It switched off its searchlight after being fired at by soldiers. The next night, at Lembery, Austria, an aircraft with a powerful light was shot at. The mayor of a town near Plock, Russian Poland, was even abducted by two Austrian pilots and flown a good distance before being released. Each side of the border accused the other, but it is noteworthy that few aircraft at that time were capable of carrying powerful searchlights.

On 24 February 1913, a large 'German' airship was seen in Poperinghe, Belgium. The Belgium-France border was said to be the haunting ground of nightly aerial phantoms equipped with searchlights. In the Netherlands six 'German' dirigibles were seen passing over Noord-Brabant. At the end of February both countries feared German espionage from the air, land and sea. Also, on 24 February at 8.00 p.m., an airship visited Dünaburg (Dwinsk), Russia. And, an Austrian balloon followed by an aeroplane came to explore Kelets, Russian Poland, but they were driven away by gunfire.

The German press had made much fun of the British 1909 and 1913 airship scares, but the laughing soon stopped when the tables were turned. On 4 March 1913, a 'Russian' airship was seen at Tarnowitz, Prussia. A burning airship was even seen to crash on the Caputh side of Lake Schwielow, Germany. A search was made for the wreckage, but not surprisingly nothing was discovered to confirm this sighting.

On the Eastern frontier regions of France there were many rumours of German aircraft flying around at night. To detect them cars were fitted with searchlights to probe the night sky. When a real aircraft was forced to land at the beginning of April, near Luneville, a crowd came out and it wasn't very welcoming![1]

Spy stories

Britain also suffered many spy scares and rumours, some of which ran in combination with the phantom airship sightings. On 13 July 1908, *The Times* (London) stated that the Secretary of War was to be asked about a rumoured staff ride made through England by a foreign power. The same paper also asked whether the Chief Constables of the eastern counties knew of any foreign spy activity in England. According to *The Observer*, German officers were said to be active off the south-east coast of England, and similar stories were spread by other sections of the press.[2]

In 1909 this trend was repeated, and *The Illustrated London News* even went as far as to publish a map of the United Kingdom showing the fifty-four invasions that had taken place since 1066.[3]

On 19 May 1909, Sir J.E. Barlow asked in the House of Commons if the Secretary for War knew anything about the 66,000 trained

German soldiers in England, or about the 50,300 stands of Mauser rifles and 7½ million Mauser cartridges stored in a cellar within a quarter mile of Charing Cross. Mr Haldane said that this story was ludicrous, and it lowered our reputation for common-sense abroad.[4]

Mr Haldane might not have wanted to say anything, but the *Daily Telegraph* did reveal that these arms were probably the 500,000 arms stored by the Society of Miniature Rifle Clubs, in a sub-basement of Lloyds Bank in The Strand.[5]

Another story said that in the garrison town of Colchester the police had been receiving many reports of foreigners who were seen to be noting the whereabouts of crossroads and buildings throughout the neighbourhood. The police themselves noted several incidents of a similar nature in May 1909.[6]

Throughout Europe there were parallel worries about foreign intrusion. A Brussels ministerial source claimed that large numbers of German soldiers were manoeuvring on the south-eastern border. In Verviers, Belgium, a number of postal officials were said to be searching the countryside on the orders of their superiors, looking for strategic and topographical information. A German newspaper in Triers advised that the town be fortified to withstand a French attack via neutral Luxembourg, as French officers had been known to have motored through the Grand Duchy with strategic aims. In reply, Luxembourg claimed that Germans had not only motored through their land, but surveyed it from the safety of airships. This controversy served to force the Belgian clerical anti-militarists to amend their objections to a pending Army Bill.

These airship and spy scares seem to support the view that foreign enemies were attempting to reconnoitre military locations. Conversely one could argue that people living in 'strategic' areas would be more sensitive to rumours related to spying activities.

The ambiguity and bizarre nature of the airship sightings, the fear of alien invasion, the existence of foreign spies and inventors, allied with secret inventors and government investigations in the 1900s parallels the modern-day UFO phenomenon, which embraces stories of strange encounters, the fear of alien (extraterrestrial) invasion, men in black, and secret government projects.

Whether these airship phantoms were the product of mass delusion or aliens cloaking themselves in the futuristic technology of that era, we can conclude that politicians and journalists were equally guilty of enhancing the public fear of invasion in order to secure more funds for military expansion. The generation of rumours of war was turned into actuality by a process of auto-suggestion. In this state of mind the European powers marched inexorably towards the most bloody and destructive war in the history of mankind.

Aerial phantoms start the war

German newspapers understandably expressed their outrage over French aircraft bombing the neighbourhood of Nuremberg on 2 August 1914. It was a lie, used to justify giving an ultimatum to Belgium and declaring war on France the following day.

The German Ambassador in Paris, Baron Wilhelm Eduard van Schoen, delivered the declaration of war, which stated: 'French acts of "organised hostility" and of air attacks on Nuremberg and Karlsruhe and of the violation of Belgian neutrality by French aviators flying over Belgium territory … ' were some of the key factors.

Germany had already declared war on Russia on 1 August, and within two days its troops had moved through Luxembourg and were pouring into Belgium, which led Britain to declare war on Germany on 4 August 1914.[7]

Thus, phantom aircraft helped set in train the tragic horrors of the First World War.

References

1.   Bullard, Thomas, *The Airship File* (Bloomington, Indiana: Privately published, 1982), pp.293–296, p.298, p.300 and pp.304–306; Bullard, Thomas, 'Newly Discovered "Airship" Waves Over Poland', *Flying Saucer Review*, Vol. 29, No. 3, March 1984, pp.12–14; Watson, Nigel, 'Airships and Invaders', *Magonia*, No. 3, Spring 1980; 'At the border of Galicia (1913)', at: souvenirsdenosgreniers.unblog. fr/2013/05/29/a-la-frontiere-de-galicie-1913/).

2. Playne, Caroline E., *The Pre-War Mind in Britain* (London: Allen & Unwin, 1928), pp. 118–119.

3. *The Illustrated London News*, 27 March 1909.

4. *Irish Times*, 19 May 1909; *Sheffield Daily Telegraph*, 19 May 1909; *Grimsby News*, 28 May 1909.

5. *Bath Chronicle*, 27 May 1909.

6. *Irish News*, 20 May 1909 and 21 May 1909.

7. Tuchman, Barbara, *August 1914* (London & Basingstoke: The Macmillan Press Ltd, 1980), p. 114 and p. 126.

EIGHT

PHANTOM AIRCRAFT OVER GREAT BRITAIN IN 1914

When war was declared, the British expected German Zeppelin airships to start their attacks immediately. To the general perplexity of the British public, no Zeppelin raiders emerged from the clouds to drop their deadly cargoes.

An editorial in the 21 August 1914 edition of *Flight* magazine summed up the situation:

Of the vaunted Zeppelins of the common enemy we hear literally nothing of a dependable nature. Rumour, ever a lying jade, has it that three of these craft at least have been destroyed in Belgium. A most circumstantial story went the rounds the other day that one of these craft had met its fate at the guns of a British cruiser in the North Sea, but the Admiralty have 'no confirmation' of the report! And so it goes on from day to day. We hear much but learn little – and we must be content in the meantime to look upon that as a necessity of the conduct of scientific war.[1]

A SECRET SOCIETY.

BERLIN ORDERS TO SPIES IN LONDON.

EXTRAORDINARY DIARY.

The intention of Germany to make an attack on England in the event of an outbreak of civil war in Ireland is emphasised by the entries in a minute book recording the proceedings of a German secret society in London.

This book has come into the possession of the authorities, and was instrumental in enabling the police to arrest a number of men on the charge of being spies. The society had its headquarters in Soho, and the meetings were usually held on Sunday mornings, when the colony of German waiters would be freed from duty.

The membership was limited to one hundred, and the duty of each man was allocated. The object was to discover any weak points in the English plan of defence and communicate them to an assigned place in London, whence they would be communicated to a German warship in the North Sea, or direct to Germany.

AN INTRICATE CODE.

The entries in the minute book were in an intricate German code, but they have been interpreted, and the full purpose of the German conspirators has been revealed.

Among the entries were the following:—

April 19.—Full attendance in response to urgent summons. Chairman announced that official cognisance had been taken by the authorities at Berlin of the Crisis in Ireland. Members notified to be ready at any moment to take up their duties as servants of the Fatherland.

April 26.—Meeting of Executive Committee. Reports read from rifle stores.

May 3.—Full membership meeting. Chairman read letter announcing sending of £2500 by G———. Posts and duties allotted.

May 10.—Executive Committee meeting. Purchase of wire-cutters and rubber gloves ordered.

May 17.—Membership meeting. Chairman announced despatch of consignment of rifle and pistol cartridges from Bremen marked as screws and nails.

May 25.—Executive meeting. Warning from chief at Berlin to be ready at any moment.

AIRSHIP DEPOT.

May 31.—Members' meeting. Chairman read letter from chief ordering establishment of a depot for airship parts at a place to be selected by this body. East coast of England selected.

June 7.—Executive meeting. Telegram received from Berlin ordering us to strike at end of July.

June 14.—Members' meeting. Parts of pistols and rifles ordered to be distributed.

June 21.—Executive meeting. Chairman reported that police are watching our movements.

June 28.—Members' meeting. Decision to disband owing to police activity. Arranged for members to be communicated with by post. Code given to each member.

There is no record of any meeting after the last date, but there is evidence of increased activity on the part of the members, whose purpose was upset by the course taken by European politics involving a widespread war.

LONDON LETTER.

October 19, 1914.

THE SPY PERIL.

Despite Mr McKenna's reassuring statements, public opinion is becoming genuinely apprehensive of the German spy peril as revealed in the unearthing of wireless apparatus, the discovery of concrete foundations, and in a hundred and one other directions. Whereas on the outbreak of the war there was a tendency to belittle the efficiency and scope of the enemy's espionage system in this country, there is now a marked disposition to treat the German menace as something very real and highly dangerous. Recent revelations of the activities of the enemy's agents in the towns of Belgium and France have succeeded in opening people's eyes to the peril of harbouring a German population in our midst. There are doubtless many subjects of Germany and Austria resident in the United Kingdom who are perfectly innocent of any designs of a mischievous kind, but on the other hand there are large numbers who should be under lock and key. Registration, as has been frequently pointed out, is useless in itself. These aliens, unless they can thoroughly satisfy the police as to their intentions, should be rounded up and placed in the concentration camps or kept under the closest surveillance; and only in this way can the peril from the spy peril be minimised. The recent "anti-German riots in some parts of London are an unmistakable indication that the public will tolerate no kid-glove methods in dealing with the menace. It is to be hoped that the authorities take the hint.

UNFOUNDED RUMOURS.

The frequency with which silly rumours of naval disasters or reverses to the British arms are circulated, and the wide currency such stories usually gain, induce the belief that this sort of thing is the work of German agents. During the latter part of last week quite a crop of these reports were disseminated far and wide. One story was to the effect that a famous British aviator had offered his services to the Germans, while the gist of another was the discovery of treachery on the part of an exalted personage who occupies a high position in official life, and his consequent incarceration in the Tower of London. Then on Saturday there was a rumour of a serious naval disaster in the North Sea, the names of two British vessels of the super-Dreadnought class actually being given in this connection. The telephone played an important part in the circulation of the latter rumour, and in at least one case the office of the Press Bureau was given as the place of call. The unfortunate part about this affair is that these stories, wildly improbable, if not altogether impossible though they generally are, obtain ready credence among the more ignorant and unthinking sections of the public, and in consequence create a good deal of uneasiness and alarm. It is obviously difficult to trace such lies back to the original source; but where the authorship is discovered it would doubtless have a salutary effect if the culprits were punished with the utmost rigour of the law.

QUESTIONS FOR MINISTERS.

The opening of the new session next month promises to be of more than usual interest if only on account of the formidable list of questions which is being compiled by members with some special grievance to ventilate or some particular suggestion they wish to raise. Naturally enough, practically all these inquiries deal with one or other aspect of the war, and most of them relate to matters arising from the administration of the various Government departments. The non-militant side of the War Office will come in for a large share of criticism, particularly in respect of the subjects of separation allowances and the accommodation of the recruits for the new armies. Other questions to be raised which concern the War Office deal with the alleged overcharging of men in the canteens and the conditions under which soldiers' uniforms and clothing are made. Mr Churchill, as representing the Admiralty, will also be closely questioned on a variety of subjects. The most interesting of these is in connection with the employment of half-trained naval volunteers at Antwerp—a point about which much has been heard of late. Other Ministers to be questioned include the Postmaster-General, who will be asked to make a statement on temporary employment in the Post-office, and Mr Runciman, who will be invited to explain what authority he had for declaring that a Zeppelin attack would be made on London at the end of October.

German spies were apparently caught planning to establish a depot for airship parts in Scotland or on the east coast of England (left). (*The Standard*, 20 August 1914)

The effect of silly rumours was a cause of concern to the Government, and it was suggested culprits who started or spread them should be punished with 'utmost rigour of the law.' (centre). (*Inverness Courier*, 23 October 1914)

HOSTILE AIRCRAFT IN SCOTLAND — £100 REWARD.—The following notice has been circulated by Lieut.-General Sir John Spencer Ewart, Commander-in-Chief, Scottish Command :—

£100 REWARD.

Numerous reports of the presence of hostile aircraft in Scotland have recently been received. If these reports are true, it is probable that the hostile aircraft have been operating from a secret base in some unfrequented part of Scotland, where they are able to obtain supplies of oil, petrol and other stores. The above reward will be paid by the Military Authorities to any person who gives information leading to the discovery of any place which is being used in this manner. Such a base would probably consist of a store of oil and petrol concealed in an unfrequented locality, possibly in charge of an armed caretaker. Information should be given to the nearest Military or Police Office.

—There have been persistent rumours that there is well-grounded reason to suppose that the Forres district has been associated with the source of the illegal practices referred to above. A reliable correspondent informs us that he saw an aeroplane hovering high above Forres on Sunday evening, and that it disappeared on the western horizon.

A £100 reward was offered to anyone who gave information that might help discover a hostile aircraft depot in Scotland. (*Forres, Elgin, and Nairn Gazette*, 21 October 1914)

Motoring journalist R.P. Hearne explored in this 1910 book how different countries were using aerial technology. He feared that the German airships posed a great threat to the security of Britain.

An imaginary dogfight is illustrated in the January 1914 edition of *Strand Magazine*. (Author's collection)

The British shores were beyond the range of German aeroplanes until Christmas Day 1914, when a raid was made on Kent. At this time, aeroplanes were not much of a physical threat, compared to the Zeppelins that could carry large bomb payloads and travel under the cover of night over long distances. The Zeppelin threat finally became real on the night of 19 January 1915, when Norfolk suffered the first airship raid on this country. Yet, from the very opening of hostilities, the War Office began to receive reports of unidentified aircraft from various parts of Britain.

These reports were dealt with by the Assistant Director of Military Aeronautics, a post held by Lieutenant Colonel W.S. Brancker; the department of Military Training; and by the Military Observation Department Five (MO5), under the control of Lieutenant Colonel Kell. (MO5 was renamed the Military Intelligence Department Five (MI5) in 1916.) Brancker liaised with MO5 and with Military Training. This information has been preserved at the PRO under file number AIR 1/565 16/15/89, entitled: GHQ Home Forces General Correspondents File: Movements and Rumoured Movements of Hostile Aircraft Etc., 3/8/14–2/1/15. Unless otherwise stated, all reports in this chapter originate from this file.

One of the first reports came from two water bailiffs on the River Eden, near Carlisle. At 2.45 a.m. on 5 August 1914, they heard an aeroplane travelling east to west, which followed the course of the river.

Soon afterwards, the War Office began to receive reports of an airship flying in the vicinity of Barrow-in-Furness. Barrow was of immense importance to the war effort. To signify its importance, the only anti-aircraft gun on the entire west coast was positioned in the local Vickers shipbuilding yard. Vickers itself was involved in building airships and from 1915 constructed non-rigid Submarine-Scout-Class airships for the Royal Navy.[2]

Sentries positioned at the approaches to the town were ordered to fire at anyone who did not answer their challenge.[3] Such precautions seemed to be necessary when, on the night of 7 August 1914, all the lights at Vickers were switched off because of an air-raid warning. A Furness Railway train was allegedly followed by an airship from Askam to Bootle, Cumbria where the airship headed out to sea.[4]

A battle between Zeppelins, aeroplanes and dreadnoughts is dramatically envisioned in *All About Aircraft* by Ralph Simmonds (London: Cassell, 1915).

The Great Yarmouth Naval Air Station commenced their war patrols on 9 August 1914. At 12.30 p.m., they received a message saying that Lieutenant Rainoy had landed at Brancaster and had reported that he had followed two German seaplanes along the Norfolk coast.[5]

That evening, at about 9.30 p.m., two privates of the 4th Battalion, The King's Own (Royal Lancaster) Regiment, were on duty at Next Ness Bridge, Ulverston, 9 miles north-east of Barrow. They heard a buzzing sound in the air and saw a flashing white light go towards Barrow. Two civilians, Henry Wilson, a chauffeur, and John Kay, the son of an ex-police sergeant, were also witnesses. They were positioned a mile from the Next Ness Bridge at the same hour.

Henry was able to see a long and narrow shape when the bright light went out. A light was seen again by Henry just after 10 p.m. when he was at Townbanks. It came from the north-west and went towards the North Lonsdale Iron Works, Cumbria.

Major Becke, Commander of Barrow Defences, reported that airships – certainly two, possibly three – had been seen during the night of 10 August over Vickers flying in a northerly direction. The anti-aircraft gun at Vickers shot at them with no apparent effect.

On 11 August, Commander Boothby, Royal Navy, in charge of the airship shed at Barrow, reported to the Admiralty Air Department:

Last night at 10:45 p.m. Military outpost at Sowerby Farm, two miles north of Barrow, sighted two airships. They were seen by a sergeant and a private. The officer was doing his rounds. On his return only one was in sight. He describes it as cigar shaped and yellowish. There appears no doubt that at least one airship is working in this district.

It appears probable that they have a temporary base in the hills. It appears to work before moonrise and has now been reported on the 6th, 7th, 9th, and 10th of this month, all on reliable evidence. The Military are sending out scouts into the hills around to try and locate its base.

It is suggested Ela [sic] or Delta be sent here to assist in the search.

Eta and *Delta* were non-rigid airships, originally built for the British Army, but now under the control of the Royal Navy, which took responsibility for all airship developments in January 1914.

Besides rumours of an enemy airship operating in the area of Barrow, there were stories of other enemy activities in circulation. These mainly focused on the concern that spies were at work to undermine the war effort. They were certainly given some credence when two German sailors who arrived on the SS *Luciston* were taken away by soldiers as suspected spies. One rumour said that a German spy had been captured at the oil works on 12 August. It was even rumoured that some spies had been shot. In this climate of anxiety and fear any 'suspicious' person was likely to be the subject of police or military inquiry.[6]

Police Sergeant Horn heard an aircraft flying over Egremont, Cumbria, at 10.40 p.m., on 11 August. He also saw a white speck moving rapidly towards the Solway Firth.

The following day, Scout Master Henry Motson, in charge of eleven boy scouts who were watching the railway line at Silk Mill Crossing near Taunton, Somerset, observed an airship coming towards them. It came from the north-west at 8.32 p.m. A few minutes later, it turned broadside-on, giving them a full view of the object, before turning round and going back. Shortly afterwards it turned and came towards them again. At 8.57 p.m., the object gradually rose and went in a north-westerly direction and out of sight. A group of boys, 3 miles further down the line towards Wellington, also glimpsed it before it disappeared. A lady informed the scout master that a friend of hers had seen it between 8.30 and 9.00 p.m. Lieutenant Colonel Brancker, at MO5 headquarters, thought this might have been an aeroplane, although no flights had been authorised for that area.

The first report from Ireland came on the 13 August. The Galway police reported that an aeroplane had been seen at Costelloe in Galway Bay. The same evening, a farmer at Hasket-New-Market, near Wigton, Cumberland, saw three or four distinct flashes that looked like searchlight beams.

A few minutes into 14 August, the same Sergeant Horn who had a sighting on 11 August viewed a light rise and fall above the Solway Firth along with PC Nelson. At 2.50 a.m., PC Kirkbridge, also of Egremont police station, saw red, green and white lights moving southwards. The Chief Constable of Cumberland and Westmorland, noted: 'I am causing every search to be made to locate it.'

A submarine entering the Humber River sighted an airship hugging the coast at a high altitude at 10 p.m. Ten minutes later, a sentry at Barrow saw a light in the sky. In the same hour, the Chief Constable of Carlisle saw a strange stationary light. And an airship making a peculiar whirring sound was seen during the evening of the 14th at Penrith.[7]

Three aeroplanes were seen flying up the Bristol Channel on 15 August. Brancker commented: 'This does not seem at all probable.'

The reports of an airship or aeroplane in the Lake District were so strong that the Cumberland and Westmorland Yeomanry at Penrith were commanded to search for the phantom aviator. They were sent to Ambleside, Keswick and Wigton on the morning of 15 August. Boy scouts helped to guard various water supplies in the area, and chains of runners were organised to keep everyone in contact.

An aeroplane had been seen resting on the hills near Eskdale and aerial noises had been heard in the vicinity. As a consequence, soldiers were sent to search this area thoroughly, but they found nothing to indicate the presence of an aircraft or any traces of one.[8]

A decision was made to send an aeroplane to Derbyshire, Cumberland and Lancashire to help the search parties. Lieutenant B.C. Hucks was given this task and his Bleriot XI was painted white so that it could be easily identified.

Action needed to be taken since, on Sunday 16 August, a number of sightings were reported. The hum of a motor was heard at Brandling Ghyll, near Cockermouth, at 2.30 a.m. A flying machine was seen at Parton, near Whitehaven, at 10.30 a.m. It was seen again at Whitehaven at 7.30 p.m. and 7.50 p.m., and like the earlier visitations it was seen at a high altitude.

At Teignmouth, Devon, an aeroplane came from the direction of the sea at 6.30 p.m. It hovered over the town and then returned seawards. Near Carlisle, the noise of an aircraft was heard at 10 p.m., and, an hour later, PC Moore saw an aeroplane going north to south.

An aeroplane was followed by two men on bicycles between Cockermouth and Uldale at midnight.

The scare in the Lake District was now at its height. People who possessed binoculars and telescopes eagerly scanned the skies. The police expended agreat deal of time and energy in an attempt to trace the source of the aviator's fuel supply and to apprehend a mysterious motor car, which was apparently being used by associates of the airmen.

On Monday 17 August, Hucks flew over Derby, Bradford, Skipton, Rochdale, Manchester, Buxton and Ashbourne. Meanwhile, the Bleasdale Moors were searched by members of the Duke of Lancaster's Own Imperial Yeomanry.

Peter Kidd, of Kilcock, County Kildare, wrote this letter to the *Irish Times* on 17 August:

> Quite a number of people round here are alarmed at the constant flight of aeroplanes generally travelling in the same direction, either on an imaginary line from Belfast to the Curragh, or towards, or a little north of, Dublin from the Curragh. They generally pass where I write about from 3 o'clock a.m. to about 5:30 a.m. Only this morning about the latter five were observed coming from the Curragh direction.
>
> Should this catch the eye of the General Commanding the troops in Ireland, I should be glad if he would ease our minds as to whether these airmen are British or foreign, by publishing a statement in your journal of Tuesday next. Should no such statement appear it is our intention to treat these gentry to the business end of our Mausers as we honestly believe that in face of a proclamation issued some days ago regarding these craft in the British Isles, that they are German spies. I am also confirmed in this view by a conversation with a prominent Meath man who also complained of their unwelcome attentions there…

The authorities forbade the publication of this letter. They said it was practically impossible for any enemy aeroplanes to visit Ireland and farmer Kidd was told not to shoot at any aircraft.

In England the more real possibility of the presence of enemy aircraft meant that shooting at them could be allowed. In a letter to the War Office, dated 17 August, Murrey F. Sueter, the Director of the Admiralty Air Department, wrote:

> I am commanded by my Lords Commissioners of the Admiralty to request that you will inform the Army Council that no objection is seen to the anti-aircraft defences at Barrow-in-Furness firing on any airship seen over or near Barrow by day or night till further orders.[9]

On instructions from Western Command, the aeroplane sheds of the Lakes Flying School on Lake Windermere were searched. During the time of the scare, no flying took place at Windermere and the police were satisfied that the flying school was not responsible for the phantom sightings.

Western Command's report about the scare was sent to the War Office on 18 August. This contained the view of the officer commanding the Cumberland and Westmorland Yeomanry that the flight paths of the craft pointed to a possible depot in the Kirkcudbrightshire Mountains.

Hucks reached Lancaster at 1.20 p.m. on Tuesday 18 August. He reconnoitred the hills between Leeds, Skipton, Settle, Bentham, Lancaster and Slaidburn, but low clouds prevented him going any further on that day.

Meanwhile, the police in Cumberland were kept busy investigating new reports. The sound of an aeroplane was heard at 2.30 a.m. in Great Orton, near Carlisle. Another aircraft was seen and heard by two colliers at Brayton Pit, Aspatria at 3.25 a.m. In the afternoon, villagers at Crosby-on-Eden were alarmed by the presence of an aeroplane.[10] A similar craft passed over Houghton, near Carlisle, on its way to the Solway Firth at 2.30 p.m. Two witnesses at Ireby, near Wigton, saw a light at 9.50 p.m., which headed towards Skiddaw.

With the help of gamekeepers and shepherds, the yeomanry searched the most likely hiding places in the Lake District, without any success. They were instructed to return to Penrith by Tuesday night.

Hucks finally reached Penrith on the afternoon of Wednesday 19 August, by way of Sedbergh, Hawes, Askrigg, Reeth, Brough and Appleby. When passing over Augill Castle, Brough, at 2.30 p.m. two observers there saw another aeroplane to the north of Huck's course travelling in the same direction. It eventually headed over the Pennines. The police in adjacent counties found no trace of the second aeroplane, and Hucks did not see it either. Hucks telegraphed his base at Farnborough, that evening:

> Many reports reach Chief Constable here [Penrith] of mysteri-
> ous aircraft seen at night so this district appears to require more
> thorough search. My engine will soon require cleaning as power
> beginning to fall off. Should like on account dangerous nature
> of country to be flown over procure another machine if possible.
> Suggest flying direct Newcastle 60 miles and take anything avail-
> able there, leaving Bleriot for attention.[11]

He left Penrith at 11.20 a.m. the next morning for Newcastle. When he got there he had some trouble with his engine, and on the 25 August was recalled to Farnborough.[12]

At 12.20 a.m. on 20 August, Private Howe of the 4th East Lancashire Royal Field Artillery was between Flimby and Siddick when he saw an aeroplane flying near the ground. It carried a red tail light and went southwards along the coast towards Workington.

A visitor to the Loweswater district on Monday 17 August, found the inhabitants scared of a 'foreign aeroplane'. A mysterious motor-cyclist was also linked with the activities of this phantom flier.

The police at Seaham Harbour in Durham reported that at 10.50 p.m. an aeroplane had passed over South Hylton, near Sunderland. It travelled southwards and showed a white light. Brancker thought that it was most unlikely that any aeroplane, hos-tile or friendly, would carry a white light.

The noise of an aeroplane overhead was heard at Seaton, near Workington, 40 minutes later. It carried a white light at the front and rear. After hovering over and about Seaton, it went in the direction of St Bees Head. This performance was repeated again at 2 a.m.

On Sunday 23 August, Mr Steele, a Carlisle solicitor, informed the police at 9 p.m. that he had seen a light moving in the eastern sky. The next evening, he saw the same light and concluded it was the planet Jupiter and not a phantom aircraft.

Seven miles north of Carlisle, at Lynhow, a red and white moving light was seen between 9.20 p.m. and 12.45 a.m. This was witnessed by Mrs Ferguson, the wife of the Mayor of Carlisle, together with three other ladies and the servants. At 11.45 p.m., a second light was seen going towards the first light until it was obscured from view by nearby trees. The coachman and head gardener told the police that they thought the light was a star.

Also on 23 August, Captain Lowthorpe-Lutwidge of Holrook Hall, near Seascale, told the police that for four nights running he had seen a strange light. This appeared in the south-east between Black Combe and Muncaster Fell. Two days later, PCs Johnson and Carson went to the hall at 11.10 p.m. When shown the light they concluded it was a star.

As this scare was petering out in the Lake District, it was just starting up in the Galloway region of south-west Scotland. Curiously, only one report from Scotland is contained in the Air Ministry file.

The first definite report from Kirkcudbrightshire came on 23 August. Two police constables, in different parts of the town, and a lamp lighter heard the drone of an aeroplane as it took a wide sweep over the town at 11.40 p.m. Two nights later, at the same time, a police constable who had experience of aeroplanes whilst at Montrose, saw an aeroplane flying overhead for 20 minutes. The machine, flying at a considerable height and carrying a light, came from the Solway Firth. It went away towards the south-west, then it reappeared for a short time when it was seen going northwards. A local newspaper thought these reports were caused by War Office aerial experiments, though this idea was soon dropped, either because it was true or the authorities did not want to fan the flames of rumour.[13]

Numerous reports were made on 24 August. The first came from Clitheroe, Lancashire. Police Constable Iain Snowden was near the Pimlico Road railway bridge at 2.45 a.m. when he noticed a light over the Big End of Pendle Hill. It kept disappearing and reappearing every few minutes. He was able to see that the light came from a platform slung beneath a sausage-shaped airship. Five minutes after Snowden first saw it, Police Sergeant Thomas Pope saw a similar light when he was at Primrose Arches. Whether this was the same light is debatable.

On the evening of 24 August, London became the centre of airship activity. At 7.30 p.m. an object like an enemy airship was seen from Hendon Aerodrome going eastwards at an altitude of 4,000 feet. At 8.45 p.m., an identical object was seen over the mouth of the Thames. An hour later, a faint light, flying high, was seen heading westwards at Hove, on the south coast near Brighton.

Nearer London, an airship was seen heading towards Eastchurch at 10 p.m. and it was also seen in the vicinity of Chatham. The next morning, a worrying telegram was sent by an intelligence officer at the Sheerness Naval Centre:

> I consider that from reports received at this centre during the past three weeks regarding movements of hostile airships that enemy has made complete reconnaissance of district and intend shortly attempt destroy dockyard etc. here and Chatham by dropping high explosives.

This reflected the feelings of personnel at the nearby Eastchurch Air Station, where there was a general belief that the Germans would lose no time in sending airships over England. The whole place was alive with sentries who kept a sharp lookout for hostile airships.[14]

Major de Wattevill at the Headquarters of Mersey Defences, Liverpool, observed in this very frank communication, dated 3 September, that:

> The airship scares continue harmlessly. The Chief Constable of Lancashire is clean off his head over them. He has enlisted 20,000 special P.C.s for the war and they have to earn their living. I am convinced that Barrow is cracked on the subject. There are so many iron foundries in Furness that at night the glare of the smoke in the sky are enough to create airships whenever the wind & clouds are right.

He attached the following listing and analysis of what he called 'a scare we had the other night':

AIRSHIP? 26th/27th August 1914.

(a)	8.45 pm	Seen at Southport – one observer; details not forthcoming.
	9.10 pm	Reported at headquarters, Mersey Defences, by Head Constable, "Zeppelin seen by two gentlemen."
(b)	10.40 pm	Airship reported observed sailing towards Liverpool from Wallasey, showing three white lights.
(c)	11.57 pm	"Airship of cigar shape flashing white light 400 feet up at Corporation Pumping Station."
(d)	1.10 am	Sentry at Seaforth fired at what was believed to be an Airship.
(e)	2.05 am	Sentry at Showick Bridge. Aircraft over New Brighton flashing lights.
(f)	2.30 am	Yellow light in the sky going towards Runcorn, seen from Wallasey.
(g)	3.15 am	Police Southport saw very bright light flashing in the sky, higher than any building, over mouth of Mersey.
(h)	9.30 am	Report from Bury – G.O.C. East Lancs Division.

SOME PROBABLE EXPLANATIONS

(1)	Perch Rock or Seaforth Searchlights (e) and (g)
(2)	Flashes from Electric Overhead Railway (b)
(3)	(c) is highly improbable; at an altitude of 400 feet an airship would be seen by more than one individual.
(4)	The discrepancy between report (a) received by Southport Police and statement (b) received at Defence Headquarters, is significant.

These reports prompted the Commander-in-Chief of Western Command to ask the War Office to send Lieutenant Hucks to Liverpool, but Brancker replied that Hucks could not be spared for this purpose.

More sightings continued to be reported. Two airships were seen travelling over Little Hilton, near Bolton, soon after dawn on 27 August. The press censor stopped this from being published at the time, but no reason was given.

F.H. Glew, a surgical radiographer in Brixton, London, wrote to the War Office saying that he heard the propellers of an airship at 1.15 a.m. on 28 August. He also saw two searchlight beams shoot from the vehicle. At about this time, sightings were made at the mouth of the Ribble River and at Bury. At Liverpool, '… an airship is consistently reported in the neighbourhood of HMS *Erin* – appearances at Barrow having ceased.'

Even the captain of this battleship was certain that aircraft were active in the area. One story claimed that on 13 August a spy was caught onboard this vessel who had important plans on his person. Whether true or not, it does show that everybody was alert to any kind of German threat.[15]

On Southport Promenade, an airship was seen at very low altitude going north to south on 1 September, between 11 a.m. and midday. The action shifted to Scapa Flow in the Orkneys on 5 September. Seaplane No 156 was sent to search for a mystery aircraft. A report had claimed that it had gone over Hoy Island in a southerly direction, but the search failed to find anything.[16]

Also on 5 September, the crew of a police boat patrolling the River Thames off Woolwich Arsenal saw an egg-shaped object pass over their boat at 9.05 p.m. The object followed the course of the river, and was in view for 2 or 3 minutes. The press attributed these sightings to the flight of a naval airship. Brancker knew nothing of such a flight.

MO5 was informed that, at 4.30 a.m. on 6 September, an aircraft was over Ashton-under-Lyne, Lancashire. It carried a green and red light and a very brilliant flashlight appeared occasionally as it went eastwards. Brancker noted:

This was not one of our aircraft, naval or military. I cannot understand why red and green lights and brilliant flashlights should be shown except with a view to signalling to secret agents below.

Why not depute some intelligent individual, perhaps a good private detective, and instruct him to set out to obtain more details about these repeated occurrences?

So far as we know, Military Training did not act upon this suggestion. An equally intriguing report came from Flight Commander Rathborne of Felixstowe Royal Naval Air Station, Suffolk. As soon as he returned from a patrol, he logged this report:

At 5:35 a.m., 6th September, whilst on patrol half way between the Sunk and Shipwash lightships, I sighted an airship, with a silver coloured envelope on the horizon. I was flying at 1,300 feet at the time. I at once started to follow her, and did so for about ten miles, when she disappeared into the haze, and I was unable to pick her up again. The estimated position of the airship is from 25 to 30 miles south of Orfordness. The airship appeared to be steering south-south-east.

Owing to haze and distance it was impossible to distinguish any details, such as cars. The shape appeared to be similar to the Astra Torres, and the sun showed up the silver colour of the envelope clearly.[17]

That evening, at 10 p.m., the loud throbbing of an engine was heard by a number of people above the village of Cononley, North Yorkshire. Although the craft itself was not visible, it was heard going towards Skipton.[18]

The Customs Office at Lowestoft reported on 7 September that a Grimsby trawler had sighted an airship while fishing 18 miles east by north of Smith's Knoll. The airship had bright lights and eventually disappeared to the south-east. Details of date or time of this sighting were not given.

At 7.15 p.m., on 8 September, two airships were seen over Brixton. An aircraft was sent from Hendon to investigate, without any success. Yet, on the ground lots of witnesses saw the airships.[19]

It is worth noting that few British flights were made at night. Major Longcroft, Commander of No. 1 Squadron, Royal Flying Corps (RFC), made this point clear in a letter dated 29 October 1914:

> I have given orders to Officers Commanding Detachments that no night flying will be done on service machines until urgent necessity arises, as I consider that as the pilots have had no previous experience, the risk of damage to machines is considerable.[20]

Military officers saw a Zeppelin-type airship travelling very fast eastwards over the Needles, Isle of Wight, at 2.50 a.m. on 9 September. That evening, there were two reports from London. At 9.30 p.m., an airship was seen passing over Putney Heath. It was suggested that this was caused by searchlights at Charing Cross. A few minutes later, a Mr Wilding saw a cigar-shaped airship, which made a buzzing sound and passed over Lee Green, headed for Mottingham. It disappeared behind a cloud and left a light smoky trail.[21]

In south-east Scotland, the aeroplane rumours continued apace. Uneasiness was prevalent in various districts to the south of Dumfries, including Kirkbean and Carsphairn, on account of the suspected passage of an aeroplane during the night of 8 September.[22]

During late August and early September, the book illustrator Hugh Thomson was touring Galloway and the Carrick in order to make drawings for a forthcoming volume about the district. He chose an unfortunate time to do his work as he was subjected to much annoyance and hindrance by the authorities owing to what he called the 'Galloway German Spy Scare'.[23]

Tragedy

A small station was set up at Hendon, north of London, to protect the city against aerial attack. For a few days after the outbreak of war there was only one unarmed aircraft to protect London, and for several months the priority was to send aircraft to France and other theatres of war. In his recollection of his war experiences, Sub-Lieutenant E.B. Beauman noted this tragic incident that occurred in September 1914:

A R.N.V.R. [Royal Naval Volunteer Reserve] Officer in charge of a small captive balloon had been posted to us, and every evening he used to ascend to a height of about 500 feet and keep a look-out over LONDON for an hour or two. One dark night, he signalled down that he observed a large hostile airship approaching LONDON at a rapid pace, flashing red, green and yellow lights.

On hearing this report, a civilian pilot – who was in reality manager of the aerodrome and had been granted the temporary rank of Flight Lieutenant – immediately went up alone in a Henri Farman. He naturally could see nothing and in attempting to land, injured himself fatally.

In the meantime, the balloon observer had signalled down that he was very sorry, but that he had discovered that the lights he had seen were not those of an airship, but were in reality the star 'Vega'.

This period was also remarkable for the number of panic messages which came in from all parts of the district from civilians who thought they had heard or seen hostile aircraft. Needless to say, none of these reports were of any value, and wasted a great deal of time.[24]

The Chief Constable of Sutherlandshire at Dornoch forwarded the only Scottish report in the files:

At twenty five minutes to two a.m. on Sunday last 13 September, Dr Henderson, who was staying with us, knocked me up, announcing that an aeroplane was passing. I immediately got up, so did my wife and daughter. There was a brilliant light fairly high in the sky – well above the line of the hill to the west of Tain. It was proceeding rapidly in a westerly direction, we all looked at it through binoculars, but we could not see anything but the light, although Dr Henderson said he thought he detected something like a wheel going round. Dr H. and I went downstairs and out to the front gate. I got the light between me and a horizontal and upright bar, and in this way saw that it was proceeding to the west and undulating, when it reached what we thought was Edderton it suddenly disappeared. Then we noticed that there was a fog around Struie Hill, and immediately after, the light reappeared, as if it had passed through the fog. A minute or two later it disappeared from view gradually. I have no doubt at all that it was an aeroplane.

The aeroplane, from the first time I noticed the light, seemed to be following the line of the Dornoch Firth. Altogether the light would have remained in my view for about 12 minutes, but Dr Henderson told me he had been watching it for some minutes before he knocked us up. It was of course nearby at that time, and he told us he detected with the naked eye, that it was not proceeding in a straight line but in waves. To make absolutely certain, however, he also tested it with and upright and horizontal before he called us. Dr Henderson also stated that he heard a noise before the light made its appearance on the bedroom window. He said it was not the noise of a gun, nor yet of a door banging, but something midway between both.

MO5 received three telegrams from the Chief Constable of Lancashire on the evening of 13 September. These noted the lights of an aircraft seen at Eccles, going towards Manchester, at 7.40 p.m. A bright light was seen shortly after 9.00 p.m. going towards Liverpool and then the subject of the third telegram said that a light passed over Lostock Hill, near Preston, heading for Chorley.

The next day, MO5 received another telegram from the Chief Constable of Lancashire. An aircraft had been seen at Newchurch at 9.20 p.m., going in the direction of Rochdale. Captain Ramsey at the War Office intelligence section told Kell:

It would greatly assist if, in cases of this kind, the source of the information were given. In many cases, where similar reports have been investigated, the information has been traced to unreliable sources.

Acting on this suggestion, Kell wrote to the Chief Constable of Lancashire for a detailed report on recent airship alarms.

A weary Brancker memoed Ramsey: 'Here we are again! I have acknowledged.'

In the centre of Birmingham, at 1.15 a.m. on 15 September, two police officers and several others saw a light going westwards. An aircraft was seen at Ince going towards Liverpool at 10.40 p.m. The best sighting occurred 15 miles east-north-east of Smith's Knoll light vessel. A brilliantly lit airship shot searchlight beams at the water. After circling a trawler and two nearby fishing vessels, it departed.

The next evening, the Chief Constable of Lancashire reported yet another airship sighting to MO5. Mr E.R. Crippen apparently saw a stationary Zeppelin at 10 p.m. near Sefton. This case was investigated by an intelligence officer, and it was discovered that the witness only described 'artificial lights' and not any type of airship. A letter from Major de Watteville sent to Captain Ramsey, dated 20 September, contained a postscript to the report:

Here is a sidelight on the Lancashire Constabulary and their ways. The most instructive point is that Mr Crippen is a personal friend of the Chief Constable and saw him on the morning of that day on which he saw the "airship". He was much impressed by the Chief Constable's opinions as to the presence of aircraft in Lancashire and straight away went and saw one.

Now Lancashire Constabulary have warned the Cheshire police; the latter had received strict instructions to look out for aircraft and are now seeing them for the first time.

Early on 17 September, two more reports were received by MO5 from the Chief Constable of Lancashire. These related to aircraft seen at Stretford, near Manchester, going in the direction of Warrington at 12.30 a.m., and to an aircraft at Barnacre, near Garstang, 35 minutes later.

An airship was seen passing over Upnor at 8.20 p.m. going towards Gravesend. This worried the War Office as they thought it was impossible for an airship to fly in the heavy winds of that evening. The Commander-in-Chief of Eastern Command was ordered to make enquiries into this matter. Detective Inspector H. Grey interviewed the three witnesses to this incident, and made this report the following day:

AIRSHIP REPORTED NEAR UPNOR

I beg to report having seen Privates Mitchell, No. 6064, and Capon, No. 6742, both of H Company, 6th Battalion, Middlesex Regiment, now doing duty in H M Dockyard, when they stated that the airship was smaller than an ordinary airship, and bulkier. That when they first saw it, it was just above the trees, a long way off at the rear of Upnor Castle … That they could not give me a drawing of the airship as it was too dark to see it properly. They could only see the shape of it on the skyline and that it was shaped like a large pear.

I also saw PC 120 Callan, who stated that he was on the caisson at Upnor entrance when his attention was drawn by some dockyard workmen (whom, he does not know) to an airship. That it was cigar shaped and that he could see its shape on the skyline, and that it was a long way off. That he could not give a rough sketch of it as it was so dark, and he could only see the outline of it. That he could not say whether there was a car attached to it or not.

Neither the privates nor the PC could give any further particulars.

I beg to add that PC Callan and Private Mitchell were both on duty at the caisson at Upnor entrance and that Private Mitchell shouted and that brought Private Capon to the scene.

Also on 17 September, the Chief Constable of Lancashire supplied two more reports to MO5: at 9.15 p.m., a Zeppelin was seen flying over Bretherton, going towards Wigan and at midnight, a light was seen going towards Coniston. Brancker received this letter from Kell on 11 September:

I have received a letter from Col. Everett, Headquarters Staff, Scottish Command, Edinburgh, to the effect that there is a strong suspicion that a hostile aircraft has a base somewhere in the wilds of the north or west of Scotland. Lights from an aircraft have been repeatedly reported at night in the neighbourhood of the Firth of Forth.

Everett asks, by direction of the Commander-in-Chief, that I should send a reliable man up to take up this matter.

As you know, I am getting nightly reports from the Chief Constable of Lancashire that enemy airships are constantly being sighted between Liverpool, Manchester, and Preston. This may be the same aircraft? I have no suitable man to send up. Could you perhaps be able to send someone who has a knowledge of these things to carry out a thorough investigation on the spot? If so, I would suggest that he reports himself in the first instance to Col. Everett, and after local investigation, he might pass down to visit the Chief Constable of Westmorland and Lancashire. We might then be able to make a connected story. If you do send an officer up, I would be glad to give him introductions to the various Chief Constables.

On Brancker's orders, Captain Cox, of the Royal Flying Corps, was sent from Farnborough on 21 September. Brancker informed Cox's commanding officer:

He will probably not receive much local assistance and should use his own initiative to get to the bottom of the rumours.

Although it has not been possible to locate Cox's report of his investigations, it is known that he sent a telegram to Farnborough on 28 September at 2.43 p.m., stating that he was proceeding to Dumfries. At 5.45 p.m., on 30 September, he telegraphed that he was going to Liverpool and Manchester the next day. He returned to Farnborough on 2 October.[25]

MO5 was informed on 25 September:

During the past few days, various rumours reported of aircraft being seen over parts of Ireland. None so far definitely confirmed on reliable authority.

These reports were forwarded to Military Training. The Constabulary at Castlecaufield, County Tyrone, provided this report of a sighting made on 22 September:

Airship reported flying south-west about 7.15 p.m. from the direction of Dungannon to Ballygawley, high, colour not distinguished. Shape Parseval or Astra Torres, propellers heard distinctly. Information believed reliable, no lights visible.

The Constabulary at Belgooly, near Kinsale, County Cork, reported on 24 September:

A private named Langlan of the South Irish Horse, states when on sentry at 3 a.m. at Heathburn Hall this sub-district, observed a cigar-shaped airship with two bright headlights pass over the place at an elevation of 5,000 feet. Came from Cork city in north west direction and going towards Roberts Cove in a south east direction. He had a view of it for twenty minutes.

On the same day, the Naval Centre, Kingstown, noted:

Following received from Howth Point, begins Mrs McGuiness reports having sighted aeroplanes at great height coming from direction of Sutton and proceeding in a northerly direction sighted at 6:20 p.m. ends Mrs McGuiness is wife of Chief Officer Howth Point War Signal Station.

A note added:

Balloon seen by Military and others passing over Howth 6:15 p.m. last night at great height travelling north. Black colour with some white markings.

Commander Stevens, of the nearby Dublin Headquarters, telephoned MO5 at 12.45 a.m. on 26 September. He said that because an aeroplane had been sighted in the south of Ireland, he wanted to search the area for any secret depots. Kell replied, saying that such action was unnecessary, presumably because he did not think it would be possible for an enemy airship to operate so far away from the Continent.

Later in the day, the Naval Base at Aultsea, on Loch Ewe, on the north-west coast of Scotland, reported a sighting at about 4 p.m. of an airship of the Zeppelin type. It was observed by four residents, flying over Gruinard Bay, 3 miles north of the base.

A special constable reported an airship near Bromley, Kent, at 2 a.m. on 27 September. Other reports were made the same night but not given much credence.

The scare began to lose its force during October 1914. At 1.30 a.m. on 2 October, the operator at the Marconi station Ceunant, near Caernarvon, North Wales, reported that an aeroplane was circling over his station. The guards were strengthened, but nothing further was heard about incidents at this location.

On 9 October, a hostile airship was seen 9 miles from Dover at 6.45 p.m., and, at 10.15 p.m., an airship was observed over Eastchurch from Shirland Hall, Sheppy.

Two aeroplanes passed over Wexford Harbour, Ireland, at about 1 p.m. on 10 October. They were high up and travelling very fast from the south-east to north-west. The same day, the Ennis Constabulary, County Clare, observed an aeroplane passing west of the town at 6.39 p.m., carrying a bright light and travelling south to north-west.

There was a report from Portsmouth on 12 October that a large airship had been seen at 8 a.m. northwards off St Catherine's Point on the Isle of Wight.

Shortly before 9 p.m. on 13 October, a meteor was heard and seen over North Cheshire. The War Office received reports referring to explosions, bombs and artillery fire for a period of two hours that covered a 20-mile radius. An official report published the next morning spoke of two hostile airships operating during the night and dropping bombs over half a county.[26]

MO5 received two telegrams from the Chief Constable of Lancashire relating to this incident:

Large red light seen at 8:45 p.m. today passing over Runcorn Bridge Arches, Widnes from direction of Weston Point near Runcorn going in a north westerly direction. Immediately afterwards, an explosion was heard in Widnes and Runcorn. No report of damage.

At 8:50 p.m. today a very strong light was seen passing over Huyton railway station going in the direction of Liverpool. As soon as light disappeared a loud explosion was heard from direction of Liverpool.

Early the next morning he telegraphed MO5 again:

Further to my telegrams 13th inst. collated reports regarding aircraft appear to indicate two operating in South Lancashire. Namely first from the Cheshire direction via Widnes, Prescott, Aintree & Formby. Second from Yorkshire direction via Aston-under-Lyne, Rochdale, Bury, Bolton, Tyldesley, Leigh, Haydock, Wigan, & Skelmersdale. Also reported from Blackburn, Borough, & Chorley.

This new deluge of reports from Lancashire instigated another search of the area. The Australian Mounted Training Corps was selected to establish a temporary base at Chipping, 10 miles northeast of Preston. Their commanding officer, Captain Rushall, wrote to Western Command on 15 October:

I have the honour to inform you that I have drawn stores as arranged by GOC Western Command and have gone into all details with the staff – also with the Preston police.

Have established a temporary base at Chipping as suggested by Major James. The large number of reports shown me by Chief Constable of Preston police dated 13th October contain very clear evidence re the presence of aircraft in this and surrounding district and Westmorland during the last few days.

Am pushing out without delay, will forward all my reports direct to GOC Western Command unless otherwise ordered.

The Major James referred to in the communication was attached to Military Training. Unfortunately, this unit now disappears from the records, so we can only assume they didn't find anything.

Leeds police stated that an airship was seen at 9 p.m. on 16 October. It passed over Worsley Reservoir at a great height, showing a red light and travelled towards Dudley Hill, Bradford.

The presence of hostile aircraft in Scotland was also being given serious consideration, as this press release shows:

A matter of considerable importance – the presence of hostile aircraft in Scotland – has been recently receiving attention by the authorities, and it is necessary that the people in the country districts should have this brought prominently under their notice. Numerous reports of the presence of hostile aircraft in Scotland have recently been received. If these reports are true, it is probable that the hostile aircraft have been operating from a secret base in some unfrequented part of Scotland where they are able to obtain supplies of oil, petrol, and other stores. Such a base would probably consist of a store of oil and petrol concealed in an unfrequented locality, possibly in charge of an armed caretaker. A reward of £100 is offered by the military authorities to any person who gives information leading to the discovery of any place which is being used in this manner. Persons who observe aircraft of any description in this district should take note of their appearance and direction, and communicate at once with the nearest military or police office.[27]

Posters were put up in country districts with that information so that everyone was aware of what to look out for.

One morning, during this week, two sparling fishermen near Newton Stewart saw an aeroplane while engaged in their work. They were attracted by the noise of the engine and it came near enough to reveal two men inside it.[28]

The Galloway Hills, which form part of the Southern Uplands, were well suited as a location for a secret base. A writer at the time described it as being more of a wilderness than the better-known highlands. The military now began a search of the region. This continued for many months and became known as 'The Glen Trool Patrol'.

Sheerness Naval Centre telegraphed that an airship had been seen at 11.30 p.m. on 18 October over the Nore, in the Thames Estuary.

On 22 October, another message was received from Sheerness stating that Mr Cullas of the RFC had seen an airship over Folkstone at 11.20 p.m. Shortly afterwards they relayed a report from Sandwich police that an airship had been seen over the town at 12.15 a.m., travelling towards Ramsgate.

The Headquarters at Dublin telegraphed on 24 October that the police at Tralee, County Kerry, had seen an airship at 5 p.m., which travelled from Brandon Head to Kerry Head before returning to Brandon Head. It was last observed seawards, going in a northerly direction.

Between 7.00 and 7.30 p.m., on the evening of 27 October, an aeroplane showing a green light was seen flying over New Bridge and Woodlands, near Dumfries, going in the direction of Castle Douglas.[29]

Two more reports came from Ireland. About 6 p.m. on 28 October, a cigar-shaped airship passed north to south over Graiguenamanagh, County Kilkenny. At 10.30 p.m., the following evening, the Killantringan lightkeeper observed an airship over mid-channel, which rapidly disappeared westwards over Belfast Lough.

The west coast of Ayrshire produced a crop of reports during the course of the week. In Girvan there had been many stories of mysterious lights and airships flying about at night. There was something of a wild panic in the Colmonell and Barrhill district in connection with stories of a mysterious aeroplane making nightly visits between 10 p.m. and 4 a.m. The machine, in each case, was said to be travelling inland and carrying a headlight. One man claimed he heard the whirring of the engine.[30] The aeroplane was also said to have been observed in the Dunmore, Maybole and Pinwherry districts. One paper suggested that the £100 reward, which the Government was offering for the location of the secret base was having a very stimulating effect on some minds.[31]

A special constable saw two airships at St Stephens, near Canterbury, at 10.12 p.m. on 1 November. One of them appeared sausage-shaped and they were heading north-eastwards before they turned towards Dover. Five other witnesses also saw them and heard a faint humming noise.

The 7 November edition of the *Dumfries and Galloway Standard* devoted a full column to a discussion about a possible German aeroplane base in Galloway. The belief in its existence was strengthened by the strange lights seen to the east of Newton Stewart in the first week of November.

The staff of Culzean Castle, between Girvan and Ayr, heard an aircraft fly overhead at 7.30 p.m. on 7 November.[32] Thirty minutes earlier, police officers at the Surrey Commercial Dock, on the river Thames, saw a large airship head towards London.

On the evening of 9 November, soldiers at Filton, near Bristol, watched an intermittent light between 10.00 and 11.00 p.m.

No reports were received by the War Office for over a month, although many sightings continued to be made in Galloway. In strong wind and heavy rain, a white light was seen going southwards at Moniaive, Dumfriesshire around midnight on 10 November. The noise of its engine must have been very loud to have alerted the witnesses to this vision.[33]

Between Dumfries and New Abbey, at 7.30 p.m. on 17 November, lights were seen over Criffel Hill. Later, at 11.00 p.m., distinct signalling was seen from Ward Law Hill in Caerlaverock. The light appeared like a large star, which changed colour.[34]

An aeroplane was seen two nights later passing over the Solway Firth, to the south of Dumfries, at 5.30 p.m. Lights were seen by three people in different parts of Dumfries at 11.30 p.m., again over Ward Law Hill.[35]

Persistent rumours of strange lights and aircraft noises, which appeared nightly at 7.30 p.m. and 2.30 a.m. were prevalent in the New Galloway district of Kirkcudbrightshire. A number of residents kept a lookout on 19 November. At each time a large aeroplane with no lights was seen flying at a great speed.[36]

Away from the south-west of Scotland, the population of Thumster, near Wick, frequently scanned the skies and occasionally caught a glimpse of the aerial phantom.[37]

The last sighting, for the time being, in the Dumfries area, took place at Waterbeck. A moving light in the south-west was seen on 22 November by a party of people.[38]

The War Office did not get another report until 11 December. On that night, a lookout at the Needles saw an airship travelling northwards over St Catherine's Point, Isle of Wight, at 9.50 p.m.

An airship passed over Bernera, Stornaway, proceeding south-eastwards, at 6.30 p.m. on 13 December. The same night, at 11.30 p.m., a civilian claimed he saw aeroplanes on Pentreath beach at the Lizard, Cornwall. The military made an immediate search but did not find anything.

When the steamer SS *Ape* arrived at its home base, Great Yarmouth, late on the evening of 15 December her master immediately reported to customs that an airship had come close to his vessel. This was when they were positioned about 5 miles east of Trusthorpe, Lincolnshire. Captain L.S. Stansfeld reported:

I arrived at Yarmouth at 3:30 a.m., today proceeded to Custom House and then to SS *Ape* and interviewed the Master, G.F. Hiles, who reported as follows:

SS *Ape* was proceeding from Hull to Yarmouth and at 4:10 p.m., 15th inst. when just south of Protector Buoy sighted a black object astern which gradually drew nearer. Weather very hazy, sky one mass of unbroken cloud, wind west-northwest fresh breeze. Course south east by south 9 knots. As the object drew nearer it was seen to be an Airship and Master drew attention of two Seamen to it. She hovered astern about one mile distant at first, but gradually closed was low down 500 to 600 feet, speed slow. She soon turned and headed in towards land, rising as she did so. A car was then observed underneath amidships, as bow canted up car swung in towards stern which showed it was not rigidly fixed to airship. As she rose speed increased and she was gradually lost sight of in haze and increasing darkness. Colour and shape could not be distinguished as upper part was always in thick haze, the car, which seemed a good distance below, was much clearer. If it had not been for the car hanging below and the whole thing moving against the wind, she might have been taken for a black cloud. However, he is prepared to take his oath she was an airship. Thinks he could just hear a buzzing noise but would not be certain, as his own engine room skylight close to bridge.

Under the hazy condition of weather would not like to state actual length but she was very large size. Considered she should have made the land in the vicinity of Mablethorpe.

The Master gave his evidence in an exceedingly clear and truthful manner and I can suggest no reason why his evidence should be doubted. I reached the Admiralty again 10:30 this morning. Weather report gives wind as west–north–west to west–south–west. 1 to 5. 16.12.14.

This report was considered to be evidence of a reconnaissance flight, prior to the German Navy's devastating bombardment of Hartlepool, Scarborough and Whitby on the morning of 16 December. No evidence has been found to support this theory, and the barometrical conditions were not right for a Zeppelin crossing at that time.[39]

Sheffield police, on 19 December, were informed that, at 6.30 a.m., two aircraft with searchlights had been seen flying over the north-western outskirts of the city.

In Ayrshire, there was a recurrence of the rumours of aeroplanes flying at night. On Friday 18 December, a Lendal Valley farmer saw the lights of three aeroplanes between 6.00 and 10.00 p.m. They came from the east and flew a considerable distance apart from each other. One of them passed so close that he could hear the throb of the engine. He observed them passing again on the evening of Sunday 20 December.[40]

They were also seen in Inverness-shire, where they caused considerable excitement in the days before Christmas 1914 in the parish of Laggan in Upper Badenoch. On 20 December, aeroplane lights were seen at Craigbuie.[41] On the same day, for 8 minutes, three lights and the sound of machinery was seen and heard by the Chief Boatman at Garron Point Harbour, County Antrim, Ireland. The airship came from the sea at 8.00 a.m. and passed over Carneal Mountain.

Seven miles to the north, at Cushendall, a teacher saw an airship with a bright light fly westwards at 7.45 p.m. on 22 December.

Three hostile aeroplanes, one displaying a blue light, passed over St Catherine's Point, Isle of Wight, Spithead and Hillsea on the morning of 26 December. Five hours later, at 10.25 a.m., an aeroplane was seen at Worthing and by an anti-aircraft detachment at Hove. But the weather was too bad to send an aircraft in pursuit. That evening, at 6.20 p.m., lights were seen coming from the sea at Dunfanaghy, County Donegal.

A sighting made on 27 December in County Tyrone, Ireland, was reported to MO5:

Headquarters, Irish Command,
Parkgate, Dublin.
30 December, 1914

Dear Colonel Kell,
Below I give report of Police Sergeant of Castlecaulfield re aircraft seen near that place on 27th inst ... Castlecaulfield. 28/12/14. I beg to report that on this date I received information that an aeroplane was seen convenient to this village at about 5.00 p.m. on yesterday evening, 27th inst. I made careful inquires and was informed by Henry Wilson and Westley Roan of Castlecaulfield, Robert Studders, Glassmullash, that while out for a walk at time stated, their attention was attracted by the noise of motor engines above them, and when they looked towards the sky they distinctly saw at a great height, and without lights, a long dark object, which they were satisfied was an aeroplane. The aeroplane remained in their view for fully three minutes, and came from the direction of Pomeroy, circling on towards Ballygawley and Dungannon, and then going in the direction of Cookstown and left their view. Those are three respectable young men, and from the result of my inquiry I am satisfied they are telling the truth, and that their statements are correct, so that I am satisfied that this is a genuine case.

Yours sincerely
I.H. Price, Major.
Intelligence Officer, GSIC.

Also on 27 December, between 8.00 and 9.00 p.m., several prominent Girvan gentlemen saw a seaplane over the Firth of Forth in the
clear moonlight. They were able to watch it for a considerable time
as it made evolutions over the Firth.[42]

A blue light was seen at Ramsgate at 6.15 a.m. on 29 December.
And, before daylight on 30 December, a milkman with his cart travelling from Dornock to Annan, saw a large biplane travelling quickly
northwards.[43]

References

1. 'Editorial Comment. The War and Aircraft', *Flight*, No. 295, No. 34, Vol. VI, 21
    August 1914, at: www.flightglobal.com/pdfarchive/view/1914/1914%20-%20
    0871.html.
2. 'Submarine Scout Class', The Airship Heritage Trust website at:
    airshipsonline.com/airships/ss/index.html.
3. *Lancashire Daily Post* (Preston), 8 August 1914.
4. *Millom Gazette*, 14 August 1914.
5. PRO Air 1/187 15/226/4, *Diary of Patrols for 9 August 1914. Royal Naval Air Station,
    Great Yarmouth.*
6. *Ulverston News*, 15 August 1914.
7. *Penrith Observer*, 18 August 1914.
8. *Cumberland News* (Carlisle), 22 August 1914.
9. PRO Air 1/653 17/122/486, August 1914–May 1915, *Instructions Regarding Action
    to be Taken Against Aircraft.*
10. *Cumberland News*, 22 August 1914.
11. PRO Air 1/889 204/5/671, August–September 1914, *Miscellaneous Telegrams on
    Aircraft and Personnel Movement from Dover.*
12. PRO Air 1/889 204/5/671, August–September 1914, *Miscellaneous Telegrams on
    Aircraft and Personnel Movement from Dover.*
13. *Dumfries and Galloway Courier and Herald*, 29 August 1914; *Dumfries and Galloway
    Saturday Standard*, 29 August 1914.
14. PRO Air 1/2387 228/11/30, *War Experiences of Wing Commander Bromet, 1914–18*
    (unpublished).
15. *Ulverston News*, 15 August 1914.
16. PRO Air 1/188, *Diary of Patrols for 5 September 1914. Royal Naval Air Station, Scapa
    Flow.*
17. PRO Air 1/187 15/226/4, *Diary of Patrols for 6 September 1914. Royal Naval Air
    Station, Felixstowe.*
18. *Craven Herald* (Skipton), 11 September 1914.
19. PRO Air 1/565 16/15/88, *GHQ, Home Forces Daily Intelligence reports for periods
    5th August – 17th September, 1914.*

20. PRO Air 1/761 204/4/155, *October, 1914 – September, 1916: Home Defence, Night Flying.*

21. PRO Air 1/565 16/15/88, *GHQ, Home Forces Daily Intelligence reports for periods 5th August – 17th September, 1914.*

22. *Dumfries and Galloway Courier and Herald*, 9 September 1914.

23. *Galloway Gazette* (Newton Stewart), 12 September 1914.

24. PRO Air 1/2386 228/11/5, *War Experiences of Lieutenant E.B. Beauman, 1914–18* (unpublished).

25. PRO Air 1/826 204/5/150 *Reports re hostile aircraft in North and West of Scotland. Asking for a RFC officer to investigate the situation.*

26. PRO Air 1/720 36/1/6 *G.H.Q. Home Forces, London, Intelligence Circular, No. 6, May, 1916.*

27. *Galloway Gazette* (Newton Stewart), 17 October 1914.

28. *Galloway Advertiser and Wigtownshire Free Press* (Stranraer), 22 October 1914.

29. *Dumfries and Galloway Courier and Herald*, 28 October 1914.

30. *Carrick Herald & South Ayrshire Advertiser*, 30 October 1914.

31. *Galloway Advertiser and Wigtownshire Free Press* (Stranraer), 5 November 1914.

32. *Ayrshire Post* (Ayr), 13 November 1914.

33. *Dumfries and Galloway Courier and Herald*, 14 November 1914.

34. *Dumfries and Galloway Saturday Standard*, 21 November 1914.

35. *Dumfries and Galloway Standard and Advertiser*, 18 November 1914.

36. *Dumfries and Galloway Courier and Herald*, 21 November 1914.

37. *John O'Groat Journal* (Wick), 27 November 1914.

38. *Dumfries and Galloway Courier and Herald*, 28 November 1914.

39. PRO Air 1/2320 223/33/3, *Airship Raids Jan–June, 1915.*

40. *Carrick Herald & South Ayrshire Advertiser*, 25 December 1914.

41. *Inverness Courier*, 25 December 1914.

42. *Carrick Herald & South Ayrshire Advertiser*, 1 January 1915.

43. *Wigton Advertiser* (Cumberland), 2 January 1915.

NINE

GERMAN AEROPLANES OVER SOUTH AFRICA

' ... a wonderful aeroplane with its fearsome headlight.'[1]

A mystery aircraft sighting was made in January 1914 by a resident of Pretoria, who was called out by his children to watch a shooting star. On going outside onto the verandah of his home, he saw a powerful light attached to what looked like an aeroplane. The light made a swishing sound as it circled over the town for a period of 90 minutes. At 11.30 p.m., it seemed to land on the nearby Law Court roof. Strangely enough, despite the long duration of this sighting, nobody else seemed to see this craft, even when it apparently made a landing. This suggests that it was a misidentification of a celestial object or perhaps a Chinese lantern.[2]

That was not the first UFO-type sighting in South Africa. During the Boer War (1899–1902) there were several sightings of what the soldiers called the 'Boer Signal':

Those who were with Butler's Brigade during the last war in this country, will remember the "Boer Signal" that followed the camp, and always appeared shortly after sundown as soon as the tents were pitched – that is, when there were any tents to pitch.

What bets were made, what quarrels took place, how men argued that the falling light was a signal to the Boers to show where the camping ground was. It took a long time to convince the men that what they saw was the planet Venus going to bed.[3]

The potency of aircraft to deter and intimidate the enemy was discovered way back in 1884, when a British balloon detachment was sent to Mafeking to aid a fighting force there. The unit stayed in Bechuanaland for a year, and the very sight of their captive balloon is said to have secured peace in the area.[4]

The Boers feared that the British would use free-flying balloons to bomb Pretoria in the opening stages of the Boer War; indeed, plans were made for such a strategy by Her Majesty's Balloon Factory, Aldershot, but they were never seriously considered.

In the actual war, the British used captive balloons, which carried one or two men, to spy on enemy positions. Their presence always upset the Boers who felt that all their actions were suddenly exposed and understood.[5] Although balloons were important at the siege of Ladysmith and for the relief of Mafeking, what seemed to be their greatest value was that: 'They were a symbol of scientific superiority on the side of the English.'[6]

The Transvaal Government feared the threat from the air so much that on, 24 October 1899, they ordered all telegraph offices to report any sightings:

Balloons – yesterday evening two balloons were seen at Irene, proceeding in the direction of Springs. Official telegraphists instructed to inform the Commander in Chief about any objects in the sky.

Pretoria received many telegrams in response. Any bright light in the sky was shot at, but their bullets had no effect, mainly since their targets were stars and planets rather than enemy aircraft. A typical telegram from Vryheid reported:

Airship with powerful light plainly visible from here in far off distance towards Dundee.

Telegraphist at Paulpietersburg also spied one, and at Amsterdam three were seen in the direction of Zambaansland to the south-east.[7]

The use of balloons in these conflicts, even though they had a very limited role, might have sensitised the population to watch out for aerial phenomena at the outbreak of the First World War. Certainly, the Germans had the perceived strength of 'scientific superiority' this time.

The sightings of numerous aerial objects multiplied in August 1914. In the first few days of the month, early one morning, the men of the Jeffreys Bay fishing fleet saw an airship heading for Cape Town.[8]

Rumours quickly spread that an aeroplane was operating in the north-western parts of Cape Province, yet the most substantial report was of an airship:

> We are all very excited on account of an airship that passes over here (Clanwilliam) almost every night. Last night [13 August?] a lot of young fellows watched for it, and when it came one of them rushed to call me, but when I got out it had passed on in the direction of Lambert's Bay [in the west]. The idea is that it belongs to German South-West Africa, and that it is sent to spy upon the seacoast.[9]

Aeroplane, rather than airship, sightings proliferated in the neighbourhood of Cape Town. At 7.30 p.m. on the night of 13 August, several residents of Sea Point saw a mysterious aeroplane flying over Table Bay.[10] A reporter from the *Cape Argus* newspaper interviewed one of a trio of ladies who claimed they saw this craft from Sea Point on the same night. She said:

> It was about twenty minutes to seven, when a friend and myself were on our way home to dinner. We were near the post office at Three Anchor Bay when I chanced to look upwards. For a moment I could scarcely believe what I saw, and my startled examination having attracted the attention of my companion,

she also looked up and saw what looked like two pieces of wood about twelve feet long gliding horizontally through the air at a great height. At the time we saw the biplane – for such it must have been – it was between Robben Island and Mouille Point. It was travelling at great speed, and we gazed at it wonderingly for about the space of two minutes, when it disappeared in the mist over the far side of Signal Hill.[11]

In the early hours of 14 August, two independent reports were made of the aircraft by witnesses on the Cape Peninsula.[12] To the north-west at Williston and Fraserburg the craft was seen heading towards the east.[13] In the evening, thirteen people saw the headlight of an aeroplane at 10.15 p.m. It was observed through the clouds over Riversdale and it went in the direction of Mossel Bay (in the south-east).[14]

An aeroplane was seen over Worcester, in the west, by fifteen people on Ashton railway station on the night of 16 August. They said it carried a strong headlight, like those used by motor cars.[15]

A report in the *Cape Argus* of 25 August mentions that an aeroplane was seen going from east to north at Oudtshoorn. This could either have been on 16 or 23 August. It also states that, at 9.30 p.m. on Tuesday night, a bright star behind clouds was thought to be the headlight of the aeroplane. The direction of the clouds made the star look as if it was going westwards. This was with on the night of 18 or 25 August.[16] At 5.30 a.m. on 17 August, the aeroplane was seen again in the direction of Mossel Bay by witnesses at Ashton Station.[17]

The aircraft made a return visit to Sea Point on the morning of 17 August. An unnamed lady saw the machine and heard its engine.[18] Later in the week, the craft's headlight was seen in the evening at Sea Point. Then it made an appearance over Signal Hill on the morning of 20 August. The *Johannesburg Star* cautioned its readers that this sighting was possibly caused by a large box-kite and that they should not be alarmed by its appearance.[19] At 5.00 p.m. it was seen on the same day by local residents. Some who viewed it through binoculars claimed it was definitely an aeroplane, but others were not so sure. The next morning, it was seen hovering over Signal Hill for a short time before shooting off towards Lion's Head. It reappeared over the hill, slipped behind it and then reappeared in the direction of Cape Town. There were hundreds of witnesses to this mysterious light that was at a considerable height above the ground. It regularly went into and out of view, and finally disappeared at 1.00 p.m.[20]

As might be expected, these sightings sparked off many more reports and a torrent of speculation. A sceptical correspondent advised the editor of the *Cape Argus*:

You would do a kindness to the public if you would further explain that the supposed Sea Point 'aeroplanes' are myths. There is a hawk or similar bird that flutters over the hill, and there is a toy kite being flown by a little boy who has spoofed the public. Do aeroplanes flap their wings, remain stationary, or are they connected to terra firma by a piece of string? These silly rumours are on a par with the idea spread around that there are 20,000 German soldiers in German South-West Africa, the actual amount being less than 3,000.

Yours etc.
H.P.S.[21]

A witness was less than pleased with H.P.S.'s explanation:

I would just like to assure 'Mr H.P.S.' that I, together with four other gentlemen, saw the aeroplane or hydroplane, last Thursday evening (20 August) at about 9.45. At the time it was seen, it was travelling at a good height over the sea in an easterly direction. It subsequently descended and disappeared from view; in the course of this flight it displayed at intervals red and green lights. We saw it distinctly with the naked eye, but had a better view of it with field glasses which we were using. I am quite aware that a box kite is to be seen occasionally at Sea Point, but then, as I have said before, a box kite is not an aeroplane, at least to ONE WHO KNOWS.[22]

To show solidarity, another of the witnesses calling himself 'One Who Knows' confirmed that he 'had the pleasure of seeing this aeroplane'.[23] H.P.S. counter-attacked by insinuating that those who roam abroad at night are more likely to see visions.[24] Support was given to H.P. S. by another letter writer calling himself 'Headlight' who felt that the four witnesses should consult the Observatory to 'tell them which particular star "caught them bending".'[25]

According to 'A.E.P.', a most extraordinary encounter with an aeroplane took place off the south coast:

> When on her journey from Durban to Cape Town on Tuesday week [18 August] the SS *Kathlawur* sighted an aeroplane and as it came nearer and nearer to the ship it appeared to be about to swoop down upon her. Eventually it came so close that it touched the wire strung from mast to mast of the vessel, and forms part of the wireless apparatus that the ship carries. One of the passengers on board asserts his belief that it was the intention of the aeroplane pilot to cut the wire, but it failed, and so hurried away. All the passengers of SS *Kathlawur* as well as the officers and crew, saw the aeroplane, while a number of Indians on board were so alarmed that they knelt down and prayed on deck.[26]

It is a pity that no other witness or witnesses came forward to support this fantastic story.

Later, on that same Tuesday 18 August, railway engineers at Kykoedie saw the headlights of a craft.[27] This was explained as the reflection of searchlights used by a man-of-war based at Simon's Town. However, one of the witnesses telephoned the newspaper and told it that the light was seen 10 miles away to the north-west of their camp. This put the light in an entirely different direction from that of Simon's Town. In addition, the light moved towards the engineers' camp and then retreated. This movement and the direction of the light made them certain it was the headlight of an aeroplane.[28]

This night, and possibly other nights as well, people in Vryberg and in farms 30 miles away saw the aeroplane going from east to west.[29] On the same night, it was also seen at Bonnie Vale and Ashton, at 10.00 p.m., and at Robertson and Calvinia.[30]

By now, the aeroplane scare was in full swing. On the 19th, it made another round of appearances. The caretaker at Wynbery Reservoir on

Table Mountain saw a light heading for Hout Bay. A few minutes later, he saw it head towards him and go out of sight behind a higher part of the mountain.[31] Just over an hour later, at 10.30 p.m., people in Simon's Town saw the aeroplane going northwards, towards Cape Town.[32]

It was also heard going over Hopefield and seen flying at Vredenburg and in the Malmesbury district to the north of Cape Town.[33]

The sightings now became increasingly widespread. For example, on the night of 20 August, a light was seen to the north of Cape Town, at Porterville.[34] At the Royal Observatory the sightings were attributed to Venus, which was very bright at that time. The astronomers claimed that several nearby residents were watching the planet on this night in the belief that they were seeing the German aeroplane.[35]

An anonymous gentleman at Robertson, to the west of Cape Town, said he and several others were called out to watch the 'wonderful aeroplane with its fearsome headlight.' He and his fellow witnesses recognised the aerial fiend as Venus behind some light clouds, but he acknowledged that it gave off the 'most magnificent flashes of light'.[36]

Some 400 miles to the east of Cape Town, another light was seen at Humansdrop, St Francis Lighthouse, and by the police at Gamtoos Ferry. In the latter case, the machine seemed to carry powerful headlights, which flashed like searchlights.[37]

At 11.20 p.m., another strong headlight was seen heading for Steynsburg by two railway employees at Providence Siding.[38] This was a good 200 miles to the north of Humansdrop. If these were sightings of aircraft, there must have been more than one aloft or a single one flew on a 600-mile curve from Porterville to Steynsburg, which would have been highly unlikely.

At Bloemfontein, Orange Free State, the usual sort of searchlight was seen in several parts of the city at night time prior to the 21st. For a change, it visited the city on the morning of the 21st. The same morning, to the north, at Mafeking, a plane was seen going from north to west just before 8.00 a.m.[39]

Bloemfontein seemed to hold the pilot's attention, as it was seen and heard to make a humming sound the next morning.[40] A local correspondent noted that fire balloons had been released in the area, but it is not certain if they were launched before or after the initial sightings were reported.[41] The *Rand Daily Mail* stated:

> That the aeroplane must be German is the popular conception. That its occupant is utilising the darkness of night to carry out his spying operations preparatory to a German invasion of the Free State is also an accepted theory. Up to the present the advent of the mysterious aeroplane has been received with a good deal of scepticism. The outcome of the investigations made, however, point to the fact that it is quite possible that an aeroplane has been seen by the persons concerned.[42]

The fear of a German aerial spy even upset a golf tournament between the Metropolitan Gold and the Royal Cape women's clubs. They were playing at Green Point links, near Cape Town, when the army arrived at the scene. An officer told the golfers to leave the course as there was an aircraft in the sky. They all saw something bigger than a sea bird at a height of 500 feet, hovering and swaying over the same spot for nearly an hour. The officer said they would shell the object if it came any nearer, but this never became necessary. Many of the witnesses thought it was a box-kite and several men took the opportunity to have a round of golf while the course was clear of women.[43]

As these antics played themselves out on the golf course, the night of 21 August still had some surprises in store. The aeroplane was seen on the Peninsula at 7.35 p.m. and at St James and the Observatory at 8.20 p.m.[44] To the north-east of the Cape at Tulbagh, 'several trustworthy people' saw the aeroplane.[45] By 10.30 p.m., it was seen at Darling heading for Cape Town.[46] A hour later, it was at Graaff-Reinet. Many residents watched it heading for the south-east, and some said they heard a loud whizzing noise.[47] For a second night at Gamtoos, near Port Elizabeth, the police officers there said it crossed the sky, and appeared in the nearby localities of Kragga, Kana and Bushby Park.[48]

The next evening, Saturday 22 August, a bright light was seen in Oxford Street, East London. The open-mouthed wonder of the

crowds as they looked at this vision in the west, inspired one reporter
to write:

> An aeroplane it was, and then there was no doubt, for according
> to various observers it went through all the tricks in an up-to-date
> airman's repertoire. It looped the loop, squared the circle, spiralled
> up and spiralled down, volplaned, tangoed to the right and one-
> stepped to the left, advanced, retired, set to partners, hands down
> the middle, did everything except come nearer and descend in the
> Recreation Ground of the Market Square. And that searchlight,
> what did that do? It waxed and waned, appeared and disappeared,
> twinkled the other eye, and signalled in the Morse Code in English,
> Dutch German, Sanskrit, Volapuk and Pitman's shorthand.[49]

The reporter was confident that East London would be safe from rains
of bombs as the visitor reappeared on the night of 26 August, and it
was Venus again playing with their furtive imaginations. Nonetheless,
the 'coincidental' fusing of the electric lights does remind us of the
alleged effects of modern-day UFOs on electrical equipment.

A whirring noise was heard at 1.00 a.m. on 23 August by a farmer
in the Kantzkop district of Natal. It seemed to pass near his house
and the witness assumed it was an aeroplane flying without lights.[50]
In the evening, 40 miles to the north of Port Elizabeth at Zuurberg, the
aeroplane was seen heading towards Blue Cliff.[51] Further north-west, a
farm at Olifantsvlei reported seeing the aeroplane going southwards.[52]

More people saw what they thought was a German airship, full of
bombs and bloodthirsty airmen, on the night of 23 August. The lights
were seen in the western and eastern suburbs of Johannesburg. The
Johannesburg Star thought that this craft, which seemed to disappear
into the Sachsenwald Plantation, was a box-kite. It warned, 'Parents
who know that their children have box kites should not allow them to
experiment with such playthings while the war crisis lasts.'[53]

On the other hand, the *Rand Daily Mail* told its readers that the
lights were really caused by Venus and Mars. They took the trouble
to visit the Government Observatory where they discovered that
none of the officials there had seen anything unusual on the night

in question. They suggested that if people viewed the stars through field glasses they would appear to move because it is difficult to keep such instruments steady without a tripod.[54]

Dundee, and nearby Dannhausser, in the Natal, were both visited by something that carried lights on the night of 24 August.[55] The most interesting report of this date came from a person who said that when he visited Old Morley district he saw through a hole in a wall two aeroplanes take off from a sea vessel. This ship was seen cruising between the Xora and St John rivers. The aircraft flew inland and then returned to the sea.[56] The *Natal Advertiser* was not very impressed with this story:

> ... how any vessel could possibly be 'observed cruising between the rivers St. John and Xora?' That particular part of the Indian Ocean is the highway between Durban and East London, and British ships are passing to and fro daily. It is, therefore, difficult to imagine how any vessel can be hovering about there fooling with an aeroplane. I have my doubts about that 'hole in the wall, in the Old Morley district'.[57]

Once more, large crowds of people at Dannhauser saw lights in the sky on the evening of Tuesday 25 August.[58] At 8.30 p.m., red and white lights on the stern of an aerial vessel were seen at Hoetjes Bay.[59]

In the area of Pretoria, stories of Zeppelins and foreign aeroplanes enjoyed a wide circulation. For example, natives in Derdepoort saw the aeroplane. One of them described it as a great big thing, with red and blue lights, and another with a big bright light which shone down to the ground.[60]

Over in Cape Province, the situation had already got out of hand. Reports of sightings came from Worcester, Swellendam, Robertson, Goudini and Nuy. In response, this message was posted on Worcester Court house:

> Notice: As it has come to my knowledge that kites and air balloons to which Chinese lanterns and other lights are suspended, are being sent up at night time in this town, notice is hereby given

that this must cease, as it causes needless excitement and unnecessary alarm at the present time.

J. W. KUYS, Magistrate, 19 August.[61]

Rumours about the aeroplane in Natal also caused problems for the forces of law and order. The natives of Durban were so frightened by the threat of destruction from the air that they were returning to their kraals (villages). In high-handed fashion, the *Natal Advertiser* noted:

> White men are able to listen to such rumours with calmness, well knowing that in ninety-nine cases out of a hundred, they have no foundation in fact; but with the natives it is entirely different. They have not all got access to the newspapers and are easily led astray by false and exaggerated 'rumours'.[62]

If the rumour was lacking foundation, why did the newspapers carry on publishing material that could only spread its acceptance? A cynical answer to that would be that newspapers thrive on sensation; but, when the sensation gets out of their control, they seek to contain it, ridicule it and divert their readers to other subjects of sensation. To allay the fears of the natives about the impact of the war between the European powers, General Botha issued a statement to them on 10 August. Part of it read:

> The Government ... trusts that the native will display their customary loyalty to His Majesty and the Union of South Africa, by going quietly about their daily work, and paying no heed to idle rumours, resting assured that the Government, as heretofore, will carefully watch over their interest in common with those of the other inhabitants of the Union.[63]

The *Natal Advertiser* reproduced the whole of the statement in order to calm matters. The next day, it advised employers not to repeat the silly rumours to their native servants. Their belief in what the white man said about 'the aeroplane' had already caused sixty 'boys' to leave the whaling companies at the Bluff, near Durban. Extra guards were put on the native compounds to stop cases of desertion, though this was rather late in the day – the railway was already trying to cope with the great number of natives wanting to go home.[64]

Elizabeth Klarer, a South African contactee, who was born in 1910, claims she saw a huge silver disc in the sky when she was a small child. The craft seemed to divert a 'planetoid' from colliding with the Earth. At her farm in the foothills of the Drakensberg she also saw a disc during a storm and a ball of light went into her home.

These events occurred during the summer of 1917. What is most interesting is that her native house-servant told her about the legends of Zulu sky gods, who had ascended into the skies and had promised to return. Perhaps these legends, combined with the fear of war, helped fuel this aircraft panic among the local population in 1914.[65]

After wondering how the phantom flier fuelled himself and his machine, and why he should conduct a reconnaissance at night when nothing can be seen, and why he should advertise his presence by illuminating the skies with his lights, the *Natal Advertiser* pontificated on the subject of rumours in general. It repeated, as another recent example, the story of a liner carrying 300 nurses, which sunk off the English coast. Having previously shown its racist biases, it now revealed its sexist colours:

> These things do not affect men very much, but we forget the women. Many a tender-hearted woman heard that particular rumour during the week, spent sleepless hours thinking of the horror of it, perhaps drawing a mental picture of the scene, perhaps only falling asleep to indulge in vivid dreams of some awful catastrophe.[66]

A report of an early morning flier came from Giebe Station, near Germiston.[67] Four hours and fifty-five minutes later, on Wednesday 26 August, it was seen at Tongvat. This sighting, at 8.55 p.m., was made from the sugar plantations on the coast.[68]

By now people, or at least the newspaper reports, were becoming more sceptical. The theory that the Cape Peninsula sightings were caused by Venus was repeated and given more credence.[69] To appease those who still feared that the German enemy might still prove a threat, on 28 August the Defence Department announced that anyone who saw an aeroplane in flight was allowed to shoot at it or use any other means to bring it down. If an aircraft was found on the ground, members of the public were told that they could try to capture it and its crew, and/or report it to the nearest police post.[70] This move was made with the confidence that no Union aircraft would be hampered by this proclamation, simply because the Union didn't have any.

UFO researchers have tried to make these sightings sound more mysterious by pointing out that, 'In that year there was not a single aeroplane capable of flying in the entire Union of South Africa; there wasn't even an airfield.'[71] UFO author, John Keel, conceded that, 'Only three or four flimsy, short-ranged biplanes existed on the entire continent.'[72]

What makes it less mysterious is that these flimsy craft were stationed in German South West Africa. In this country, the population had even collected £5,000 for a special aeronautical fund that was sent to Berlin, and in return they received two aircraft in April 1914.

One was a Roland double-decker biplane, which was capable of a 16-hour overland journey, and was stationed at Keetmanshoop. The other was an Automobil ind Aviatik double-decker. This was stationed at Karibib, a good 300 miles north of Keetmanshoop. They were fitted with a 'signal mirror and light', which could indicate their presence at a distance of 18 to 31 miles so that they could be tracked if they got lost.

The Commandant of the Troops, Lieutenant Colonel von Heydebreck, was in charge of these craft. Rather than being used for spying or bombing, the aircraft were intended as mail or diamond carriers, or for providing medical assistance for people in outlying districts. A civilian aircraft used for exhibition flights, owned by the Rudolf Hertzog confectionary company, was also based in the territory, but this did not have the capabilities of the military craft.[73]

A British aviator travelled on a ship with three German aviators to German South West Africa in April. He said that, since then one of these, Mr Bruno Buchener, had made a flight from Swakopmund on the west coast to German East Africa, and eventually arrived at Dar es Salaam. Lieutenant Alexander von Scheele established a base between Windhoek and the coast for the purpose of conveying diamonds. The third aviator was Herr von Zech, a representative of Aviatik Co. All of them were experimenting with their aircraft, especially in relation to how they coped with the tricky tropical conditions. They found that it was better to fly at night when it was a lot cooler. The British aviator confirmed that night flying was better because:

> … the bright skies of the Southern Hemisphere also make it pos-
> sible to discern the contour of the country, particularly so in the
> case of the Peninsula, where land and sea unite. You can always
> distinctly make out the coast line in the darkest night, the differ-
> ence between land and water being unmistakable.[74]

When asked about the aeroplane scare, the aviator was not that certain it had been caused by enemy aircraft. If it had been a plane, it would need petrol supplies throughout the country. Indeed, the distance from the nearest point in German South West Africa to Cape Town would have easily stretched the capabilities of their pilots and machines to their limit just for one or two trips. It is just conceivable that they could have been responsible for the sightings in the northern regions of the Union. However, the majority of the sightings took place in the regions of Cape Town, Port Elizabeth and Durban, which are all at the furthermost points from the German territories.[75]

As noted before, one witness said they saw two aircraft leave from a sea vessel, but this would be a particularly dangerous mission for an enemy to conduct. Even if the naval patrols were avoided, why take the risk of flashing a searchlight at the ground and advertise its presence?

Near the end of September 1914, a press report noted that there was only one aircraft left in German South West Africa. The aircraft, flown by Lieutenant Buchener to Dar es Salaam, was the exhibition aircraft owned by the Rudolf Hertzog Co. Early in August, the Roland biplane at Keetmanshoop had been wrecked beyond repair. This meant that just the Aviatik biplane was available to terrorise the whole of the Union of South Africa.[76]

These facts lead us to speculate that either some mysterious force was mimicking night-flying aircraft – a view that some ufologists would support – or simply objects, such as kites or planets, caused the witnesses to misinterpret them as aircraft. To support the latter case, we must remember that many witnesses did not know how many aircraft Germany possessed and were not likely to calculate the problems that would have to be overcome to visit them at night on a regular basis. The salient fact for them was that the Union was at war with Germany, which owned aircraft in the German territories, so it was easy to put two and two together to conclude that they would be using these machines to spy out their nation. With this knowledge, rumours encouraged by misperceptions of celestial phenomena and/or the activities of hoaxers, along with the propagation of the stories by the press and by word of mouth, would seem to be the major factors for this scare.

H.C. Marais, a correspondent to the *Pretoria News*, was aware that the Union could be the victim of balloon-flying jokers. But he thought that balloons could be used to their own advantage against the Germans:

Balloons may be made automatically dirigible, and they may even be so governed by certain machinery carried by themselves as to be destroyed after a certain time in the air. There is no insurmountable difficulty to send balloons off with certain prevailing winds to carry news to German South West Africa. A computation of the air-current, the adjustment of the clock-explosive, and a balloon may carry a batch of very instructive letters and drop them in German South West Africa, if the explosion be well timed.[77]

If we look at the reports, which appeared at the end of the panic, we can see that they had very little substance. In the last week of August, the aeroplane was said to have been seen in the district of Rustenburg.[78]

Several witnesses saw it hovering over Graaf-Reinet on the night of 29 August. It remained in the sky the entire night, but nobody shot at it because they were worried that it might be one of their own aircraft. The long duration of this sighting indicates that they probably saw a star or tethered balloon or kite.[79]

To the north of Vryburg, a light that flashed on and off was seen going towards the north-east.[80] On 30 August at 8.35 p.m., a gunshot disturbed the peace at Skinner's Court, Pretoria. Alfred Allen and a few other inhabitants of the hotel ran outside to find Mr Conje, who had fired off the shot to alert everyone to the presence of an aircraft in the sky. Mr Allen said he saw it flash its searchlights over the Leper Asylum, then it travelled away in a north-west direction towards German South West Africa, at an estimated speed of 50mph. This case should be treated with some suspicion. Conje was also the surname of a prominent military leader in the Boer War. The references to a Leper Asylum and to German South West Africa also indicate that someone was using this story to poke fun at the aeroplane reports.[81]

Ten people at the Wesleyan Masse, Brandfort, in the last week of August, saw something strange in the sky just after 9.00 p.m. The local correspondent believed this was a sighting of Venus setting. He pointed out that every 30 seconds it changed to red, then green, then back to its 'natural colour'.[82] Also at Brandfort, it was discovered that an 'aeroplane' had in reality been a kite with bicycle lamps fixed to it.[83]

On Monday morning, 31 August, people at Middleton, and passengers on a train, saw an aeroplane heading for Cookhouse, near Somerset East.[84] A writer in the *Natal Advertiser* complained about the vagueness of this report; but, no doubt with a shrug of his shoulders, he wrote, 'What is the good of worrying? Here I am, wasting time, when I ought to be moulding bullets.'[85]

Far to the north-west, in Sydenham, a suburb of Durban, that evening at 9.00 p.m., twenty Indian employees thought they saw the aeroplane.[86] Two hours later, in Bellair, Durban, a person heard a buzzing sound coming from the sky. He went outside with some field glasses and saw an indistinct shape in the sky, which carried a light.

It went out of view behind some hills, heading in the direction of Isipingo. At the same time, a train driver and his fireman saw the aeroplane as they passed through Bellair.[87]

The aeroplane passed over Sea View, near Durban, on 2 September at 9.00 p.m. Five women and two men saw it going towards the west. At its rear it carried a light.[88] And it made another appearance at Vryburg.[89] At Verulam, to the north of Durban, it was claimed that the aeroplane passed the district every two or three days.[90] On around 3 September, it was seen to the south of Vryburg at Taung and Pokwani.[91]

On Sunday 6 September, there were a couple more sightings. Just prior to dusk at Warmbaths, near Waterberg, Transvaal, several 'whites' witnessed something flying overhead. It was thought to be travelling at a height of 1,800 feet. The sound of the craft could be clearly heard, and one of the witnesses said it looked like a flying car. Another witness said he didn't shoot at it, because he feared it might drop a bomb on him.[92] At 9.00 p.m., probably one of the best sightings was made at Durban. The vehicle came from the sea and flew over the racecourse. The noise of its engines brought many people outdoors. They saw that it carried three lights and travelled at a rapid rate.[93]

One plantation's sugar crop was found to have been burnt after a visit from this craft the previous night. Unfortunately, by now interest in the subject had waned, so despite having 'some authenticity behind it' no further details were supplied.[94] As a consequence, we are left to wonder if this was a case of aerial sabotage, land traces or sheer coincidence. Since modern-day UFOs are claimed to leave burn marks and similar types of traces on the ground after making landings, it would have been helpful if the report indicated what type of blaze occurred at the plantation.

An aerial vehicle with a headlight and a tail light was seen hovering over Utrecht on the night of 11 September. It finally headed south, towards Dundee.[95] In the second week of September, the aeroplane was still being seen in the district of Vryburg.[96] On 13 September, two Kaffirs tending their sheep ran home after being frightened by a light over Vryburg.[97] The next day it was seen, and heard making a humming noise, at Impendle, Natal.[98]

The last crop of sightings around Durban led a Pieterm Aritzburg optician and meteorologist to look for an answer to the aeroplane problem. His solution was not very original, as it was his view that it was caused by a planet, which was presently low on the horizon at 8.00 p.m. It was made more mysterious by evening winds that blew moisture into the western skies, making the planet appear and disappear behind the cloud coverage.[99]

The Annual Report for 1914 by the Secretary of Justice in the Union of South Africa even included a report, made on the 27 October, of a bright light associated with a buzzing sound, observed at Port Shepstone, Natal.[100] The Secretary of Justice had received many reports about the aeroplane during August, but he seemed to regard them as the product of 'the early exciting days of the War' when people 'saw visions and dreamed dreams … '.[101]

The 1914 scare was reviewed by Edgar Sievers in his book, *Flying Saucer uber Sudafrica* (Sagittarius Verlag, Pretoria, 1955).[102] In response to this, an old farmer contacted the author to say that while near Greyton, Natal, he saw the aeroplane one September evening in 1914. The machine was resting on the ground, and not far away he saw two 'German spies' filling a pail at a brook.[103] Why he didn't report it at the time, particularly since he believed he saw the activities of enemy agents, is hard to explain. As with other cases where people report events many years after they occurred, we must be cautious of the effects of wishful thinking, or a case of false memory.

When the South African forces invaded German South West Africa, they did come under attack from a single Taube monoplane. It dropped shells on them from a high altitude in late December 1914, but they found it was easily kept at bay by artillery fire.[104]

References

1. *Cape Argus*, 22 August 1914.
2. *Johannesburg Star*, 26 August 1914.
3. *Natal Advertiser*, 29 August 1914.
4. Walker, Percy, *Early Aviation at Farnborough: The History of the Royal Aircraft Establishment. Volume 1. Balloons, Kites and Airships* (London: Macdonald, 1971), p.12.

5. Walker, p.34.
6. Lynch, Colonel Arthur, 'The Role of the English Military Balloons in the South African War, by Colonel Arthur Lynch of the Boer War', a lecture given in Paris, 27 March 1902, published in *L'Aeronaute*, April 1902; Walker, pp.35–36.
7. de Souza, C.W.L. (ed.), *No Charge For Delivery* (Cape Town: Books of Africa, 1969), p.160; Farwell, Byron, *The Great Anglo-Boer War* (Toronto, Canada: Fitzhenry & Whiteside, 1976), p.57; Raugh, Harold E., *The Victorians at War, 1815–1914: An Encyclopedia of British Military History* (Santa Barbara, California: ABC-CLIO Ltd, 2004), p.44; Holman, Brett, 'The Boer War in airpower history', Airminded website at: airminded.org/2010/04/19/the-boer-war-in-airpower-history/.
8. *Cape Argus*, 21 August 1914; *Cape Times*, 22 August 1914.
9. *Cape Times*, 15 August 1914.
10. *Cape Times*, 15 August 1914.
11. *Cape Argus*, 14 August 1914; *Rand Daily Mail* (Johannesburg), 19 August 1914; *Johannesburg Star*, 21 August 1914.
12. *Cape Times*, 15 August 1914.
13. Creighton, Gordon W., 'Saucers and South Africa', *Flying Saucer Review*, Vol. 8 No.4, p.20, quoting from *The Annual Report of the Secretary of Justice of the Union of South Africa, 1914*, chapter 8.
14. *Cape Times*, 21 August 1914.
15. *Cape Times,* 18 August 1914; *Rand Daily Mail*, 21 August 1914.
16. *Cape Argus*, 25 August 1914.
17. *Cape Times*, 18 August 1914; *Rand Daily Mail*, 21 August 1914; *Johannesburg Star*, 21 August 1914.
18. *Cape Times*, 22 August 1914.
19. *Johannesburg Star*, 21 August 1914.
20. *Cape Times*, 22 August 1914.
21. *Cape Argus*, 24 August 1914.
22. *Cape Argus*, 26 August 1914.
23. *Cape Argus*, 28 August 1914.
24. *Cape Argus*, 29 August 1914.
25. *Cape Argus*, 31 August 1914.
26. *Cape Argus, 31 August* 1914.
27. *Cape Times*, 20 August 1914.
28. *Cape Times*, 21 August 1914.
29. *Cape Times*, 19 August 1914; *Rand Daily Mail*, 19 August 1914; Creighton, p.20.
30. *Cape Times*, 20 August 1914.
31. *Pretoria News*, 20 August 1914; *Cape Times*, 20 August 1914.
32. *Cape Times*, 20 August 1914.
33. Creighton, p.20.
34. *Cape Times*, 22 August 1914.
35. *Cape Argus*, 21 August 1914.
36. *Cape Argus*, 22 August 1914.
37. *Cape Argus*, 21 August 1914; *Cape Times*, 21 August 1914; *Johannesburg Star*, 21 August 1914.
38. *Rand Daily Mail*, 24 August 1914.

39. *Cape Times*, 22 August 1914; *Rand Daily Mail*, 22 August 1914.

40. *Rand Daily Mail*, 24 August 1914.

41. *Cape Times*, 5 September 1914.

42. *Rand Daily Mail*, 24 August 1914.

43. Clark, Jerome and Farish, Lucius, 'The Phantom Airships of 1913', *UFO Report*, Vol. 7 No. 6, December 1979, p.63; *Johannesburg Star*, 26 August 1914.

44. *Cape Times*, 22 August 1914.

45. *Cape Times*, 22 August 1914.

46. *Cape Times*, 26 August 1914.

47. *Cape Argus*, 24 August 1914.

48. *Cape Times*, 22 August 1914; *Natal Advertiser*, 22 August 1914; *Rand Daily Mail*, 22 August 1914.

49. *Cape Argus*, 27 August 1914.

50. *Cape Argus*, 28 August 1914.

51. *Cape Argus*, 25 August 1914; *Cape Times*, 25 August 1914; *Johannesburg Star*, 25 August 1914.

52. *Johannesburg Star*, 25 August 1914; *Cape Times*, 26 August 1914.

53. *Johannesburg Star*, 24 August 1914.

54. *Rand Daily Mail*, 25 August 1914.

55. *Cape Argus*, 28 August 1914.

56. *Natal Advertiser*, 31 August 1914.

57. *Natal Advertiser*,, 5 September 1914.

58. *Cape Argus*, 28 August 1914.

59. *Cape Argus*, 26 August 1914.

60. *Pretoria News*, 26 August 1914.

61. *Johannesburg Star*, 25 August 1914; *Rand Daily Mail*, 26 August 1914.

62. *Natal Advertiser*, 27 August 1914.

63. *Natal Advertiser*, 27 August 1914.

64. *Natal Advertiser*,, 28 August 1914.

65. Klarer, Elizabeth, *Beyond the Light Barrier* (South Africa: Howard Timmins' Publishers, 1980), pp.17–24; Evans, Hilary, *Gods, Spirits, Cosmic Guardians* (Wellingborough: Aquarian Press, 1987), pp.151–153; Drake, Dr Raymond, *Cosmic Continents* (Madras: Guardian Press, 1986), pp.207–208.

66. *Natal Advertiser*, 29 August 1914.

67. *Johannesburg Star*, 26 August 1914.

68. *Cape Argus*, 28 August 1914.

69. *Johannesburg Star*, 28 August 1914.

70. *Cape Times*, 29 August 1914; *Rand Daily Mail*, 29 August 1914.

71. Clark, Jerome and Farish, Lucius, p.63; Creighton, pp.18–21.

72. Keel, John, *UFOs: Operation Trojan Horse* (London: Abacus, 1973), p.121; Lore, G.I.R. and Deneault, H.H., *Mysteries of the Skies* (London: Robert Hale, 1969), p.103.

73. *Cape Times*, 21 August 1914; Dale, C., 'Aircraft in the German Colonies': s400910952.websitehome.co.uk/germancolonialuniforms/hist%20aircraft.htm.

74. *Cape Times*, 22 August 1914.

75. *Pretoria News*, 2 September 1914; *Cape Times*, 5 September 1914.

76. *Pretoria News*, 21 September 1914.

77. *Pretoria News*, 2 September 1914.

78. *Rand Daily Mail*, 1 September 1914.

79. Creighton, p.20.

80. Creighton, p.20.

81. *Pretoria News*, 31 August 1914; *Cape Argus*, 1 September 1914; *Rand Daily Mail*, 1 September 1914.

82. *Johannesburg Star*, 31 August 1914.

83. *Cape Times*, 5 September 1914.

84. *Cape Argus*, 31 August 1914; *Natal Advertiser*, 1 September 1914; *Cape Times*, 31 September 1914; *Rand Daily Mail*, 1 September 1914.

85. *Natal Advertiser*, 5 September 1914.

86. *Cape Argus*, 5 September 1914.

87. *Natal Advertiser*, 1 September 1914.

88. *Natal Advertiser*, 4 and 5 September 1914.

89. Creighton, ibid., p.20.

90. *Cape Argus*, 5 September 1914.

91. Creighton, p.20.

92. *Rand Daily Mail*, 10 September 1914; Creighton, p.20.

93. *Natal Advertiser*, 7 September 1914.

94. *Cape Times*, 18 September 1914.

95. Creighton, p.20.

96. *Cape Times*, 11 September 1914.

97. Creighton, p.20.

98. Creighton, p.20.

99. *Cape Times*, 18 September 1914; *Johannesburg Star*, 18 September 1914.

100. Creighton, ibid., pp.20–21.

101. Creighton, p.20.

102. Creighton, pp.18–21.

103. Creighton, pp.18–21. Gross, Patrick, URECAT – UFO Related Entities Catalog, at: ufologie.patrickgross.org/ce3/1914-09-safrica-greytown.htm.

104. *Cape Times*, 19 and 22 December 1914.

TEN

PHANTOM MOTOR CARS, COSSACK ARMIES, SIGNALS AND SPIES

Along with the wider social context of the aircraft scares, we should also take into account the other rumours that circulated either in parallel or in conjunction with them, or rumours that had similar stimuli but were interpreted differently.

In Germany a great wave of patriotism swept the nation. Fear of enemy agents grew so much that in Leipzig a mob attacked a German artillery officer because he had a dark complexion and black hair. His appearance suggested to the crowd, who beat him about the head with umbrellas and sticks, that he was a Russian in disguise.[1]

Such public indignation towards anyone who looked remotely like a Russian was fuelled by an order published in the *Leipziger Volkszeitung*, supplied by Von Laffert, the General in Command of Leipzig. He asked people to look out for any foreigners, 'especially Russians', who might be acting suspiciously.

In contrast, the Director of the Stuggart police was more sceptical of the population's powers of discrimination. He noted:

The populace is going absolutely mad. The streets are crowded with old women of both sexes [*sic!*] who have nothing else to do but disgrace themselves. Each sees in his neighbour a Russian or French spy, and imagines that it is his duty to thrash both him and the policeman who intervenes, till the blood flows; if not that, then at least to cause an enormous crowd to gather in giving the alleged spy over to the police. Clouds become airmen, stars are mistaken for airships and the dross-bars of bicycles are thought to be bombs; bridges have been blown up, telegraph and telephone wires cut in the middle of Stuttgart; spies have been shot and water supplies poisoned! It is impossible to imagine what will happen when serious events really come.[2]

An example of one of these stories came from Metz, on 3 August. It was claimed that a French doctor, with two officers in disguise, were caught trying to put cholera bacilli into the water supply. This was later found to be a pure invention, though not in time to prevent panics about infected water supplies from erupting elsewhere in Germany.[3]

Spies riding in motor-cars also became quite a fashion. One report alleged that eighty French officers disguised as German officers attempted to drive towards the Rhine province in twelve cars.[4] The most influential story noted:

Several motor-cars with ladies in them, taking gold to Russia, are on their way across Germany. They must be stopped and a communication sent to the nearest military or police station. The occupants of the motor-cars carrying gold to Russia are said to have transferred the precious metal to cyclists dressed as bricklayers.[5]

Soon the whole German population seemed to be on the lookout for French and Russian motor-cars loaded down with gold. The comedy of the situation soon turned to tragedy:

In Leipzig a doctor and his chaffer have been shot, while between Berlin and Koepenick a company of armed civilians on the look-out for Russian motor-cars tried to stop a car. The chauffeur was compelled to put the brakes on so suddenly that the motor dashed into a tree, with the result that the occupants – several persons connected with the army – were hurled onto the road and received dangerous injuries.

In Munich a chauffeur was shot dead by a sentinel because he did not stop soon enough. Even children are not spared in this degrading fear of spies. Near Buren (Westphalia) the twelve-year-old daughter of a town councillor Buddeburg in Bielefeld was returning with her mother from Marburg in a motor. Somebody must have telephoned that the car was suspect, for the Landwehr Society placed armed sentinels at various points in the road. They cried 'Halt!' to the chauffeur; just as the car was stopping, shots were fired, and the girl sank dead in the arms of her mother.[6]

Almost in despair it was reported that:

This fatal hunt for motor-cars has claimed yet another victim. Recently an Austrian countess was shot while working for the Red Cross, and now a cavalry captain and his chauffeur have been killed by a forest-keeper on the lookout for a Russian automobile.

The General Staff has again and again issued the most urgent demands that this unhappy hunt for foreign motorists – which has already caused the death of several good Germans – should cease. It is unadulterated madness to search for enemy motors in our land. Neither enemy officers, nor cars loaded with gold, are driving around in Germany.[7]

This rumour and others did provide the chance for the population to do something concrete against the perceived enemy, even though it was in reality a disastrous nonsense.[8]

British rumours

Britain also suffered similar waves of rumours, which had varying degrees of veracity. There was the North Sea battle rumour, which produced an eyewitness report of a (non-existent) battle between French and German fleets off the Yorkshire coast. The masts of nineteen sunken German ships were even reported to be visible off Spurn Point by one steamer captain! At Scapa Flow a seal was mistaken for the periscope of a German submarine, causing Admiral Sir John Jellicoe to send the whole fleet to sea, leaving the North Sea open to attack from the Germans and showing that the implication of just one rumour could easily cost hundreds, if not thousands, of lives and irrevocably change the fortunes of war.[9]

Snow on their boots

The Russians also featured in British rumours, but this time they were seen as saviours rather than gold-smuggling enemies. The story spread in the last fortnight of August 1914 that a Russian army was being shipped from ports at Archangel to northern Scotland. From there the troops were allegedly sent by train to English south-coast ports and then on to the Western Front in France and Belgium.

This rumour took such a hold on the nation's consciousness that it was still believed long after the war ended. Although most of the accounts were of the 'friend of a friend' kind, there were people who claimed to have seen and spoken to the Russian soldiers on the troop trains.[10]

The story spread equally throughout urban and remote regions of Britain. In the Yorkshire Dales:

> The oldest inhabitant is absolutely certain of the accuracy of the news, and comments gleefully on the demoralisation which will be produced among the Germans when they find Cossacks fighting against them on the western as well as the eastern frontier.[11]

As proof, many swore they saw the troop trains passing through stations on the way to the south coast, and it was alleged that twenty-seven trainloads of Russians had passed through Carlisle to Southampton.[12]

Unbridled by wartime censorship, the *New York Times* revealed that 72,000 Russian troops landed at Aberdeen on the night of 27 August 1914 and were transported by train to the ports of Grimsby, Harwich and Dover. Their information came from the passengers and crew of the Cunard liner *Mauretania* when it docked in New York on 3 September.[13]

Some of these stories claimed that as many as 500,000 troops could be in transit, and any unusual train delays or movements were attributed to their transportation. Mr G.R. Gifford saw 10,000 Russians marching down the Embankment, London, on their way to catch a train at London Bridge Station. A resident in north London saw a train full of Russians halted by signals at the bottom of his garden, and correspondents in Leith, Warwick, Tewkesbury, Gloucester, Dorking and Dover confidently reported seeing them.[14]

A wounded Russian soldier was claimed to have been treated at St Albans, and thousands of them were seen camping on Woolwich Common and Chiswick Green.[15] There were some amusing aspects to these claims, including the story of a Russian who jumped off the train at Malvern to order 300 'lunch sky baskets', the fair-haired hungry giants who ordered food at the pastry cook's shop in Oban, and the railway station chocolate machine that was put out of order because it was clogged with roubles.[16]

One person, Mr W.H. Champion, a Cardiff mining engineer, claimed that he had travelled on a steamer from Archangel to Newcastle along with 2,500 Cossacks who were destined for France. He even said he took photographs of the Cossacks but they were subject to an embargo by the press censor.[17]

The official Press Bureau finally responded to these claims by issuing this statement at 11.10 p.m. on 14 September 1914:

> There is no truth whatever in the rumours that Russian soldiers have landed or passed through Great Britain on their way to France or Belgium.

This scare was aptly summarised by the *Fleetwood Express*:

> Everybody has heard by now of the individual who saw Russian soldiers passing through a mainline station in this country and knew for certain that the occupants of the carriages of the train were Russian because there was snow on their boots![18]

More mystery cars

The nefarious activities of motor-cars were not restricted to the gold-carrying cars in Germany. A debate in the British House of Lords brought to public attention that motor cars were distributing anti-British propaganda in Ireland. The Earl of Desart said he was informed in September 1914 that a large motor car had travelled through three counties distributing this kind of literature, and the police were informed about it but nothing was done to stop it.[19]

THE SPY MENACE.

CAPTURE IN HIGHLANDS.

MOTOR CAR WITH WIRELESS.

Of late numerous and circumstantial reports of the presence of hostile aircraft in Scotland have been received by the military and police authorities. If these reports are true, it is probable these aircraft have been operating from a secret base in some remote and unfrequented part of the country, where they are able to obtain supplies of oil, petrol, and other stores. Such a base would probably consist of a concealed store of oil and petrol in charge of an armed caretaker.

Last week an important arrest was effected in a remote part of the Highlands near the East Coast, the arrested person having in his possession a motor car carrying a portable wireless apparatus, besides arms and ammunition. There can be no doubt whatever that the movements of British warships have been reported to the enemy by means of wireless or signal lamps used by spies to communicate with hostile submarines and supposed "neutral" trawlers. —"Glasgow Herald."

A motor car was captured containing wireless equipment in the Scottish Highlands, indicating that it was used to signal to enemy shipping or aircraft. (*The Inverness Courier*, 23 October 1914)

A YARMOUTH HOUSE WRECKED BY ZEPPELINS   A "GRAPHIC" PROPHECY OF 190   ANOTHER VICTIM OF THE YARMOUTH RAID

The Zeppelins have come at last, for three of them visited the Norfolk coast on Tuesday night and dropped bombs in the darkness. The middle picture at the bottom shows that "The Graphic" anticipated an air raid so long ago as May 22, 1909, though the present raid was made more fearsome by explosive bombs which killed four peaceful people—two of whom were women—at Yarmouth and at King's Lynn. Several bombs fell near Sandringham, and it is not improbable that the Royal estate was the objective of the airmen.

The British 1909 phantom airship scare was remembered as a prophecy of the aerial attacks of the First World War. (*London Graphic*, January 1915)

It is all too easy to forget just how much of a shock it must have been to witness death raining from the skies for the first time; another image of the houses in Yarmouth bombed by Zeppelin L3 on 19 January 1915. (Library of Congress)

In October 1914, in association with rumours of a secret base from which hostile aircraft were operating in Scotland, it was reported that in a remote part of the Highlands a person was arrested who owned a motor car that carried a portable wireless apparatus. The car also contained arms and ammunition, leaving no doubt that 'the movements of British warships have been reported to the enemy by means of wireless or signal lamps used by spies to communicate with hostile submarines and supposed "neutral" trawlers.'[20]

Many Zeppelin raids were linked with the activities of motor cars that seemed to be guiding them to their targets at night. The Admiralty sent out cars to search for a motor vehicle carrying lights associated with a Zeppelin seen on 23 January 1915 near Oxted. This was only a few days after the L3 and L4 had bombed Great Yarmouth on the night of 19 January 1915, killing four people in the process.

The L10 Zeppelin raided Northumberland on 15 April 1915. The following night, three airships raided the east coast of England, including the L6 Zeppelin that bombed Maldon, Essex. A 'mystery' car was seen travelling ahead of the Zeppelin. It was seen by two 'London ladies' passing through Lathington going towards Maldon. Mr and Mrs Woods saw the car headlights illuminate their bedroom and then heard the engine of a slow-moving car. Just a few minutes later, at about midnight, an old couple who lived a few miles away, in the village of Mundon, also heard the car passing by. Half-an-hour later, these independent witnesses heard the car make its return journey and noticed that its headlights were not so bright.

Strangely enough, the car should have passed a police station on its way to Maldon, but the officer on duty only saw a car containing people he knew going in the opposite direction at 12.30 a.m. The witnesses seemed to think that the car extinguished its lights and went into a field to pick up men who were signalling to the Zeppelin to identify its target.[21] Several miles to the east of Maldon, at Walton-on-Naze, a military patrol saw a powerful motor car going at a tremendous speed at the time the L6 was seen at Harwich. They tried challenging the car but it continued without slowing down, and they shot at it, to no avail. Efforts were put in place to track down this vehicle.[22]

Enemy signalling in Great Britain

Rumours about the presence of spies and signalling to enemy aircraft or ships became increasingly prevalent, and as a consequence became the subject of *Intelligence Circular No. 6*, which concluded that 89 per cent of the cases had a satisfactory explanation.[23]

Whatever their source or reason, such rumours and reports were a nuisance to the war effort. Munition factories lost output because they had to extinguish their lights every time there was the possibility of an air raid, and communications became congested with worthless stories. As a consequence, the War Office issued this circular in March 1916:

> On tracing the source from which these rumours have emanated it has in many cases been found that officers and soldiers, as well as civilians, who have heard reports or rumours regarding the possibility of air attack from other than official sources, have idly and recklessly repeated such reports.
>
> Further, statements received at General Headquarters during the past few weeks reveal the fact that observers reporting the presence of hostile aircraft have in repeated instances been unduly influenced, if not led to absolute hallucination, by the unnecessary communication to them by higher authority of information pointing to the very doubtful presence of aircraft in their vicinity.
>
> Reports and rumours thus repeated acquire precision and become magnified in circulation; they soon assume the form of definite statements that hostile airships have been actually seen in various localities.

The War Office compilation of reports for January 1915 tends to confirm the above statement. It should also be borne in mind that there was a high expectation of Zeppelin raids at the very commencement of war, so anything in the sky was given the closest attention.

The *Intelligence Circular No. 6* outlines the fact that at the start of the war reports of enemy signalling quickly spread and increased in number throughout the autumn and winter of 1914/15.[24] At first every case was taken seriously but experience revealed that many 'arose out of excited imaginations, or were based on impossible evidence'. These consisted of three main categories:

1. Lights or other methods (such as the use of carrier pigeons or wireless telegraphy) being employed to signal or communicate with the enemy.
2. The above activities associated with petrol or supply depots for the use of hostile submarines [and aircraft] on our shores.
3. Concrete gun-platforms prepared by enemy forces and disguised as the foundations of factories or tennis courts.

At first reports of illicit signalling were not officially recorded, but this report estimates that a maximum of 2,000 were made in the Scottish Command area down to a few hundred in the Southern Army, Home Forces command area.

The circular was produced to give information about how to treat and investigate such incidents, based on the experience gained up to that time. It notes that all cases should be investigated to eliminate the 'possibility of enemy agency in this country' and to clear the 'names of harmless people who, by reason of such reports, come to be viewed with grave suspicion and, even in some cases, to be ostracised by their neighbours.'

Another purpose for taking these reports seriously was to help calm any public agitation:

In fact, it may be said that investigating officers will, in many cases, have a real duty to perform in treating the informants sympathetically, in spite of a possibly ridiculous story, and thereby restoring peace of mind to an agitated body of people.

It goes on to note that out of all the reports only eight seemed to suggest the activity of enemy agents and that convictions had been secured in three cases. Though it does concede that:

The possibility of an arrangement existing for enemy agents to exhibit lights at certain fixed places in order to enable hostile aircraft to locate their position over this country cannot be dismissed.

The investigating officer is advised to weigh each case according to its level of probability:

There can be no comparison in importance between a case of reported signalling on the East coast by means of rockets or powerful lamps to seawards on a night of Zeppelin or submarine activity, and another report made inland of a boy signalling into the sky with a bicycle lamp which would in all probability never be observed from any aircraft at any likely altitude.

The circular provides several case histories of typical enemy signalling activities, and lists the types of lights in the sky that can be mistaken for enemy signals, such as planets, meteors, flares and distant shell bursts. It also provides a list of broad principles for investigating officers. This states that they should begin by analysing whether the informant has any personal animosity or *prima facie* prejudice towards anyone blamed for signalling to the enemy. If satisfied with the validity of the informants' claims the officer is told to find out if there are any natural causes for the reported signalling, and in 'Appendix I' a list of suggested questions is provided to determine the nature and cause of 'rocket and floating light' sightings. The document is very reminiscent of the projects conducted by the United States Air Force in our own era that tried to determine the validity and meaning of flying saucer and UFO sightings.

References

1. *Leipziger Volkszeitung*, 3 August 1914.
2. *Leipziger Nevesten Nachrichten*, 9 August 1914.
3. *Deutsche Tageszeitung*, 3 August 1914; *Berliner Tageblatt*, 4 August 1914.
4. *Berliner Tageblatt*, 3 August 1914; *Kölnische Volkszeitung*, 3 August 1914.
5. *Das Kleine Journal* (Berlin), 5 August 1914.
6. *Leipziger Volkszeitung*, Supplement 1, 7 August 1914.
7. *Leipziger Volkszeitung*, 15 August 1914.

8.   Smith, Thomas F.A., *What Germany Thinks* (London: Hutchinson, 1915).

9.   Tuchman, Barbara, *August 1914* (London & Basingstoke: The Macmillan Press Ltd, 1980), pp. 319–320.

11. *Yorkshire Observer* (Bradford), 31 August 1914.

12. *Workington Star & Harrington Guardian*, 4 September 1914.

13. *New York Times*, 4 September 1914; *Workington Star & Harrington Guardian* 5 September 1914.

14. *The Star* (London), 8 September 1914.

15. *Manchester Guardian*, 9 September 1914.

16. *Liverpool Courier*, 10 September 1914.

17. *The Star*, 14 September 1914.

18. *Fleetwood Express*, 16 September 1914.

19. 'The Spy Peril', H.L. Deb 18 November 1914, Vol. 18, cc65–83, at: hansard.millbanksystems.com/lords/1914/nov/18/the-spy-peril.

20. *Inverness Courier*, 23 October 1914, p. 3, col. 3.

21. *The Times* (London), 19 April 1915, p. 5, col. 5.

22. *Evening Despatch* (Birmingham), 17 April 1915, p. 5.

23. PRO Air 1/720 36/1/6 GHQ Home Forces, London, *Intelligence Circular No. 6*, May 1916.

24. PRO Air 1/720 36/1/6 GHQ Home Forces, London, *Intelligence Circular No. 6*, May 1916.

ELEVEN

SIGHTINGS IN THE USA

'A foreign war contrivance, never seen before on this side of the Atlantic.'[1]

Long before it entered the First World War on 6 April 1917, the United States was not immune to sightings of strange aerial objects that were regarded as German aircraft. At some unspecified date in 1914, two men saw three lights about 20 feet above the ground, which did not cast any shadows. The lights flew over the Indiana landscape, '… in an unusual manner; appearing at times as though intelligently controlled, searching for something or carrying out a pre-arranged assignment.'[2]

The same witnesses claimed that, from 1915 to 1917, similar lights had been seen in the north-western counties of Indiana, which were reported by the local newspapers.

From newspaper research it has been discovered there were several reports of incidents in New Jersey, Wisconsin and Minnesota during January and February 1916. These involved sightings of phantom aircraft, saboteurs and snipers, combined with rumours of German spying activities. Michael T. Shoemaker studied this scare and noted:

The flap conforms to [Jacques] Vallee's 'control mechanism' hypothesis to the extent that it incited considerable suspicion of German sabotage and anti-German sentiment; thus it can truly be

said that this flap contributed, at least in a small way, to an atmosphere that provoked US entry into war.[3]

One of the first sightings was made by Carl L. York who resided
on the banks of the St Croix River, west of Grantsburg, and on the
boundary line between Wisconsin and Minnesota. His experience
occurred on 5 January 1916 at 7.00 p.m., but he did not report it
until two months later:

> I was outdoors and I heard a low humming noise like that of
> a humming bird, and I stood and listened. Happening to glance
> toward the sky, I saw a light like that of an automobile searchlight
> almost straight drove me, [sic] and going southwards along the
> course of the river, but I could not make out any sort of a machine
> as it was very dark. The light kept on down the river and a few
> minutes more disappeared below the horizon.[4]

A sound in the sky and then a sighting of a light became a common
feature of many of the following incidents. The scare in New Jersey
began on 10 January, when a glazing house at DuPont's gunpowder
plant, Carney's Point, exploded. This was an important munitions
factory that had quickly expanded to meet the needs of the war
effort, and at this time employed 25,000 workers.[5]

The next morning, another DuPont plant at Hagley Yard,
Wilmington, was rocked by two explosions that destroyed some
powder mills. The next day, another powder mill was destroyed by
explosion at the same plant.[6]

What seems almost coincidental was a sky quake, which shook
buildings in Cincinnati, Ohio on 12 January. Flashes were seen in
the sky, but, so far as we know, these were not associated with aerial
spies. This incident might indicate that some geophysical mechanism
could have been at work in a variety of localities on that day or series
of days.[7] On 14 January, at the Gibbstown gunpowder plant, only 14
miles from Carney's Point, an acid house exploded.[8]

So many explosions in DuPont factories making gunpowder for
the Allied Forces in such a short space of time and within such a

small area obviously led to fears that German agents or sympathisers were at work.

In the week that followed, people began to see phantom aircraft in the area. Mame Zehner, a resident of Philadelphia, said that just before dark she saw a black object cross the sky. And an aircraft was seen circling over the Gibbstown plant by residents of Paulsboro.[9]

There was an attempt to keep such reports secret, but several stories of phantom aircraft were published in the press at the end of the month, making it apparent that something odd was going on in the skies over New Jersey.

Not long after the explosions at Hagley Yard, a railroad employee was going home early in the morning when, '… he saw an airplane flying over the powder plant along the Brandywine [Valley].'[10] A week later, the sound of an aircraft was heard over the same valley. At the close of January, the aircraft was heard again in the area.

During the same period, an aircraft was seen over Sixth and Broome Street, in the centre of Wilmington. It did not seem far from an office block used by DuPont.[11] An aerial object was also observed over a rifle factory in Eddystone.[12] This was part of the Baldwin Locomotive Works and it further highlights the fact that sightings of aircraft were concentrated around industrial and military locations.

The captain of DuPont's security police at Carney's Point, Albert J. Parsons, claimed he saw a strange light in the sky on two nights after the Gibbstown explosion on 14 January. The captain had served with the US Marine Corps for three years, and he had been working at the DuPont plant for three months. He was described as, '… a young man of more than ordinary intelligence, apparently. He is clean cut, well dressed, a good talker and of more than usual brain power, if appearance counts for anything. Under the cross fire of questions from the newspaper men, he was cool and collected and told his story in a straightforward and unassuming manner.'[13]

Parsons kept watch nightly for any unusual aerial activity and his vigil was rewarded on the 31 January:

On the high ground at the labour camp at Carney's Point, two miles from the river and three miles from Deep Water Point … at about 8.45 p.m., a white light appeared suddenly over the Deep Water Point section of the plant. It shone steadily at an estimated height of 1,500 feet.

Parsons continued:

> For a few minutes, the light seemed to move hardly at all. But finally it floated down until apparently it was within a few hundred feet of the river. That's what made me think it was a hydro-aeroplane.[14]

Later, he admitted he had not seen the outline of the flying machine, nor had he heard the whirr of its motor.[15] Several other witnesses at the Deep Water Point did, however, say that they heard the buzzing noise of its engine.[16] A guard told Parsons that a night engineer at a pumping station 3 miles from Carney's Point saw the same aircraft on the same night. The machine descended and disappeared from view, but the witness was not sure whether it had landed or gone behind the horizon. Unfortunately, the name of this man was not given and the sighting never substantiated.[17]

When pressed for more details of his sighting, Parsons said, the light, '... moved at times and then appeared to be still and then it seemed to be going up and down or moving in a semi-circle.'[18] This motion has been compared by Michael T. Shoemaker to the 'falling-leaf' motion of UFOs described by modern-day witnesses.[19] Parsons added: 'The machine circled the works for about 15 minutes when it disappeared in a south easterly direction.'[20]

One of the more sinister parts of this account is that at that time the Italian ship *Bologna* was loading explosives at the Deep Water Point and was directly beneath the aircraft.[21] On the same night, an airship was seen over Coatsville, Pennsylvania, where another DuPont gunpowder plant was located.[22] Earlier on that afternoon, J.M. Smith, a Philadelphia salesman, was going to a funeral when he noticed 'the throbbing of an engine'. Looking up, he saw, 'swooping over my home, not more than 250 feet in the air ... a big aeroplane'. This rapidly flew towards the Frankford Arsenal. Mr Smith was upset by this intruder, indeed he averred: 'I'm a good American citizen, and I think this sort of thing should be stopped.'

Officials at the arsenal said the witness only saw a blackbird and the local newspaper high-handedly asserted, 'It's a dull day when some eagle-eyed resident … does not see an aeroplane whizzing over his home, bent on an errand of mischief.'[23]

The blackbird or birds must have stayed out late on 31 January, because in the evening a DuPont official's friend saw an airship.[24] At Wilmington, Edward P. McKay, a plumbing inspector, heard the chugging of an engine fly over his home at 11.00 p.m.[25]

Understandably, DuPont wanted to dismiss these sightings as the product of overwrought imaginations. With regard to Parsons' report, Charles B. Landis, the head of DuPont's publicity department, said:

> In view of the fact that aeroplanes do not usually carry lights, we are constrained to believe Parsons's imagination may have conjured what he saw.

He might have added that blackbirds do not carry lights either![26] A more interesting part of Landis' statement was this revelation: 'There are known to be six aeroplanes in the vicinity, but all are said to be out of commission at present … '[27]

Multiple fires destroyed five buildings at DuPont's Carney Point plant on 28/29 January 1916, and a prowler who was suspected of starting them was quickly arrested. Not long afterwards it was claimed the fires were purely accidental, making us wonder if this was said to allay public fears and reduce the spread of rumours at these factories.[28]

Mystery aircraft swung back into view on 3 February 1916. At about 4.00 p.m., several people saw one fly over Glenolden and head towards South Philadelphia. The witnesses were members of Mount Zion church, Darby.[29] Possibly the same craft, was seen by William S. Taggart, who said a monoplane, 'came from behind the … water tower at South Philadelphia.' This occurred at 5.20 p.m. and, after circling over the City Hall, it disappeared into the dusk.[30] On the morning of that day, at 10.23 a.m., there was a 50 per cent solar eclipse visible from New York and an hour later, an earthquake with its epicentre in Schenectady, New York, broke windows within a 25-mile radius.[31]

The next day, a fire erupted in the DuPont's Carney Point plant photographic studio. That night and the following night, people at Woodbury declared they had seen 'some foreign war contrivance, never seen before on this side of the Atlantic' at about 9.00 p.m.[32]

On the night of 6 February, Robert M. Baird at Hagley Yard saw an aeroplane hovering over Wilmington. What was possibly the same object was seen by C.A. Bell, who watched it as he walked in Rockford Park. The machine was clearly visible and it began to display a light just before it flew out of view.[33]

A great distance away, at Tacoma, Washington, a DuPont plant blew up on 7 February.[34] A few days later, an aeroplane was seen by railway conductor Archie Reavie and a brakeman, as they were travelling between Wills and Winnebijou, Wisconsin. The vehicle carried several lights and passed over the railway tracks twice. It flew at a low altitude and the pilot of the machine was clearly seen operating the controls. When the train stopped at the water tank, the engine crew said they had also seen the aeroplane. One of the witnesses said:

> It might be that someone is practising with the machine with the intention of flying over to Barksdale and dropping some bombs on the Du Pont powder plant. I'm sure I don't know how to explain it.[35]

The Eastern states of America again became the focus of attention on 13 February 1916. Just before sunrise, a gigantic aircraft flew over New Jersey. The craft carried red head and tail lights and a powerful searchlight, which paid careful attention to munition plants owned by Ingersoll-Rand Co., the Edison Cement Co., and Taylor-Wharton.[36]

That evening, aircraft were seen over Wilmington, but like the sightings on the same night in London, Ontario, they were explained as misperceptions of Venus and Jupiter.[37]

Two lights were also seen at Queen Anne, Clayton and Dover, in Kent County, Maryland. Mr Knight and his family, near Dover, saw a red and a white light come towards the Earth after changing position several times.[38] A later report explained that an oddly shaped cloud plus Jupiter and Venus caused witnesses on the same night to see 'a Zeppelin or some other aerial warcraft' at Kent Island, opposite Annapolis.[39]

A week or so prior to these events, a rapidly moving airship with red and green lights was seen going westwards over White Bear Lake, Minnesota.[40] The week before, on 13 February, farmers in the neighbourhood of Nash, Wisconsin, said they saw an aircraft, and farmers several weeks earlier had seen one near Maple Ridge.[41] Although these reports were discounted by the press as being visions of the ubiquitous Venus and Jupiter, the witnesses were convinced that the aircraft was searching for the Barksdale, Wisconsin, DuPont plant. Since many of the sightings occurred near this plant, it is worth noting that it manufactured dynamite and the more powerful triton explosive. The workforce, consisting of 1,400 to 2,300 men, was mainly resident in Washburn and conveyed the 5 miles by special trains to the plant. Six men had been killed by explosions at Barksdale, but there had been no incidents of this type since 1907. The plant was protected by barbed wire, arc lamps and searchlights. Each worker was provided with an identity card with their photograph on it which had to be presented every time they wanted to enter the plant. Given these precautions, the only means of attack that might be effective was either by air or by internal sabotage.[42]

People in Laurel, Delaware, saw two lights on the night of 14 February 1916. Some who watched them claimed:

> They were drawing nearer and predicted an explosion when they met. Others quoted the scripture and said it was a true sign that the war would soon be over.[43]

Those who enjoy conspiracies might connect these lights with a sudden attack of thirty-nine fires scattered throughout Philadelphia from 8.00 p.m. on 14 February until noon the following day.[44]

Also, on 15 February, a fire destroyed a distillation house at the Gibbstown gunpowder plant.[45] That night, three lights were seen to the east of Middletown, Delaware. Some said it made several changes of position over the Delaware River and that it made a whirring sound.[46]

An observer in the fire tower at Ellis fire station, Ashland, Wisconsin, saw a large light at 8.30 a.m. This was either on the morning of 17 or 18 February. The most important aspect of this sighting was that the many spectators who were alerted by the fireman saw the light moving behind the Barksdale DuPont plant. No one at the plant or in nearby Washburn saw this, but the Methodist minister of Washburn, the Rev. A.M. Harkness, said that the guards at the plant had been doubled. A very sinister aspect of this localised scare was a rumour that workmen had received anonymous letters, which warned them to leave the plant before 1 March, as it would be destroyed on that date. These threats caused one man to quit his job, but no one else left, and nothing did happen on the date in question.[47]

Meanwhile, in New Jersey, fires occurred at the Carney's Point plant on 17 and 24 February, while the Deep Water Point suffered an explosion on 22 February.[48]

To the north-west of all this unusual activity, another mystery aircraft was seen near a chemical plant in Tionesta, Pennsylvania:

> Nearly 100 skaters … were startled by the appearance of an aeroplane in the sky, plainly discernible in the clear moonlight as it made several circles over the plant of the Maybury Chemical Company. The machine, which the skaters say was a large one, remained in sight for several minutes and then sped northward, finally disappearing from sight.[49]

An airship carrying red and green lights and making a whirring noise was seen by two night watchmen at 2.00 a.m. over Couderay, Wisconsin.[50] On the same morning of Tuesday 22 February, another mystery fire came into view. A train was sent to collect the body of an employee who had been killed at the Kaiser Camp 5 near Sawyer, Wisconsin. As the locomotive approached the Stinson spur, the footplate crew heard 'an engine sound' and saw a light in the sky that flashed from red to green. When they stopped to watch this, two doctors on the train also saw and heard this craft head towards the west.[51]

More excitement was generated by the sight of three lights in the west on the night of 23 February at Hawthorne, Wisconsin. This was connected with the idea that the machine was part of a plot to blow up the Barksdale DuPont plant.[52]

A few nights later, several residents of Duluth heard an aircraft and saw moving lights.[53] However, the greatest attention was given to sightings made on the morning of 26 February. Just before dawn, at approximately 5.00 a.m., employees of the Great Northern Railway terminal at Allouez Bay, Superior, Wisconsin, heard a purring sound and saw lights in the sky. Although there was a strong northerly gale, the aircraft circled at an altitude of less than 3,000 feet.

The witnesses assumed the pilot was making a detailed survey of the ore docks, yards and shops. Furthermore, the grain elevators at Superior, which contained millions of bushels of wheat for the Allied Forces in Europe, were thought to be a target for the pilot's observations. Shortly after 6.00 a.m., the aircraft climbed higher into the sky and by 6.20 a.m. it had disappeared in the direction of Minnesota Steel Co., which was in the west at Duluth.[54]

That night, red lights were seen at South Range at 9.00 p.m. And, moving lights were seen over the West Ed freight yards at Superior. Both of these sightings involved single witnesses.[55]

The aircraft seemed to remain in the vicinity of Superior on the night of 27 February. Yet another train crew reported seeing and hearing an aircraft going westwards. This time the outline of the craft was seen as the train was going along the Omaha line. When they got to the South Shore depot, a railway agent was shown the craft, but he could only see two lights. This took place at 9.00 p.m. and at about the same time an employee of Pittsburgh Coal dock saw a similar aircraft heading westwards.[56]

Pedestrians walking along the Broadway, Superior, saw a moving light in the west at 8.30 a.m. on 28 February. A train crew also saw a similar light in the west at the South End yards, Superior. Just after midnight, the Johnson family in Duluth saw two aircraft circle over their home. The lights then headed towards Superior where they circled over the coal and grain elevators. Finally, they disappeared in the direction of the Minnesota Steel plant. Mr Johnson exclaimed, 'Can't something be done? We are afraid of bombs. There were two of them. We saw the red lights of both – and they separated.'[57]

The same night, lights were also seen at Highwood and St Paul, Minnesota.[58] A few days earlier, a witness at Marengo, Wisconsin, said he saw the aircraft and plainly saw the pilot inside it.[59]

The best sightings of the mystery aeroplane were made on the morning of 29 February. These observations were particularly important since they occurred the day before the threatened destruction of the Barksdale plant.[60] All of the reports came from night watchmen at the docks and elevators along the St Louis bay front, Superior. Their stories are remarkably similar, which might suggest a hoax, nonetheless their reports do contain some intriguing features. John Tullvson, the head watchman at the Globe elevators, said:

I was making my last round outside the elevators and was going to ring in for the last time at 4:30 o'clock when I heard a roaring noise in the sky. I looked up and there was a big aeroplane, flying along very fast. There were three men in it and there was a long rope hanging below with something fastened on its end.

It was a big machine. I should say it was 50 feet wide and 100 feet long, and there were three lights, one on each end and one in the middle. One of the men was sitting up near the front of the machine. He was probably running it. The other two were back from him a little way and seemed to be looking around. It was about 600 feet up in the air.[61]

Later that day, a second night watchman at the Great Northern elevator, who was known to a member of the *Superior Telegram* newspaper staff, admitted that he also saw this aircraft.[62]

On the same morning, at 6.00 a.m., the crew of the Northwestern freight train run heard a purring sound, and saw two lights moving rapidly near the ground. The shape of the aircraft was not seen because it was still dark, but the train crew was convinced that what they saw near Birch, Wisconsin, was neither produced by balloons or stars.[63]

On the night of 29 February, numerous witnesses saw green, red and white lights circling over Duluth. They appeared at 8.30 p.m. and remained in view for half an hour, then at 9.30 p.m. they reappeared. Duluth police headquarters received twenty-seven telephone calls from witnesses. At Superior, hundreds of witnesses thought they saw an aeroplane, although patrolman John Thurber said the lights were attached to toy balloons. To support this view, he said he saw red, white and blue stripes painted on the side of one of the balloons.[64]

John and Henry Rowe, in the town of Bemidji, Minnesota, to the north-west of Duluth, also saw some aerial activity. John said:

It was shortly after 9:30 o'clock Tuesday night while I was return-ing from the firemen's meeting with my father that I noticed two lights in the sky travelling very fast toward the west. We stopped and watched the lights which remained the same distance apart and came to the conclusion that it was an aeroplane. We could not hear the working of the machinery. We watched the lights until they disappeared in the west. The craft appeared to be coming from the east, probably from Duluth, and was headed toward Grand Forks and the west.

I believed that it is the same craft that has been seen around Duluth.[65]

This mystery was deflated by John Dormady, foreman of the Missabe Docks, Duluth, and his colleague Albert Daldec who claimed it was nothing more than a toy balloon.[66]

There are several problems with this solution. For example, they state that they saw the yellow lights of the balloons, but all the other reports speak of red, green and white lights and no one else reported seeing yellow lights. It was discovered that at least half a dozen toy balloons had been sent up from various parts of Superior, on the night of 29 February. Though one report noted that they were easily identified as balloons and that the sightings made on previous nights were still a mystery.[67] Three balloons were sold to a customer at Iron River, Wisconsin, 'a week ago', which seemed to account for many sightings made near the Barksdale plant.[68]

By now there was a certain amount of scepticism about the substance of some of the reports. A pupil at the Superior Normal School said that he saw the aircraft over the Great Northern railroad yards at 3.00 a.m. on the morning of 1 March. The purring of the machine alerted him to this spectacle, and he was able to observe two men inside the vehicle. One of his tutors told him: 'You must have had an awful nightmare.'[69] The local Rotary Club even offered a $100 reward for the mystery aeroplane so that they could use it to advertise their forthcoming exposition.[70]

Unlike other scares, where reports declined and disappeared after the 'revelation' of one or more mundane answers to the mystery, sightings continued in the area, and some of them were more detailed and mysterious than those we have already surveyed.

On Wednesday night, 1 March 1916, hundreds of people watched the skies in Superior but nothing was seen. At nearby Duluth, a light was reported, though most thought it was carried by a balloon. An aircraft did appear to large numbers of people at Bemidji. Behind the lights, some saw the outline of the craft and others heard the whirr of its motors. Another sighting in the area was made by a railway brakeman called Clarence Foucault. He was positive that the object he saw going eastwards was not a balloon. He explained:

We were near Funkley when I heard the whirl of the motor of the aeroplane. It was about 9:45 o'clock; the engine had stopped and I was just turning the switch when I heard the whirl of the motor. I looked up and saw the outline of an aeroplane north of Funkley. I raised my cap and could very plainly hear the motor. The machine was travelling at a high rate of speed.[71]

Twenty miles south of Superior, at Hines, a most unusual event occurred during the evening of Thursday 2 March. The details were given by Mr F.A. Porter in a letter to the *Superior Telegram*:

I have read in the Telegram about the little scare, in and around Superior, from the lights seen lately in the sky.

I noticed an article about it being a toy balloon but this evening a monstrous flying machine landed in my field to do some repair work as near as I could see. I tried to approach them and one of the men came out to meet me and requested me to go away, and as I returned to the house they sailed away in the direction of Superior.

Judging from his language he was undoubtedly a German. People can laugh if they wish but what I've seen I know to be true.

Yours truly
F.A. Porter
Hines, Wisconsin, 2 March 1916.[72]

To confirm the reliability of this witness, Mr William Williams, the owner of the livery stable at Hawthorne, reported:

F.A. Porter resides just north of the new Webster farm at Hines. He is known personally by John Connell and Ed Althapor, both of Hawthorne, who say he is entirely reliable. He has lived at Hines for some time.[73]

In the days following Porter's sighting, a resident of Hines saw the aeroplane pass overhead on two different occasions. At Hawthorne, more moving lights were seen on the night of 4 March. The previous night, an airship that beamed down shafts of light on to Mounds Park, St Paul, was visible for half-an-hour.[74]

When the sightings were at their peak in the eastern states, it was suggested that an 'airship' built by Robert Glendenning and stored at Essington, Philadelphia, was responsible. The problem with this explanation is that it had been out of commission since November 1915. Glendenning was a Philadelphia banker who bought a Curtiss flying boat and used it to provide flying lessons free of charge to college students who were willing to volunteer to join the military if the USA declared war on Germany.[75]

At the end of February, it was suggested that a hydroplane owned by Jack Vila had caused the present crop of sightings, but it was discovered that the plane had gone into storage for the winter.[76]

The balloon or star/planet hypotheses did not seem to convince everyone either. In an attempt to get to the root of the matter, the DuPont plant at Barksdale engaged detectives to track down the flier. A spokesman for the company said:

> Of course, anyone has a perfect right to go flying around in an aeroplane at night if he enjoys it these cold nights, but we are just curious enough to want to know what it is all about. One thing we are convinced of: and that is that there is no intention of the aviator to damage the Barksdale plant. If there was it would have been done long ago and not after everyone knows of the aeroplane and is on the lookout for it.[77]

Whatever investigations were made, a new spate of sightings occurred in the more southerly parts of Wisconsin. On 10 March, at 11.00 p.m., Mrs Geo. Rheingans heard an engine. Looking out from her home in Eagle Point, she saw two lights heading northwards.[78] On the night of 12 March, Mr Wise of Stone Lake reported that a machine carrying fifteen lights was seen going north-westwards, towards Superior. He telephoned this news to Birchwood, where respectable residents saw a similar craft.[79] On the same night, at Exeland, Wisconsin, a bright light was seen at 9.30 p.m. It circled over the village; but when the Soo Line train pulled into the station on its journey from Superior to Chicago, the craft extinguished its lights. When the train resumed its journey the light of the aircraft came on again. At about 9.55 p.m., the light went away towards the north-west. Mr Christensen observed this with his wife and two lodgers. He noted that an aeroplane had been seen in the vicinity at least four times during the past month.[80]

Just after midnight, on the morning of 13 March, the 'chug chug' sound of an aircraft engine was heard over Madison, Wisconsin. Some alarmed citizens tried to ascend the state capitol dome to get a view of this uninvited visitor, but some scaffolding prevented them from doing so.[81]

What was explained as a balloon was observed at St Paul at 8.30 p.m. on 14 March. For 90 minutes, Mr and Mrs Hanson watched a red and white light head towards the north-west. On the night of 19 March, scores of people saw lights over the St Paul State Fair grounds. At this moment a 'secret inventor' confessed that he was responsible for these sightings. Fred Parker, owner of the Hamline Manufacturing Company, said he was perfecting a gas that contained seventeen chemicals. In conjunction with an anonymous colleague, the two inventors hoped to make this gas counteract the effects of the hydrogen gas inside a balloon envelope so that it could descend without having to discharge the hydrogen. They experimented at night in a balloon, to try to keep their efforts secret. Mr Parker said:

> Maybe this explanation will relieve us of the escort of automobiles we have had the past few nights. Maybe you reporters thought we didn't know you were tracking us over the country last night, but we could see your lights as easily as you could see ours.
>
> And if the thing works as well tonight as it did last night, not even the fear of bullets will worry us. We have been expecting an attack, but we provided against danger by hanging lights 200 feet under the balloon. So if the lights had been used for targets we would escape injury.[82]

The lights also warned them when they were too close to the ground. The balloon was tethered by a 6,000ft-long cable so that they did not get lost in the heavens. The story does sound rather dubious. Even if his story had any validity it did not explain the sightings made elsewhere.

Far away, on the southern border of Wisconsin, a weird object with an equally weird crew appeared on 21 March. Perhaps Fred Parker's cable had snapped or another group of inventors was at work? This was the story as presented in several newspapers:

> When residents of this city [Monroe] Tuesday sighted a large dirigible balloon passing over the place, John Burkhart, Gordon Baltzer and Henry Freithe gave chase in an automobile.

After having followed it several miles they lost track of it, but, continuing to Clarence bridge between Juda and Brodhead, they discovered the airship had been brought to earth in a field. Its two occupants were examining their craft as though something had happened to the mechanism. When questioned by their pursuers they spoke with a foreign accent and declined to give their names or tell from where they came.

They said they had been alight several hours, and inquired the way to Superior, Duluth, St Paul and Minneapolis. The balloon was equipped with an apparatus which enabled the aeronauts to supply their own gas and it had a propeller by which it could be guided against the strongest wind. When the dirigible again ascended, it disappeared in the direction of Superior.[83]

Several witnesses were positive that an aircraft with bright red and green lights, which moved eastwards over St Paul at 7.30 p.m. on 28 March, was not a balloon. Mr Parker was not at home that night, so he might have been experimenting with his balloon again – that's if it existed beyond his own imagination.[84]

Another landing report was made in April 1916. Sometime prior to the 11th, Ernest Sodve, the son of the Grey-Wertin company's Pine Island caretaker, saw an aeroplane land on ice-covered Lake Vermilion. A report noted:

When he approached the machine, one of the two occupants shouted through a megaphone telling him to stay away, which he did. After resting on the ice for twenty minutes the machine arose and sailed off in a northerly direction, apparently bound for some point beyond the Canadian frontier.

The two men in the machine were dressed in heavy padded clothing and wore goggles, according to Sodve.[85]

In an area where American troops were said to be operating, a mystery aeroplane was seen going over Santa Rosalia and heading for Parral, Mexico. This happened on 12 April 1916.[86] After this, sightings were to be scattered by geography and time, in a rather random fashion.

What was described as an 'elongated oval device' was seen one morning in May or June 1916. This craft hovered near some hills south of Rensselaer, Illinois, for a few seconds and then shot quickly into the sky.[87] Something that looked like a dirigible was seen through field glasses at 11.00 p.m. on 19 July 1916 at Huntingdon, West Virginia.[88]

The following year was a relatively poor year for sightings. Charles Fort mentions an explosion over Colby, Wisconsin at 6.25 p.m. on 4 July 1917. This was linked with a stone that fell from the sky. On the same day, an 'extraordinary' meteor was seen over France.[89] In the late summer, John Boback saw an elliptical object – the size of an automobile – at 12.30 p.m. It was standing in a pasture near railway tracks in the Mount Braddock area of Youngstown, Pennsylvania. Lights inside the craft could be seen through portholes arranged around the top part of this structure. It quickly climbed into the sky and throughout the observation it made a swishing sound.[90]

A recollection of a sighting by Edwin Bauhan in early 1918 shows how outside factors conditioned the interpretation of a phenomenon in the sky. At the time of the observation it was regarded as a 'Zeppelin', then as the years passed the witness brought it into line with the UFO mythology. Nonetheless, what he saw at Rich Field military installation, Waco, Texas, does sound fascinating:

As we were coming from the mess hall after our meal, we suddenly saw approaching the camp what seemed to be a Zeppelin at first glance. It came directly overhead and was no more than 500 feet high, so we got an excellent view of it. It had no motors, no rigging, it was noiseless. It knew where it was going, steering from southwest to northeast. It was not white, but rose or sort of flame colour. It could be said to be cigar-shaped. I could observe no windows, though there could have been some.

We all experienced the weirdest feeling of our lives, and sat in our tent puzzling over it for some time. Through the years I came to the conclusion that it was controlled from some other planet, had no one in it, and was being used as an instrument of observation.[91]

This could have been a sighting of a particularly large and bright meteor that attracted their attention at a time of stress. Another 'solid object' seen over Butte, Montana, by Maurice McKenney during the summer of 1918, could have been a balloon.[92]

References

1. *Evening Bulletin* (Philadelphia), 7 February 1916, p.1.
2. Lore, G.I.R, and Deneault, H.H., *Mysteries of the Skies* (London: Robert Hale, 1969), p.103.
3. Letter from Michael T. Shoemaker to Nigel Watson dated 19 December 1987.
4. *Superior Telegram*, 11 March 1916, p.1.
5. DuPont website, at: www2.dupont.com/Phoenix_Heritage/en_US/1892_detail.html.
6. *Evening Bulletin*, 10 and 12 January 1916, p.2; *Daily State Gazette* (Trenton, New Jersey), 11 January, p.1.
7. Fort, Charles, *The Complete Books of Charles Fort* (New York: Dover, 1974), p.520; *New York Herald*, 13 January 1916.
8. *Daily State Gazette*, 15 January 1916, p.1.
9. *Evening Bulletin*, 26 January 1916.
10. *Evening Journal* (Wilmington), 3 February 1916.
11. *Every Evening* (Wilmington), 3 February 1916, p.1; *Evening Bulletin*, 3 February 1916, p.1.
12. *Philadelphia Inquirer*, 4 February 1916.
13. *Morning News* (Wilmington), 4 February, 1916.
14. Ibid.; *Evening Bulletin*, 3 February 1916, p.1; *Philadelphia Inquirer*, 4 February 1916, p.1; *Early Evening*, 3 February 1916, p.1; *Evening Journal*, 3 February 1916.
15. *Philadelphia Inquirer*, 4 February 1916, p.1.
16. *Evening Free Press* (London, Ontario), 4 February 1916; *Early Evening*, 3 February 1916.
17. *Morning News*, 4 February 1916.
18. *Early Evening*, 4 February 1916, p.7.
19. Shoemaker, Michael T., 'UFO Saboteurs', *Fate*, December 1985, p.60.
20. *Every Evening*, 3 February 1916, p.1.
21. *Every Evening*, 3 February 1916, p.1; *Morning News*, 4 February 1916.
22. *Evening Journal*, 3 February 1916; *Philadelphia Inquirer*, 4 February 1916, p.1.
23. *Evening Bulletin*, 1 February 1916, p.3.
24. *Every Evening*, 3 February 1916, p.1; *Evening Journal*, 3 February 1916, p.1.
25. *Evening Journal*, 3 February 1916, p.1.
26. *Philadelphia Inquirer*, 4 February 1916, p.1.
27. *Evening Bulletin*, 3 February 1916, p.1.
28. *Evening Bulletin*, 29 January 1916, p.1 and 31 January 1916, p.1.
29. *Evening Journal*, 3 February 1916; *Evening Bulletin*, 4 February 1916.

30. *Every Evening*, 4 February 1916, p.7; *Evening Bulletin*, 2 February 1916, p.3.
31. Letter from Michael T. Shoemaker to Nigel Watson dated 19 December 1987.
32. *Evening Bulletin*, 7 February 1916, p.1; *Philadelphia Inquirer*, 8 February 1916, p.1.
33. *Philadelphia Inquirer*, 8 February 1916, p.1; *Evening Journal*, 7 February 1916, p.1.
34. *Philadelphia Inquirer*, 8 February 1916, p.1
35. *Superior Telegram*, 12 February 1916, p.3.
36. *Every Evening*, 15 February 1916, p.9.
37. *Evening Bulletin*, 14 February 1916, p.2; *Every Evening*, 15 February 1916, p.9
38. *Every Evening*, 14 February 1916, p.7.
39. *Every Evening*, 15 February 1916, p.2.
40. *Superior Telegram*, 3 March 1916, p.7.
41. *Ashland Daily Press*, 15 February 1916, p.1.
42. *Ashland Daily Press*, 2 March 1916, p.1.
43. *Every Evening*, 15 February 1916, p.14.
44. *Evening Bulletin*, 15 February 1916, p.1.
45. *Philadelphia Inquirer*, 16 February 1916, p.4.
46. *Every Evening*, 16 February 1916, p.13.
47. *Superior Telegram*, 19 and 21 February 1916, p.4; *Minneapolis Sunday Tribune*, 27 February 1916, p.1.
48. *Every Evening*, 18 February 1916, p.1; *Evening Bulletin*, 22 and 24 February 1916, p.1.
49. *Philadelphia Inquirer*, 20 February 1916, p.1.
50. *Superior Telegram*, 1 March 1916, p.12.
51. *Minneapolis Sunday Tribune*, 27 February 1916, p.1; *Superior Telegram*, 28 February 1916, p.4.
52. *Superior Telegram*, 26 February 1916, p.10.
53. *Minneapolis Sunday Tribune*, 27 February 1916, p.1; *Philadelphia Inquirer*, 27 February 1916, p.12.
54. *Superior Telegram*, 26 February 1916, p.1; *Minneapolis Sunday Tribune*, 27 February 1916, p.1; *Philadelphia Inquirer*, 27 February 1916, p.12; *Ashland Daily Press*, 28 February 1916.
55. *Superior Telegram*, 28 and 29 February 1916, p.5.
56. *Superior Telegram*, 28 February 1916, p.3.
57. *Superior Telegram*, 29 February 1916, p.5.
58. *St. Paul Dispatch*, 4 March 1916, p.1.
59. *Ashland Daily Press*, 29 February 1916, p.1.
60. *Ashland Daily Press*, p.5.
61. *Superior Telegram*, 29 February 1916, p.5; *Ashland Daily Press*, 1 March 1916, p.2.
62. *Superior Telegram*, 1 March 1916, p.12.
63. *Ashland Daily Press*, 29 February and 1 March 1916.
64. *Ashland Daily Press*, 1 March 1916.
65. *Bemidji Daily Pioneer*, 1 March 1916, p.1; *St. Paul Dispatch*, 1 March 1916, p.1.
66. *Ashland Daily Press*, 1 March 1916, p.1.
67. *Superior Telegram*, 1 March 1916, p.12.
68. *Superior Telegram*, 1 March 1916, p.12.; *St. Paul Dispatch*, 1 March 1916, p.1.
69. *Superior Telegram*, 1 March 1916, p.6.

70. *Superior Telegram*, 1 March 1916, p.5.

71. *Bemidji Daily Pioneer*, 2 March 1916, p.1; *Superior Telegram*, 3 March 1916, p.7.

72. *Superior Telegram*, 4 March 1916, p.12; *St. Paul Dispatch*, 4 March 1916, p.1; *Wisconsin State Journal*, 5 March 1916, p.2.

73. *Superior Telegram*, 6 March 1916, p.5.

74. *St. Paul Dispatch*, 4 March 1916, p.1.

75. *Every Evening*, 3 February 1916, p.1. Ellis, Walt, 'An outline of the history of the Philadelphia Seaplane Base … ' at: phillyseaplanebase.com/seaplanebase.html.

76. *Wisconsin State Journal*, 2 March 1916, p.1.

77. *Superior Telegram*, 8 March 1916, p.12.

78. *Daily Independent* (Chippewa Falls, Wisconsin), 13 March 1916, p.3.

79. *Superior Telegram*, 14 March 1916, p.4; *Wisconsin State Journal*, 15 March 1916, p.6.

80. *Superior Telegram*, 15 March 1916, p.3.

81. *Wisconsin State Journal*, 13 March 1916, p.1; *Superior Telegram*, 15 March 1916, p.7.

82. *St. Paul Dispatch*, 20 March 1916, p.1.

83. *Superior Telegram*, 24 March 1916, p.5; *Bemidji Daily Pioneer*, 27 March 1916, p.2.

84. *Superior Telegram*, 29 March 1916.

85. *Superior Telegram*, 11 April 1916, p.8.

86. *Superior Telegram*, 12 April 1916, p.3.

87. Lore and Deneault, pp.103–104.

88. Fort, pp.210–219.

89. Fort, p.521.

90. Lore and Deneault, pp.104–105.

91. Lore and Deneault, p.105.

92. Lore and Deneault, p.105.

TWELVE

THE 'SCAREOPLANES' OF CANADA

Canada entered the First World War in late August 1914. Remote from the horrific realities of the conflict, there was a joyful nationwide celebration that they had joined the fight. As the war progressed, Canada was gripped with a fear of German sympathisers, enemy agents or German–Americans secretly crossing the border. Either under orders directly from Germany or as independent operators, it was feared they would disrupt Canada's war efforts.

As the *Ottawa Evening Journal* put it:

> It is known in Ottawa that there are German societies and sympathizers in the United States who have contemplated action of some kind against Canada. Early in the war Germans at various centres in the United States were drilling under arms with the object in view of making a descent upon Canada to destroy canals and railways, or perhaps even take part in the war on a more extended scale. Representations were made by the Canadians Government to Washington and the organization was stopped.[1]

The Anti-German League was formed to stop the use of German products and prevent immigration. Along with schools and colleges no longer teaching German, these were just some of the symptoms of the wave of animosity towards Germany that swept Canada. Miners at the Crow's Nest Pass Coal Company, in Fernie, British Columbia, refused to work with alien workers in August 1915. This led to them being sacked and put in an internment camp. Whenever there was an industrial accident, fire or explosion it was attributed to enemy sabotage.

We do know for certain that the German Secret Service did want to inflict damage on Canada through the use of enemy agents. For example, on 3 January 1915 the German ambassador in Washington received this coded message from the German Foreign Minister Arthur Zimmerman:

> Secret: Reference my 357. General Staff anxious vigorous measures should be taken to destroy Canadian Pacific [railway] for purpose causing lengthy interruptions of traffic. Acquaint military attache with above and furnish sums required for enterprise.[2]

This resulted in a plot to dynamite the Selkirk tunnel, near Revelstoke, British Columbia, but one of the men recruited into the scheme tipped off the Canadian Authorities. A railway bridge near Vanceboro, Maine, was dynamited on 1 January 1915, which caused minor damage, and on 22 June 1915 a factory at Walkerville, Ontario, was destroyed. Otherwise, a multitude of plots were foiled by the Canadian Authorities in liaison with the British Secret Service in the USA.

There were no German plans to spy on, infiltrate or bomb Canada using aircraft, yet many saw Canadians 'German' aircraft and believed they had hostile intentions. These sightings began in September 1914. At the beginning of the month, for several nights, a phantom aircraft was seen flying over McKitrick grounds, on the outskirts of Hamilton, Ontario. The three male witnesses said it always came from, and returned in the direction of Aldershot.[3]

Three aeroplanes made an appearance at Petrolia, Ontario, at 9.00 p.m. on 3 September 1914. They were plainly illuminated by moonlight, and they all swept the ground with powerful searchlights.

Chief of Police Fletcher reported:

> Hundreds saw the machines, whatever they are, but I cannot find anyone who heard the noise of the motors. They seemed to be up too high. I saw the machines myself and watched one of them for two hours. I could not swear, though, that it was an aeroplane. All I can say is that it looked like one to me.[4]

When viewed through binoculars, green and red lights seemed to be attached to the side of the aircraft. The length of the sighting seems too long for conventional aeroplanes of that period to have been the cause, and suggests that balloons, kites or even stars might have been responsible.[5]

Also on 3 September, at Sarnia, Ontario, where previous sightings indicated to residents that an aircraft was being operated from Michigan, USA, an aeroplane was seen in the direction of Port Huron.[6]

A policeman flashing his torch at the rear of the City Hall, London, Ontario, whilst on night patrol on 5 September, led several people to report the appearance of an airship in the vicinity.[7]

An airship was seen by guards at Welland Canal from 8 to 11 September. The canal provided a vital link between Lake Erie and Lake Ontario, making it a very tempting target for any enemy saboteurs. A rocket was dropped from an airship that carried red lights on one of these nights. The next day, the wreckage of the rocket was found, but no details were provided about this evidence. An airship was seen flying low over St Catharine's by guards at Lock Seven on the 11th, and they plainly saw its framework. One explanation was that they saw biplane-shaped clouds.[8]

An aircraft also visited Pipe Lane Road, Springbank, on the nights of 8 to 10 September. One of the residents, Mr Fred Bridge, emphasised that:

> This is no cock and bull story. I have seen the planes and know what I am talking about. With my neighbours, I have seen the flashlights which sweep the countryside and have heard the roar of the motors. Last night, [10 September] three of them came down

over Springbank from the direction of Hyde Park and passed around the south of the city … It is my opinion that every farmer in the community should be given a rifle and service ammunition by the Department of Militia, so that these spy aviators might be brought down.[9]

Such views were not limited to Mr Bridge; indeed, only a few days later, on 17 September, the Canadian order-in-council ruled that all aircraft had to obtain permission to fly within 10 miles of a city. The aerial transportation of wireless and photographic equipment or firearms and explosives was banned. Canadian soldiers were allowed to shoot at any aircraft violating these rules, and a real aircraft was shot at as it flew over Sault Set. Marie Canal. This prompted the US State Department to warn its aviators not to stray near the border with Canada, otherwise they could easily be shot down by the Canadian forces who were on a high alert for anything suspicious that moved in the sky.[10]

The dangerous nature of flying over Canada was further underlined when a Burgess-Dunne biplane was being flown to Quebec City, for shipping to Britain. E.L. Janney, the commander of the Canadian Aviation Corps, was at the controls, under the supervision of American pilot Clifford Webster, when they had to land to obtain more fuel. On landing they were both arrested by Canadian customs officers who thought they were German spies. They were released once the customs officers got orders from Ottawa.

On 26 September, an aeroplane returned to the vicinity of Sarnia at 6.00 p.m. Guards at the Point Edward wireless station saw it hovering westwards over Port Huron, and they would have shot at the aircraft if it had got close enough.[11]

Orders were given to the local militia to shoot at an aircraft that invaded the skies over Windsor, Ontario, on the nights of 27 and 28 September, but yet again it never got close enough to be in any danger, whatever it was.[12]

The traffic literally stopped in the streets of Toronto, when crowds of pedestrians blocked the roads as they gazed into the sky. The focus of their attention was a strange object flying overhead on the morning of 10 October. It was later revealed to have been a kite with a mannequin suspended from it.[13]

The sound and lights of what was presumed to be an aircraft were heard at Niagara Falls in the second week of October. Another aircraft was seen a few days later, which came from the direction of America and hovered over the Sault Ste Marie locks.[14]

Several sightings at London, Ontario, were regarded as being due to balloons, and there were rumours that a fire had been started by an aerial visitor.[15] A more outstanding sighting was of a fast-moving light flying over the Welseley Barracks, London, Ontario, on the morning of 21 October. Sergeant Joseph stated that, at 5.50 a.m.:

> I and three members of the guard were sitting around the camp-fire when we heard the purr of engines and looking up saw the aeroplane coming from the north east of the barracks. It had a bright light and was travelling rapidly. It came practically over us and the ordnance stores, and then turned to the east and south. There was no use firing at it, for it flew too high and too rapid a rate. It was an aeroplane, of that we are sure.[16]

This sounds like a meteor, except they do not turn in the sky.

An aircraft seen over the straits at Victoria, Vancouver Island, British Columbia, at midday on 26 October was thought to be an American machine operating from Port Townsend.[17]

Several people wrote to the Minister of Militia, expressing concerns about enemy infiltrators. Mr Hunt wrote from Slate River, Ontario, saying that aeroplanes are visiting the locality on virtually a nightly basis. It was his view that a German settlement in Minnesota might use aircraft to bomb the grain elevators at Fort William and Port Arthur. William J. Moe reported that he had seen two airships going northwards in the last week of October, at Franklin Centre, Quebec. He regarded them as being connected to the German Secret Service, but a reply by Hon. J.D. Hazen, the Acting Minister of Militia, stated they were probably American aviators straying over the border.[18]

Further sightings of aircraft were made in the last few days of October, at Fullerton, Logan, Hibbert and Mitchell, Ontario.[19] There was a curious sighting of red, yellow and green lights by guards at Toronto power station on 18 November. They were seen in the south-east on the American shoreline. The lights flashed and moved around in different patterns, giving rise to the conclusion that they were produced by enemy agents signalling to each other.[20]

Toronto was again the target of aerial visitations for several nights at the beginning of December. A resident of Indian Road said:

I woke at four the other morning and heard the unmistakeable 'chut-chuttering' of an aeroplane. There is no mistaking the noise, like a blind being drawn down – and never reaching the window sill.[21]

On 4 December, the office of the *Toronto Daily Star* 'was deluged with reports which included window and picture rattling, purring noises and everything but bombs' from residents who heard this activity between 4.00 and 4.30 a.m. that morning.

The explanation for these noises was provided by the Canadian Stewart Company, who claimed it was the noise of their cyclone dredger. As their spokesperson put it: 'When that big draught pipe gets within a couple of inches of the water line there is something doing.' He added that they operated a 65ft-tall Gantry Crane at night that carried a light on top, and it made a noise like an aeroplane as it moved up and down the docks at the foot of Frederik Street. So 'it would make a good imitation of a Zeppelin all right'.[22]

January and February brought a few sightings of lights in the sky from Toronto, Niagara Falls, Montreal and Virden, Manitoba.[23] These were nothing compared to a visitation by aircraft seen at Brockville, on 14 February 1915. A report by the *Toronto Globe* revealed how this drama unfolded:

Four aeroplanes passed over the city at 9:15 to-night and sped in the direction of Ottawa. The city was wildly excited by the sight of the aircraft, which seemed to burst into sight almost right over-head. The first machine was flying very rapidly and very high. Very little could be seen, but the unmistakeable sounds of the whirring motor made the presence of the aircraft known. Five minutes later the second machine could be heard. In crossing the [St Lawrence] river three fire balls were dropped. They were dropped at one minute intervals. In dropping they left a streak of light from where they had been thrown out, and it was this that attracted the attention of the residents. Hundreds of feet, the three lights fell. They dropped into the river and extinguished. It is not thought that they were explosive, although, if they had been, they would not have exploded in the river. They were apparently dropped to show the airmen their direction. A few minutes later, another machine passed over the east end of the city. In another interval, a machine came over the other end of the city.[24]

Fifteen minutes later, the Mayor of Gananoque telephoned Police Chief Burke to say that two aircraft had been heard flying over their town. Since the aircraft seemed to be heading for Ottawa, Burke telephoned Sir Arthur Percy Sherwood, the head of counter-intelligence in Canada. Given that this could be an enemy attack, Sherwood gave the order to black out the lights of Ottawa. He especially feared that the lights of the Parliament Buildings would be like a beacon to the potential attackers. At 11.15 p.m. the lights of the Royal Mint, Rideau Hall and the Parliament Buildings, were switched off followed by all the city lights. This was the first ever black-out of a Canadian city and in the darkness the population prepared for the horrors of modern warfare to rain down on them. To counter the attack, soldiers who were preparing for overseas service, were drafted to the rooftops with orders to shoot at any aircraft they saw.

No aircraft that the newspapers dubbed the 'scareoplanes' turned up at Ottawa that night. Though to the west of Brockville, aircraft were seen in the early hours of 15 February. At Richmond Hill, north of Toronto and 190 miles from Brockville, lights were seen hovering over the area. At 4.20 a.m., three moving lights were seen moving westwards at Guelph, a distance of 235 miles from Brockville.[25]

The whole Brockville incident was deflated when the remains of a paper balloon was found near the Eastern Hospital by Police Constable Storey of the Brockville Police Department. Later, the remains of another balloon, armed with flares and fireworks, was discovered. Word soon spread that the balloons were sent aloft by American pranksters in Morristown, who had been celebrating the hundredth anniversary of the end of the war of 1812.[26]

In opposition to the balloon theory, the Dominion Observatory claimed that the wind direction on that night would not have sent balloons towards Ottawa. The Canadian Parliament discussed the matter on 15 February, where the issue of whether or not there had been an aerial invasion was avoided. The government would have looked foolish if they had had to admit simple balloons had caused this scare, so perhaps as a way of saving face the government instigated another night of blackouts in the city and riflemen were once more stationed on the rooftops.[27]

The balloons or aircraft did not return to Ottawa on the 15th, but a fast-moving light that made a peculiar noise and was described as undoubtedly an 'aeroplane' was seen going in a north-westerly direction at Morden, Manitoba.[28]

In Buffalo, USA, an aircraft plainly visible at a height of 2,500 to 3,000 feet was seen by thousands of witnesses at 8.00 a.m. on 19 February 1915. It travelled at a terrific pace towards Canada and then abruptly changed course towards Fort Erie on the Canadian shore.[29]

That sighting was virtually forgotten until Lieutenant E.H. Bequer, of the British Royal Flying Corps, made some startling revelations. He was in charge of the chaotic process of loading horses at the East Buffalo stockyards, when he told a reporter about his aeronautical adventures. The subsequent newspaper story featured these revelations:

> … he was in the machine which sailed over Buffalo three months ago. He called attention to a recently healed bullet wound, claiming a ball had gone through the calf and slightly splintered the bone. Another flesh wound scar in the abdomen showed, he said, where another bullet had hit.

According to Bequer, he started the flight which carried him over Buffalo from a transport about 20 miles off Long Island. He landed only once in the United States, a couple of hundred miles from

New York City because of engine trouble. Passing here, he said, he was about 3,000 feet up.

The trip across the continent after leaving Buffalo, he said was continually over Canadian territory. It took only four days and he did not consider that anything remarkable for the powerful army machine. Desire for absolute secrecy in the preparation to check the aeroplane plot unearthed by the secret service at Vancouver, he said, was responsible for the flight.

> It is true that an aeroplane was seen over Vancouver Island, British Columbia on 26 October 1914. Mr Napier Denison saw it at noon from the Gonzales Hill observatory. It headed for Trial Island, then turned back towards the straits. The machine, at the time, was thought to have come from Port Townsend where US military manoeuvres were taking place.

Lieutenant Bequer recounted that:

> I had been there three days waiting at my station on Vancouver Island for the threatened raid. When the machine finally turned up and I went out to meet it, we clashed only about 30 miles from Vancouver. They got me in the leg. That interfered to some extent with my manipulation of the controls, but we kept at it. When the bullet hit my abdomen, however, I reckoned I was beaten. Yes, I ran, as fast as my machine would go. Where the other machine went I don't know.[30]

On sober reflection, it does seem highly unlikely that someone would fly the vast distance from Long Island to Vancouver to tackle these aerial spies. Such a flight would easily have drawn attention to itself, and it would have required several refuelling stops along the route. So much for a secret mission!

Most likely the story was spun to impress the locals, although if he was trying to prove how brave and tough he was, why didn't he say he beat the enemy flier despite his injuries?

Another possibility is that he was covering up secret shipments of aircraft from Buffalo to Toronto when the US was still neutral.

(The US declared war on Germany on 6 April 1917.) An aircraft factory and flying school for Curtiss JN-3 aircraft – nicknamed 'Jennies' – was set up in Buffalo to supply the war effort in Europe, and there were other local air bases as well.

Whatever the truth, this was certainly one of the most bizarre stories of the First World War. The varying nature of what was 'seen' in the sky was underlined by sightings during February 1915 of coloured lights on the French-dependent island of St Pierre. They were regarded as representing the colours of the Republic, and a reversal of Great Britain's national colours. They helped reinforce the prevailing political attitudes of the people on the island.[31]

On the mainland, aerial invaders were still foremost in people's minds. There were several sightings of aircraft lights associated with engine sounds during March in Manitoba.[32] Also in March, on the 27th, a farmer called Cognac thought he heard an aircraft passing over Sabrevois, Quebec. This story got passed on by Major Hector Bissonette to the military authorities in Ottawa. In response, F.G. Robinson of the Thiel Detective Service was sent to interview the two men. Robinson found Cognac to be fairly intelligent and regretful about causing so much fuss, whilst Major Bissonette was found to be 'an extremely nervous individual and apparently easily alarmed'. The result of the interviews was that Robinson decided that there should be no newspaper publicity for this story, in case it generated another aeroplane scare like the one in Ottawa.

The next significant sighting was of a large aircraft on 28 June 1915. The throb of its engines was heard over Sandwich County Jail, which held William Lefler who had conspired with two Germans from Detroit to blow up buildings and was charged with dynamiting the Walkerville plant where uniforms were manufactured for the army. The fear that the aircraft was part of a plot to release him from his imprisonment, led to the mobilisation of the Sandwich Regiment of Fusiliers. The aircraft was also seen in Windsor, Ontario, for 15 minutes, heading northwards towards Detroit.[33]

Windsor had another 'alien aeroplane' visitation on 2 July. The commanding officer of the 21st Regiment of the First Division reported this in a telegram to the Military Secretary, along with a request for an 'armoured aeroplane' to be sent from Toronto. His request seems to have been ignored.

The owners of the Montreal Flying School sent several letters to the Department of Militia and Defence during July 1915, warning that enemy aviators were operating from a base in the Laurentian Mountains. From their investigation of rumours of aircraft in the area they concluded that at least two machines were being flown 'under the control of experts'. They requested funding for a biplane to track the aviators to their lair as they posed a threat to the 'Vickers Works and the various Power Plants at Bebeil, Vandreuil, Dragon, and Brownsburg'. After looking into the matter, the military concluded that the Flying School had started the rumours in order to get further funding for their own activities.

On the night of 4 or 5 July 1915, a large aeroplane was seen to land near Noyan Junction, Quebec. Two men got out of it, and checked some papers and plans before taking off in the direction of Montreal.[34]

A few days later, sightings were reported at Rigaud, and Montreal:

Judge Choquet, whose summer home is at Rigaud, said to-day that he had seen two aircraft hovering about in the proximity to a nearby factory. From Mississquot County had come previous reports of strange aeroplanes seen at night, and Montreal South, on Thursday [15 July] evening, reported an aeroplane evidently searching the shipping in the harbour.

Mayor Boyer, of Rigaud, corroborates the report given by Judge Choquet with regard to the mysterious flyers. For several evenings, he states, one or more aeroplanes have been seen floating high above the lake of Two Mountains and near the Rigaud factory. He states that on each occasion the aircraft departed in the direction of the frontier. The first time the aeroplane was seen orders were given at the Rigaud factory that all lights be extinguished. Every precaution is being taken to protect the place from possible attack.[35]

The phrase 'floating' gives the impression of balloon-like craft rather than powered aeroplanes. Certainly, many sightings of this period were of balloons, as is further confirmed by this report:

The military guard at Point Edward wireless station brought down two paper balloons which were passing overhead on Sunday night [18 July], so it leaked out this afternoon [20 July]. The balloons were first seen coming from the northwest, and passed over the station. The sentry, not wishing to take a chance, and thinking them aeroplanes, turned out the guard, with the result that five shots were fired before the balloons took fire and fell to the ground. It is estimated that they were travelling about 30 mph at the time, and were up about 1,500 feet. The hitting of both balloons shows remarkable skill of the guards with their rifles.[36]

This indicates that aircraft reports continued to be suppressed, but on occasion did 'leak out' to the media.

It was also reported that between 10.55 and 11.05 p.m. on 20 July, two aircraft were seen over the Ross Rifle factory in Quebec. Indeed, this was one of several sightings in the area during July:

Aeroplanes have been seen over the city of Quebec and the surrounding district … fully creditable persons have seen them manoeuvring over the citadel, the Plains of Abraham and over the harbour.[37]

Also on 20 July, F. Laberge, the town clerk and notary of Chateauguay, with a score of people saw an aircraft go southwards then return to the town. The strangest part of this story related to a suspected spy:

A German officer who has been living at Chateauguay, and who has been under surveillance, disappeared the night the aeroplane was sighted, and it is generally believed that he took this means of getting across the border to the United States. A number of Chateauguay citizens declare they heard signals from the earth and answering signals from the aeroplane and saw the machine alight in a field, and rise again a few minutes after. Next day the officer was gone.

A remarkable fact in connection with this report is that on Tuesday afternoon, at about 4 o'clock, the German officer in question went to a local notary and said he was leaving for New York and wished to make his will before going.[38]

The German had lived in the town for five years and rather recklessly made no secret of his German sympathies. Not surprisingly, he had been put under surveillance after the outbreak of the war. The aircraft that presumably whisked him away to New York first appeared at 9.30 p.m. Inhabitants heard the sound of its engines and saw its searchlight sweep the ground as it moved over the town. At 11.00 p.m., it landed for a few minutes near the lake shore and then flew away.

The German was lucky to get away – that's if he did use this means to escape Canada – as anything odd in the sky was shot at, especially if it appeared near a factory or military installation. As a good example, in August the foreman at the Standard Chemical Company factory at Donald, Haliburton County, Ontario, fired twelve shots at an aircraft:

> It was well on in the evening when the residents first noticed the mysterious ship in the air, their attention being attracted by a strong ray of light which seemed to come from a powerful headlight. The searchlight had the strength of a strong automobile headlight and cast a ray all around the vicinity. After remaining stationary for a short time, the machine (for such it appeared to be) sailed several feet away, and the villagers heaved a sigh of relief, but their joy was cut short and their fears increased when the machine returned and hovered around the chemical plant. It was then that foreman Jones proceeded to warn it off by firing several shots at the mysterious stranger. For an hour or so it shadowed the village and then retraced its flight beneath the stars to its hidden and unknown destination.[39]

Niagara Falls was no stranger to mystery aircraft. Toy balloons caused a minor scare there on 12 May 1915 and there were further sightings in the last few months of the year.[40] A lot of the activity seemed to be centred on the Welland Canal, and included two airships passing over the canal on 10 October. Aeroplanes were seen on the night of 21 December and the morning of the 23rd, inciting people to wonder if these were part of a plot to dynamite the Welland Canal, or whether they were German spy planes or aircraft being shipped from the Curtiss factory in Buffalo to Toronto.[41]

In the New Year, the Welland Canal still attracted mystery aircraft. An exceptional sighting was of a 'monoplane' that had a powerful headlight and twenty-seven red and white lights along its body. This was seen going over Stamford on 13 January 1916 before it circled and went off in a westwards direction.[42]

A big fire at Ottawa was attributed to the appearance of two aeroplanes that flew over Grantham at 8.00 p.m. on 3 February. Another aircraft appeared at St Catharine's the next day, and on Saturday 5 February, two or three aircraft were seen by members of a train crew. They were seen flying low over the Grand Trunk railway tracks south of the St Lambert end of the bridge. They were at an altitude of only a few hundred feet, as they circled over the track for a period of 20 minutes. A rifle shot was fired at them as a warning, and this encouraged the aircraft to rise in the sky and fly southwards to the American border.[43]

Linked with this sighting was the activity of a man who was seen earlier that day on the ice underneath Victoria Bridge. Guards feared he was planning to dynamite the bridge and they shot at him. On the same day, there was an explosion at the Jardine Munitions Factory, Hespeler, Ontario. The military authorities interviewed the train crew who saw the phantom aircraft, and as a result the guards on the bridge were reinforced and plain-clothed officers were deployed at strategically important buildings and factories.[44]

Hundreds of people in London saw the mystery flier on the night of 13 February 1916, but the sightings were explained as being caused by Venus and Jupiter.[45] Another crowd viewed a biplane circling over Windsor on the afternoon of 6 July 1916. Observers using binoculars plainly saw the pilot flying the aircraft in ever widening circles over the city, yet guards made no attempt to shoot at it. This seems to show that the authorities knew about this flight, but failed to let the press or public know about it.[46]

In the late afternoon of 25 August 1916, hundreds of people watched an aircraft circle Victoria Park and Niagara Falls, and 'believing the aviator was about to drop bombs, were thrown into a near panic.'[47] Fortunately, no bombs were dropped because this was a training flight going to Buffalo.[48]

Victor Carlstrom, a pilot employed to secretly fly aircraft from the Curtiss factory in Buffalo to Toronto, could easily have been responsible for many sightings. Certainly on the morning 31 August 1916, he caused a scare by flying in the direction of the Grand Trunk Railroad and flying over Niagara Falls, St Catharine's and Stamford. Sightings on the 13 January 1917 and 12 August 1917 were also probably due to these shipments.[49]

A biplane was seen circling, by two independent witnesses, over Oak Bay, Victoria on the morning of 16 January 1917, before it headed for the American coast. This led to the British Ambassador making a formal protest to the United States Government about infringing Canadian air space.

Captain Tweedale, the District Intelligence Officer, was not impressed by the report of two aeroplanes flying over Victoria in the last week of January 1917. The female witness claimed she heard the two pilots talking in a foreign language. Tweedale noted that it was 'so absurd and impossible that no credence can be placed in it'.

More credible were a spate of sightings on 11 February 1917 at Vancouver Island. A craft travelling at a speed of up to 70mph and at an altitude of 400 to 500 feet was first spotted at 7.00 p.m. It was then seen flying over Qualicum Beach at 8.00 p.m. before being seen carrying lights headed for Esquimalt. At 8.30 p.m., a guard at the Esquimalt Navy Yards saw it circle over the harbour before going southwards towards the Olympic Range America. It made Tweedale think that:

> It would be easy to take aeroplane parts and explosives into some secluded spot in the [Olympic] mountains, after landing them in some port on the West Coast as mining machinery and put them together in some secluded spot, and when this was done and they have a sufficient quantity of explosives ready, to fly over our harbour and destroy the ships therein, besides the powder works on James Island, chemical works in Victoria, Parliament Buildings, etc. As we have no means of defending ourselves should this be

carried out, these German agents who are certainly informed of this fact would be taking little risk ... The only other theory is, that these strange machines come from Seattle in the pay of German agents unknown to the United States Authorities.

There were very few sightings in 1917 but two came at the very end of the year. What looked like a Zeppelin, travelling at a speed of 20mph, was seen at St Felicite, Quebec, on 23 December. A telegram dated 27 December 1917, from Newport Point, Quebec, reported the presence of an aeroplane with lights flying over the St Lawrence River for three nights running. That seems to be the last mention of these mystery fliers.

As a tragic footnote, historian Brett Holman notes that when two ships – the SS *Mont-Blanc* loaded down with explosives and the SS *Imo* – collided near the coast of Halifax, Nova Scotia, it created one of the biggest ever non-nuclear explosions. This event was so traumatic that:

> Survivors proved incapable of understanding what was hap-pening. Many hallucinated, their eyes tricking them into seeing German Zeppelins attacking them from the air. A man on the outskirts of the town claimed to have heard a German shell whistling past him. Such visions had been stimulated over the preceding months by rumours of the possibility of a German attack. Residents with German-sounding names were set upon. Some survivors still believed that the Germans had something to do with the disaster.[50]

This underlines the prevailing fear and suspicion of German attack from the air and the fact that in an extremely stressful situation these came to be perceived as real events.[51]

It is significant that the number of sightings dropped after the USA declared war on Germany on 6 April 1917. After that the fear of German agents coming over from America faded away. Perhaps there were further mystery aerial sightings but the media and authorities were no longer interested in them.

References

1. *Ottawa Evening Journal*, 15 February 1915, p.1.
2. Government material is from the National Defence files at the Federal Archives, Ottawa. They are from Series (Record Group) 24, volumes: 2033 (HQ 6978-2-95), 2037 (HQ 6978-2-78), 2037 (HQ 6978-2-79), 2038 (HQ 6978-2-111), 2038 (HQ 6978-2-107) and 2039 (HQ 6978-2-112).
3. *Free Press* (London, Ontario), 12 September 1914.
4. *Free Press*, 5 September 1914, p.2.
5. *Free Press*, 5 September 1914, p.8.
6. *Free Press*, 5 September 1914, p.16.
7. Ibid., 12 September 1914.
8. *St. Catharines Standard*, 12 September 1914.
9. *Free Press*, 11 September 1914.
10. *Toronto Globe*, 18 September 1914.
11. *Free Press*, 28 September 1914.
12. *Daily Mail and Empire* (Toronto), 30 September 1914.
13. *Toronto Star*, 10 October 1914.
14. *Toronto Globe*, 20 October 1914.
15. *Free Press*, 21 October 1914.
16. *Free Press*, 21 October 1914.
17. *Daily Colonist* (Victoria, B.C.), 27 October 1914.
18. National Defence File: HQ 6978-2-79.
19. *Daily Mail and Empire* (Toronto), 3 November 1914.
20. *Buffalo Express*, 19 November 1914.
21. *Toronto Daily Star*, 4 December 1914.
22. *Toronto Daily Star*, 4 December 1914.
23. *Free Press*, 11 January 1915; *Niagara Falls Evening Review*, 30 January 1915 and 4 February 1915; *St. Catharines Standard*, 5 February 1915; *Manitoba Free Press* (Winnipeg), 29 January 1915.
24. *Toronto Globe*, 15 February 1915.
25. *The Standard*, 13 November 1982; *Free Press*, 15 February 1915.
26. *Free Press*, 15 February 1915; *Toronto Globe*, 16 February 1915; *New York Times*, 16 February 1915.
27. *Toronto Globe*, 16 February 1915.
28. *Manitoba Free Press*, 17 February 1915.
29. *Niagara Falls Evening Review*, 19 February 1915.
30. *Free Press*, 19 May 1915.
31. *Daily News* (St John's, Newfoundland), 27 February 1915.
32. *Manitoba Free Press*, 16, 25 and 27 March 1915.
33. *Free Press*, 29 June 1915.
34. *Free Press*, 6 July 1915.
35. *Free Press*, 19 July 1915.
36. *Free Press*, 21 July 1915.
37. *Free Press*, 21 July 1915.
38. *Free Press*, 22 July 1915.

39. Quoted in *Peterborough Ontario Examiner*, 1 November 1969.
40. *Niagara Falls Evening Review*, 13 May 1915.
41. *Niagara Falls Evening Review*, 14 and 20 October 1915; *The Daily Record*, 22 December 1915; *St. Catharines Standard*, 23 December 1915.
42. *Niagara Falls Evening Review*, 15 January 1916.
43. *St. Catharines Standard*, 4 February 1916; *Daily Record*, 5 February 1916; *Niagara Falls Evening Review*, 9 February 1916; *Evening Free Press* (London, Ontario), 7 February 1916; *New York Times*, February 1916.
44. *Evening Free Press*, 7 February 1916.
45. *Evening Free Press*, 14 February 1916.
46. *Evening Free Press*, 7 July 1916.
47. *Niagara Falls Evening Review*, 26 August 1916; *Daily Record*, 26 August 1916.
48. *Daily Record*, 28 August 1916.
49. *Daily Record*, 31 August 1916, 1 September 1916 and 13 August 1917; *Niagara Falls Evening Review*, 31 August 1916; *Daily Standard*, 14 September 1916.
50. Bourke, Joanna, *Fear: A Cultural History* (London: Virago, 2005), p.70.
51. Holman, Brett, 'The Zeppelins of Halifax,' Airminded blog at: airminded. org/2007/12/06/the-zeppelins-of-halifax/.

THIRTEEN

GREAT BRITISH SIGHTINGS IN 1915

The Day of the Dupes

The rumours of mystery aircraft in Galloway, Scotland, reached their climax in January 1915, and the south-east of England had a similar scare. A War Office report noted that 'real' aircraft raids had made the public more sensitive to the threat from the air:

> False alarms in January 1915. The aeroplane raids of Boxing Day and Christmas Day 1915, in Kent, and of January 19-20 in Norfolk had their aftermath of false alarms of raids, most of them of a wild and senseless nature which did not say much for the intelligence of the 'observers'. Very few of these people seemed to have asked themselves whether it was possible for enemy airships to be in the positions assigned to them, and there seems to have been no very clear idea of what an airship looked like or indeed of the difference between an airship and aeroplane. Some people were under the impression that the word 'Zeppelin' was the German for an 'aeroplane'.[1]

On the morning of 3 January 1915, warnings were issued that two Zeppelins and three cruisers were off the German coast, steering west. It was estimated that if they held on their course, they would be off the British coast by 2.00 p.m. This gave rise to an extraordinary crop of rumours:

> At 1:35 p.m. the police at Beckton informed the guard over the oil tanks there that two Zeppelins had been seen at Chelmsford. At 1:45 p.m. a naval biplane (Sopwith No. W 104) which descended at High Halstow reported two Zeppelins over Chelmsford going towards London. They also said that the Zeppelins were supported by 4 or 5 cruisers.

An hour later, the scare continued to grow. The corporal of the guard at Stevenage reported at 2.40 p.m. that an airship had flown over Barking moving very slowly, and that firing was going on between Woolwich and Purfleet. Another report said that the two Zeppelins had appeared over Crowborough, Sussex, going westwards, at 2.00 p.m.

The military guard at the West India Docks reported another aeroplane over Purfleet at 9.06 p.m. At 9.57 p.m., it was reported over Guildford (although this could be explained as a British aeroplane returning to Farnborough). A Zeppelin was seen over Boston at 9.35 p.m. This first 'Day of Dupes' was then over. However, we can see that the Zeppelin alert caused many to think that they saw the enemy approaching, and that this caused complications and confusion for the British defence forces.

An airship was seen heading up the Thames towards London at 11.30 p.m. on 21 January.

Then another crop of rumours spread after there was a warning that a Zeppelin was leaving the German coast on 23 January. The stationmaster at Martham heard an aircraft hovering overhead from 10.00 to 11.00 a.m., before it flew away northwards. At 11.55 a.m., a Zeppelin was reported over Breydon Water. In the evening, at 10.00 p.m., three 'cigar-shaped objects' were seen passing over Tilbury by the alien officer and three customs officials there. And, at 10.30 p.m., the Armoured Car Section of the RNAS at Oxted saw an airship half a mile to the south, going east to west. This was seen in conjunction with a 'motor car carrying two brilliant headlights and a light on top'. The Admiralty sent out cars to search for it, but their search proved unsuccessful.

A patrol at Purley Oakes railway station on 24 January reported seeing an enemy airship at 11.00 a.m. It travelled from the south to the north-north-west at high altitude.

The Kaiser's birthday on 27 January was expected to be a good occasion for a big raid on Britain. Accordingly, orders were given for special vigilance to be observed from 5.00 p.m. on the 26th. This resulted in a further night of wild rumours. At 6.45 p.m., a sentry thought he saw an aircraft crossing the beam of a searchlight at Waltham Abbey. The guard at Grosvenor Bridge, London, saw an aeroplane going westwards at 6.55 p.m. At Grays, Essex, a 'hostile' aircraft was seen at 9.30 p.m. An airship that was thought to have dropped bombs was reported by the stationmaster at Abbey Wood at 11.15 p.m. He thought the target for this invader was Farleigh, near Maidstone.

On the night in question, it is possible that a Zeppelin from Belgium did make a reconnaissance over the Dover Straits. It was seen at Dunkirk heading for England at 10.40 p.m., though it seems unlikely it was responsible for the Abbey Wood or the earlier 'aircraft' sightings.

On the morning of 31 January, an airship was seen at Micheldever. A few minutes later an aeroplane was seen following the same flight-path as the airship.

February started with a brand new batch of rumours. They did not require any advance warnings or any factual foundation whatsoever to inspire them.

On the first day of the month, five Zeppelins were seen at Hornchurch heading for London. Less than an hour later, at 7.23 p.m., three Zeppelins were seen at Dover. Three rounds were fired at them as they headed towards Deal.

The guard at the Surrey Commercial Docks reported that five Zeppelins had passed over Romford at 7.30 p.m. This was inspired by the original 'sighting' at Hornchurch. The passing on of the message resulted in an officer of the Home Counties Royal Field Artillery at Slough ordering all lights to be put out in the town at 10.00 p.m., '… as five Zeppelins were over London.'

The police rightly queried this order and were told that there was no truth in this rumour. An aeroplane was seen at Purfleet, heading for London, at 8.20 p.m. So it was quite a hectic night for airship spotters in the London area.[2]

The first sighting of 1915 in south-west Scotland was on 4 January. An aeroplane was seen in the district of Gatehouse of Fleet between 6.45 and 7.15 p.m. After circling for a time it disappeared in the south.[3]

The following evening, at 8.55 pm, it was again seen in the district when a coachman at Castramont saw it hovering, before it went over High Creoch.[4]

A dairyman travelling from Lincluden to Dumfries on 12 January observed over the town a red light in the sky, which immediately changed to yellow before disappearing. At the same time, he saw another light, of some brilliance, to the south of Dumfries over Criffel Hill, and after it made some 'unusual movements' it disappeared.

One local newspaper attributed the frequent sightings in Dumfries and Galloway to frequent intakes of whisky.[6] The rumours, however, continued during the second and third weeks of January.[7]

In spite of the continued military searches, no secret German base, or any other type of secret base, was found in the Galloway region. The 20 January 1915 edition of the *Dumfries and Galloway Standard & Advertiser* did provide this intriguing statement:

It may now be stated that as the result of a systematic search conducted in the mountainous regions of the Stewarty, circumstances have been discovered, we understand, which strongly confirm the suspicions that enemy airships have made frequent visits to the district for obtaining supplies, and with a view, it is conjectured, of receiving news conveyed to them by wireless telegraph or flash-light signals and transmitting it to Germany.

Commenting on the aeroplane reports, the *Annandale Observer and Advertiser* for the 22 January, wrote:

> Further and more complete search has now established its (the aeroplane's) existence beyond doubt, and there is good ground for believing that a base exists in Galloway, and there are also reasons for suspicion that the enemy has been making use of the mysterious machine or machines for the purpose of receiving and transmitting messages to Germany. In the course of the search further and equally sensational discoveries have been made, but of which is not permissible to write. The whole affair is well in hand, and when and if it is allowed to be published it will read like a romance.

It has not been possible to ascertain what had been uncovered by the military search parties in Galloway, even though these newspaper reports suggest that something of importance was found.

On 22 January several Kirkconnel miners on their way to work at Gateside Colliery, at 6.00 a.m., saw an aeroplane travelling from the north-east going westwards.[8] An hour later, the residents of North Street, Annan distinctly heard the noise of an engine and clearly saw an aeroplane making for the Cumberland hills.

Wild stories continued. Six Germans, it was claimed, had been caught in the Kells Hills and lodged in Jessiefield. On 18 January, rumour said that 800 soldiers had surrounded and captured spies signalling to the enemy on the Durisdeer hills in Upper Nithsdale.[9]

Lighting restrictions were imposed on Wigtownshire in February due to the continued rumours. On the first of the month, at 10.00 p.m., two Dumfries gentlemen observed a scarcely visible reddish light that gradually brightened until it resembled the glare of a motor headlamp. It then slowly faded and disappeared.[10]

Two men in Stranraer saw a long-shaped light on 13 February at 12.30 a.m. When it reached a great height, it burst and the whole of Loch Ryan and the surrounding district were brilliantly lit up.[11]

Several lights were seen at Annan and Dumfries at 5.30 a.m. on 23 February.[12] Then, on the 25 February, at 9.00 p.m., flashing red and green lights were seen over the Lowther Hills. Occasionally one light appeared that illuminated a large area of countryside.[13]

For some odd reason there were no more reports until Saturday 1 May 1915. On that night, Sergeant Ringland of Stranraer police observed a Zeppelin flying over the town. As a precautionary measure, he had the town's gas supply turned off. On 3 March, an enemy aeroplane was said to have flown over Loch Ryan.[14]

The *Report on the Dartmoor Floating (or Balloon) Light* is one of the most intriguing documents of the First World War. The four-page document was produced by Lieutenant Colonel W.P. Drury who was an Intelligence Officer based at the Plymouth Garrison, Devon. It deals with several sightings of lights that might have been connected with enemy activities. He began on 28 June 1915 by interviewing Miss Cecilia Peel Yates who lived at Dolbeare Cottage, Ashburton. She told Lieutenant Colonel Drury and his colleague Lieutenant Colonel C. Brownlow that a few mornings previously:

> … just before dawn, having been awakened by the barking of dogs, she saw from her bedroom window a bright light in the sky, bearing N., and apparently suspended a short distance above the earth. It was too large and bright for a planet, and, as she watched, it swung to the N.E., and disappeared. Haytor is due North of Ashburton and 4 miles distant as the crow flies.

They were dismissive of this report, even though Miss Yates stuck to her story under cross-examination, as it seemed so improbable. They revised this opinion when Mrs Cave-Penny and her daughter also saw lights on Dartmoor at their isolated home in Sherril, near Hexworthy. On several occasions they saw a white light rise from the east side of Hexworthy Mine.

Lieutenant Colonel Drury and his colleague interviewed the two witnesses on 12 July 1915. The report notes:

> The light sometimes rose above the skyline, at others it showed against the moon of Down Ridge, on which the mine is situated. On each occasion it rose from the same spot and followed the

same course. Mrs. Cave-Penny is a rather excitable, irresponsible Irish lady, but we had no reason to doubt her evidence in the main, and her daughter's testimony (which fully corroborated that of her mother) was most clear and definite. This floating light against Down Ridge has been reported from the Hexworthy district on several occasions since, the last being a few nights ago.

More lights were seen in the middle of August, including sightings by Mrs Whitley at her home Barton Pines, which overlooked the seaside town of Paignton. Her friends also saw this light, and even her sceptical husband saw the 'floating light' that would travel above a row of fir trees in their garden. Mr Falkland Ricketts of Gatcombe Manor was also a witness to these lights on several occasions. This led Drury to start his own UFO hunt:

> I obtained the sanction of the G.O.C., to watch one of the three points enumerated until I saw the light myself. I selected the Dartington Point, and, accompanied by Mr. Brownlow, began to watch from a position immediately opposite near the main Totnes-Newton Abbot road. On the third night we both saw the phenomenon precisely as it had been described at Hexworthy and Barton Pines.

He went on to describe their sighting in more detail:

> About 9.30 that night [September 4th] we observed a bright white light, considerably larger in appearance than a planet, steadily ascend from the meadow to an approximate height of 50 or 60 feet. It then swung for hundred yards or so to the left, and suddenly vanished. Its course was clearly visible against the dark background of wood and hill, though, the night being dark, it was not easy to determine whether it was a little above or beneath the skyline.
>
> We were within a mile of the light and both saw its ascension and transit distinctly. The Dart flows between Dartington and our post of observation, and, … it was impossible to reach the meadow from which the light arose.

Drury made several night-time floating-light expeditions before and after that date, but he never saw the light again. He did, however, note that the light was seen on a line that ran from Down Ridge to Barton Pines, which passed through Buckfast Abbey. Forty unnaturalised Germans of military age were living at the Abbey and were possible suspects, and it suggested to him that some type of captive balloon with a light attached was being used. Drury considered that the purpose of the balloon was either for 'some form of illicit signalling' or to lift a wireless aerial aloft, but even today we do not know what caused these sightings.

The reports in the press had by now faded away, probably due to stricter censorship that was introduced in June 1915. The eagerness for news of any kind still meant that all sorts of rumours were spread and given credence. In the 15 September 1915 edition of the *Evening News* (London), this enthusiasm for such stories was ridiculed. It said that one piece of wonderful nonsense was repeated by a man who knew a relative of a relative who saw a Zeppelin land on Hampstead Heath. As proof of this, another man was supposed to have collected some horses to take away the wreckage.

The well-known aviator, Claude Grahame-White, was said to have been either killed or injured in a very 'serious accident'. Equally valid stories about German spies circulated, and nearly every village in Kent knew of a nearby village that had witnessed the shooting down of a Zeppelin. With some cynicism, the newspaper observed: 'No flying gasbag ever falls in the particular village in which the walking gasbag has his being.'

Rumours surfaced again in February 1916, shortly after a major airship raid on the night of 31 January, but not much information was disclosed about them. No raids were mounted against Britain in February, but on 2 February, enemy airships were independently reported over Birmingham, Derby and Manchester where lights in railway stations and munition factories were extinguished. Zeppelins were reported throughout the North and the Midlands in the following days with the result that lights were put out in factories and stations in Nottingham, Bath, Gloucester and Worcester.[15]

Only two well-documented reports are known for certain, both relating to the night of 31 January 1916, when nine real German airships carried out a raid against England. None of them went as far south as Essex, but the War Office did receive a report that one of them was heading towards London and would reach the capital at 8.10 p.m. if it kept its present speed and direction.

Hainault Farm fighter aerodrome, 4 miles north of Romford, Essex, was warned about the possible arrival of this craft. In response to this news, Lieutenant R.S. Maxwell took flight in his BE 2c No 2087 biplane at 7.40 p.m. to see if he could make visual contact with the Zeppelin. In his report on this mission he stated:

My engine was missing irregularly and it was only by keeping the speed of the machine down to 50 m.p.h., that I was able to stay at 10,000 feet. It was at this time that I distinctly saw an artificial light to the north of me, and at about the same height. I followed this light north east for nearly twenty minutes, but it seemed to go slightly higher and just as quickly as myself, and eventually I lost it completely in clouds.[16]

The famous British aviator, Claude Grahame-White gets ready to fly. (*All About Aircraft* by Ralph Simmonds, London: Cassell, 1915)

THE STRAND MAGAZINE

Vol. xlii.   JULY, 1911.   No. 247.

The Aerial Menace

Why There is Danger in England's Apathy.

By CLAUDE GRAHAME-WHITE.

A YEAR or so ago, when the first crude aeroplanes were flying yards instead of miles, and when no flight of any kind was possible unless there was practically a dead calm, there were clever men who smiled when air-craft were spoken of as possible weapons in time of war. Now, in 1911, a man whirls through the air at sixty-three miles an hour, lunching in London and having tea in Paris, and amazing the whole world by bridging the distance between the two capitals in a monoplane in three hours less time than is taken by the fastest train and the quickest turbine steamer.

And this only half reveals the phenomenal progress which the aeroplane is making. A weight-carrying machine, bearing aloft a pilot and two passengers, can fly across country for several hours without descending, at a speed in excess of that of the fastest motor-car. An aeroplane can now soar aloft until it hovers more than two miles above the earth ; and, instead of being chained to the ground by every breeze that blows, a skilled pilot can now fly with safety in a wind blowing at a velocity of twenty-five miles an hour, while, if the

Aviator Claude Grahame-White warns of the danger of fleets of aircraft dropping bombs on London. (*Strand Magazine*, No. 247, July 1911)

Sub-Lieutenant Reginald Warneford bombed and destroyed a Zeppelin over Ghent in June 1915, for which action he was awarded the Victoria Cross and the Legion d'Honneur. Though of course a member of the RNAS, Warneford had initially joined the army and he was quickly adopted as a poster boy for recruitment to the Sportsman's Battalions. To destroy one of the Zeppelin monsters was clearly viewed as an almost superhuman achievement. (Library of Congress)

At the same time Second Lieutenant Claude Ridley, in another BE aircraft, also spotted a moving light over London, but he quickly lost sight of it in dense cloud. Apparently, both pilots had spotted each other's aircraft without realising it.[17]

Another of the capital's fighter aerodromes was at Rochford, some 22 miles east of Hainault Farm. Flight Sub-Lieutenant J.E. Morgan took off from here at 8.45 p.m. He was assigned to patrol between Southend and Rochford. At an altitude of 5,000 feet, he saw, slightly ahead and to his right, about 35 yards away, ' ... a row of what appeared to be lighted windows which looked like something like a railway carriage with the blinds drawn.'

Believing he had come upon a hostile airship, Morgan took out his Webley Scott service revolver and fired several shots at it. Whereupon, 'the lights alongside rose' so rapidly, it seemed that his own aircraft was diving. By now he had lost his bearings, and he had to make a crash landing on Thameshaven marshes.[18]

A Zeppelin was briefly glimpsed in the light of searchlights a few minutes later at 9.00 p.m. by a fourth RFC pilot, Flight Sub-Lieutenant H. McClelland, who had taken off from Chingford. His report was scrutinised by the Third Sea Lord, Rear-Admiral F.C.T. Tudor, who commented:

> Night flying must be difficult and dangerous, and require considerable nerve and pluck, but this airman seems to have been gifted with a more than usually vivid imagination.[19]

Whether the expected presence of a Zeppelin triggered their imaginations or not, it certainly looked real enough to be shot at by Morgan and was witnessed by three other pilots. Whatever they saw remains a mystery, and goes down in history as the first officially recorded dogfight with a UFO.

References

1. PRO Air 1/565 16/15/89.
2. PRO Air 1/561 16/15/62. *December 1914 – August, 1918: Reports of False Alarms or Rumoured Air Raids in England.*
3. *Dumfries and Galloway Courier and Herald*, 6 January 1915.
4. *Dumfries and Galloway Courier and Herald*, 9 January 1915.
5. *Dumfries and Galloway Standard and Advertiser*, 13 January 1915.
6. *Nithsdale News and Advertiser*, 8 January 1915.
7. *Dumfries and Galloway Standard and Advertiser*, 20 January 1915; *Dumfries and Galloway Courier and Herald*, 20 January 1915; *Galloway Advertiser and Wigtownshire Free Press*, 21 January 1915; *Annandale Observer and Advertiser* (Annan), 22 January 1915.
8. *Dumfries and Galloway Saturday Standard*, 23 January 1915.
9. *Dumfries and Galloway Courier and Herald*, 23 January 1915.
10. *Dumfries and Galloway Standard and Advertiser*, 3 February 1915.
11. *Galloway Advertiser and Wigtownshire Free Press*, 18 February 1915.
12. *Annandale Observer*, 26 February 1915.
13. *Dumfries and Galloway Courier and Herald*, 27 February 1915.
14. *Galloway Advertiser and Wigtownshire Free Press*, 6 May 1915.
15. Jones, H.A., *The War in the Air. Volume Three* (Oxford: The Clarendon Press, 1931).
16. PRO Air 1/611 16/15/286 *Report from Officer in Command, Royal Flying Corps, Hainault Farm, 2 February 1916.*
17. Cole, C. and Cheeseman, E.F., *The Air Defence of Britain 1914–1918* (London: Bodley Head, 1984), p.87.
18. Cole and Cheeseman, pp.88–89; Morris, Captain Joseph, *The German Air Raids on Great Britain 1914–1918* (London: H. Pordes, 1969), pp.88–89: PRO Air 1/438 15/300/1. *Rochford Station (Naval): report on night landing ground, 1916.*
19. Cole and Cheeseman, pp.88–89; PRO Air 1/720 36/1/6 *GHQ Home Forces Intelligence Circular No 6, May 1916*; Clarke, David, 'Britain's First Military UFO Encounter?', *Flying Saucery Presents* … website, at: www.uk-ufo.org/condign/hist1916.htm.

FOURTEEN

NORWAY

Norway was the location for many sightings from 1914 to 1916, and they seem to have been generated by a mixture of 'real' aircraft, phantoms, misidentifications and rumour. One report even includes the sighting of an angel in the sky, which shows that these sightings were not always interpreted as enemy aircraft.

To the south of Stavanger a biplane was seen circling the area on 2 August 1914 just as the First World War was about to tear Europe apart. The next day, a high-flying aeroplane was seen in Moi Ranen, Helgeland. At Bovbjerg, what was thought to be Zeppelin II was seen on 17 or 18 August in the morning.[1]

A white light was seen at Alta going towards Talvik by many independent witnesses on 17 September 1914. It looked like a very bright star against the background of an overcast sky, and at times it changed colour from white to red and blue. It was viewed between 9.00 and 10.00 p.m. and it varied its height and moved relatively slowly until it zoomed out of sight. It was observed through binoculars from the steamboat *Sina* and confirmed the impression that it was attached to an airplane.[2]

At Knaplund nine or ten people saw a cigar-shaped craft and heard its engine. It appeared at 9.00 p.m. on 22 October 1914, and went eastwards.[3]

In November 1914 several sightings of a 'Zeppelin' were made in Helgeland. The most detailed observation was at Mindlandet, Tjolta where twenty to thirty people saw an airship on 21 November.

The craft flew towards Skjarvaer lighthouse where it descended from an altitude of 700 metres to 400 metres, and progressed to illuminate it and a passing ship with its searchlight. Hr. Vogt who was the chief on a navy guard ship stationed at Sandnessjøen, Helgeland, explained these sightings as observations of stars and meteors.[4]

On one occasion Hr. Vogt and a friend walked from Sandnessjøen to a local rectory with a bright lantern, and had inadvertently caused a scare of their own. People at the rectory had spotted their lantern light and quickly thought it was an approaching aeroplane. Speaking in 1934, Hr. Vogt thought the war had made people more aware of strange lights in the sky.

At 8.00 a.m. on the morning of 20 December 1914, many reliable witnesses, including the sheriff of Solum, saw an airship at a dizzying height. It moved inland, then turned southwards and went away over the sea.[5]

There was a break in sightings until 13 July 1915, when four women heard the loud noise of an aircraft engine. It was reported that, 'the two women who were a little ahead of the others saw an airplane come rushing right over them with a course in a north-westerly direction'. An officer's wife, who saw the machine, is certain that she could not have been mistaken that it was an airplane, since she had often seen airplanes in flight. But now comes the strange part:

> The woman had been able to observe the machine only a moment when the motor stopped working and the machine fell down like lightning in a slanting direction, pointing toward Volhufjorden. She saw all this quite clearly, and her impression was that the machine and flier were on their way to destruction.'

They reported the matter to the sheriff at Østre Sidre, but extensive searches did not find any trace of the expected aircraft wreckage.[6]

Sometime in 1915 at Bergen, Henr. Angel Hansen saw an object as big as the moon in the north, at about 11.00 p.m. It had a brown-red colour and was very bright, and two or three times it descended and ascended in the sky before speeding away westwards.[7]

Another incident of this period was remembered by Bjarne Westvard who was 6-years-old at the time. One day in the summer of that year, he saw a dark bell-like object land on a hill near Sulitjelma. Shortly afterwards two grey-skinned, 3-foot tall humanoids dressed in dark overalls appeared and started walking towards the witness. One of the humanoids stopped and smiled at him. They then returned to the hill and the UFO took off into the sky.[8]

A Zeppelin displaying a bright light was seen over Christianaford for a minute on 20 August 1915, before it turned southwards. It was seen through binoculars during a thunderstorm at 9.40 p.m.[9]

Many reliable witnesses saw a large airship with six lights and a searchlight at Dyfjord on 13 January 1916. In the same month the captain of the steamship *Ofoten* saw a Zeppelin at a height of 500 metres over Rolvaer.[10]

In March and April 1916, aircraft carrying lights were seen at Vesterålen, Jæren and Stafjorden where the drone of motors was plainly heard.[11] On 16 April, several pupils at the Sytavanger Folkeskole saw a red light behind a black cloud. The pupils, who were aged between 9 and 11, saw an angel with a cross and later a message in the sky.[12]

Sightings resumed in June 1916. On the 14th, a hydroplane was seen to land on a fiord at Steilene. A boat was lowered from it, and this was used to tow it towards Slemmestad. On the evening of the 24 June, a biplane was seen over Ulriken at great height, heading out to sea.[13]

In December 1916, a dark Zeppelin-like object was seen moving swiftly by Norwegian fishermen who were working their nets at Svalbard Island. It flew over the Arctic ice, and went in the direction of the North Pole. That seems to have been the last sighting in Norway during the First World War.

References

1. *Morgenbladet*, 3 and 6 August 1914, p. 3.
2. *Morgenbladet*, 24 September 1914.

3.   *Morgenbladet*, 23 October 1914, p.4.
4.   *Morgenbladet*, 25 November 1914, p.2.
5.   *Morgenbladet*, 22 December 1914, p.3.
6.   *Morgenbladet*, 16 July 1915, p.4.
7.   *UFO-NYT*, March 1972, p.118.
8.   *Rapportnytt*, April 1981, p.3.
9.   *Morgenbladet*, 25 August 1915, p.4; *Gjengangeren*, August 1915.
10. *Morgenbladet*, 15 January 1916, p.2 and 19 January 1916, p.2.
11. *Morgenbladet*, 24 March 1916, p.4 and 5 April 1916, p.4; Ibid., 23 April 1916, p.4.
12. *Stavanger Aftenblad*, April 1916.
13. *Morgenbladet*, 27 June 1916, p.2.

FIFTEEN

AUSTRALIA

Following the declaration of war in 1914, most countries had their own crop of phantoms in the sky. As newspapers, journals and government files are increasingly being made available online it is easier for more people to look for references to any reports of this kind. And, 'new' cases are being found all the time.

One example of a recent discovery is a letter written by the French Chief of Staff dated 16 August 1914. In it he notes that a bright object had been viewed at Corbeil, south of Paris. On 12 August, it was seen in the north-west at a great height giving off a silver light, and on the following night it was in the direction of Versailles, moving in a north-west–north-east direction.[1]

Historian Brett Holman has recently discovered a great deal of First World War reports in the Australian media and archives, which shows there is probably much more information to be gathered from other countries and time periods.[2]

His research indicates that there was a brief aeroplane scare in October 1914 in New South Wales, when it was wondered why an Australian aircraft was flying at night, and if it was German, why didn't it drop a bomb or two? Unlike other countries, Australia suffered the most intense aircraft scares in the closing years of the conflict.[3]

Australia seemed a place where the population would be safe from any aerial invaders. Logically, it would be virtually impossible for enemy aircraft to fly there as they would need to make several refuelling stops in hostile territories, and why would any enemies risk such missions when these machines were needed in other theatres of war?

If Australia was attacked by aircraft, it would have had little protection from them as most of its own machines had been sent to fight in the Middle East and Europe, and only a few training aircraft were retained. This vulnerability was largely ignored or forgotten until the airship scares came along.

During 1917, an aeroplane was seen by a coach driver along with some other people in Gippsland. It circled at a great height and nothing much was thought of it until a crop of sightings occurred in 1918.[4]

The first sightings of 1918 occurred on 21 March, when, at noon, Mrs Tilley of Ouyen, north-western Victoria, saw two aircraft flying northwards. Four further witnesses confirmed this sighting, and in the afternoon Police Constable Wright was patrolling near Nyang, 30 miles from Ouyen, and reported that:

> I saw two flying machines pass overhead. They were up an [sic] great height & appeared to be about twenty yards apart. I did not hear the noise of the machines. They proceeded in a Westerly direction & as the sky was particularly clear the machines were easily discernible.[5]

On 18 April, a balloon or Zeppelin was seen by a teenage girl in Bunbury, Western Australia. Harry McDonald, a mechanic at South Yarra, reported:

> On the 21st April 1918, with my wife I was staying at my wife's uncle's place, Mornington Junction, and from 9.15 to 10.30 p.m. standing at the side of Mr Clipperton's place watching towards over Langwarrin Camp, I saw an object at a low altitude over the camp, then this object travelled out to sea towards Port Phillip Bay. This object was emitting intermitent [sic] flashes of red, green, and white light, with a flash; sometimes a few seconds elapsed between these flashes, and sometimes up to 2 or 3 minutes. The altitude varied

considerably, the low altitude appeared near the water, and then it would rise and appeared to come towards us and then would go away. I cannot give any information regarding noise.[6]

On 30 April, a man saw what he thought was a seaplane travel over Hobart, and on 2 May employees at the butter factory, Kongwak, Gippsland viewed an 'aeroplane' overhead for three hours. Sightings then continued until the end of the war.[7]

The so-called aeroplanes took on all sorts of shapes and appearances, some of which sound implausible. On spotting 'a dark square object' in the sky, Chief Officer Elms on board SS *Koolonga* said, 'God spare my days, that's a b...y Aeroplane!'. Though from that description what he and his fellow crew members saw off Kangaroo Island, South Australia, seems like an unusual aeroplane.[8]

At Hunters Hill, Sydney, A.K. Moore, a former naval officer, said he saw four biplanes late one afternoon. They had 'butterfly shaped wings, which gave them the appearance of huge insects. When these aeroplanes banked he got a good view of them and they appeared to be of a different construction to our machines.'[9]

Mrs Conway went one better by stating that on one moonlit night she saw an aeroplane. She told Yarra Glen police that it flew over Christmas Hills and, 'that there were two persons sitting side by side in the aircraft, that they had caps pulled down over their ears.'[10]

There were about 200 sightings in 1918, half of them made between mid-April and mid-May. Sightings were mainly made in rural rather than urban areas and concentrated in the south-eastern area of Australia.

There were two major news stories that triggered these and the following sightings. Sensational headlines in the newspapers for 16 March 1918 declared that the *Wolf* German raiding vessel had been sailing off the coast of Australia without being detected by any Australian defence forces. It returned to its home port at Kiel in February 1918, and it was claimed it had sunk several cargo ships on its fifteen-month-long cruise. More significantly, the vessel carried a Friedrichshafen FF.33 seaplane, nicknamed the *Wolfchen*, and it was alleged that it had flown over Sydney Harbour without anyone hearing or spotting it. It also made the media wonder if the seaplane was responsible for the Gippsland sighting in 1917.[11]

The publication of this only a few days before PC Wright's and other sightings indicates that it brought to the forefront the real danger of German aircraft. The second and not least major news story was that the Germans were gaining ground in their spring offensive against the Allied forces. Air raids on London and Paris reinforced the idea of the possibility of aerial invaders over Australia, and as the *Sydney Morning Herald* put it, 'there are no more civilians, in the sense of non-combatants. All are now recognised as taking their part in the war.'[12] Indeed, the *Ouyen Mail* clearly saw a link since, 'it is a remarkable coincidence that Constable Wright and the four others should have seen the machines the very day the present big offensive started.'

Later on in June 1918, the Healesville police noted that suspicious flashing signals from a nearby hill always coincided with major German movements in France.[13]

In New Zealand, mystery aeroplane sightings were certainly triggered by the news of the visit of the *Wolf*. The 8 April 1918 edition of the *Poverty Bay Herald* observed that:

Since the disclosure of the boast by an officer of a German raider that he had passed over Sydney in a seaplane, the authorities in New Zealand have had to cope with quite an epidemic of reports about mysterious aeroplanes circling around the more remote parts of New Zealand. In every case careful investigation has to be made, and in every case the report has been found to be without foundation. Some of these reports have found their way into the newspapers, causing somewhat of a scare, and it is intended to prosecute under the War Regulations any person who in future circulates without good cause any such report likely to cause public alarm. If New Zealanders see any more mysterious visitants in the sky their best plan will be to carefully verify the sight, and quietly inform the nearest police or defence officer, avoiding any public mention, for fear that it comes under the scope of the numerous possible offences against these comprehensive War Regulations.

The impact of the *Wolf* story in Australia is underlined in a letter from James French, Maffra Shire secretary, to the Intelligence Department, which informed them that an aeroplane was seen by the stationmaster at Maffra. After describing this as 'going at a good bat with bright lights, making very little noise and there was no mistaking it', he went on to relate:

> For some time the residents of Seaspray on the Ninety-Mile Beach see bright lights westward of that place; supposed to be in the Carrajung Hills, and it was from here that Mr. J. M. Maclachlan, M.L.C., saw the raider 'Wolf' standing out for many hours one day ... It is quite evident that the material is carted into the bush and the planes are there fitted up. A friend of mine here met a lady from Healesville, who said she frequently noticed cars going up into the bush in that direction loaded up and returning empty.[14]

In response to these sightings, every boat and ship available was deployed by the Royal Australian Navy (RAN) to reinforce its patrols of the eastern and southern coastline, and its coastal batteries were reactivated.[15]

Major-General J.G. Legge, Chief of the General Staff, confessed that:

> These raiders are knocking about and some of them have sea planes. Supposing one came over Melbourne and said 'I will drop bombs on your banks I will give you such and such a time to send your money down to a certain place on the beach. If you do not do that I will blow you to smithereens'. You have not got a single gun here to shoot at them and you would either have to have your public buildings knocked about or give them your money. That is the position at present.[16]

Two days later, on 20 April 1918, two armed aircraft were also dispatched to find the aerial invader. Captain Frank McNamara VC made daily searches in an old F.E.2b biplane over the coastal areas of south Gippsland with a view to spotting floating mines, enemy signalling or hostile seaplanes. The other aircraft was sent to Two Fold Bay on the New South Wales coast. Both searches were equally futile and by 9 May 1918 they concluded that the majority of reports had no foundation in reality.[17]

Ironically, these aerial patrols caused people to mistake them for enemy aircraft and generated even more reports.[18]

On the 24 April, Senator Pearce was quoted as saying, with reference '... to the rumours, which were in circulation ... there was nothing that need alarm the public, but it had been thought advisable to take certain action [sic] of a precautionary nature to guard against any interference with our shipping.' He acknowledged that aeroplanes had reportedly been 'seen in certain places in Victoria' and he explained how Allied aircraft markings can be distinguished from German markings. On this date, the Censorship Office prevented any more reports of aircraft sightings being published in the press.[19]

Reports had begun to slow down by now, although the public continued to report any sightings to their local newspapers or police station. The Navy Office, in a communication to the Admiralty on 27 April 1918, certainly thought that the phantom aircraft sightings were due to enemy activities:

Reports are being received daily of Aeroplanes seen in Victoria and South Australia ... King Island indicated as a possible base ... Aeroplanes may be in connection with some inland organisation.[20]

This led them to think that if:

... all the reports as correct, and assuming that some or all of the aircraft are from vessels at sea, there must be at least four such vessels ... If the aircraft come from land bases, the number of bases must be at least four, and almost certainly several more than four.[21]

The idea that a spy ring in Australia had aided the *Wolf* and was working on other schemes to attack the country mixed these sinister activities with the arrival of the phantom aeroplanes. These possibilities led to a reward of £2,000 being offered to anyone who could help catch the saboteurs who were suspected of sinking the SS *Cumberland*, off Gabo Island.[22] It was wondered if there was

> … somewhere in this country a wireless apparatus at work that might keep a German rover in the Pacific aware of all that is going on amongst Commonwealth shipping. There is every likelihood of such being the case. What one thinks of is a well-appointed wireless station in some out of the way place, among unfrequented hills, probably, the operator being fed with information by contingents of German spies in Melbourne, Sydney and Brisbane.[23]

Some of the aeroplane activity did seem to indicate a link with spies. At 2 a.m. on 18 April, Mr Sutton a drover near Macarthur saw two signal rockets fired from the ground followed by the landing of an aeroplane. He and two other witnesses saw the pilot emerge from the machine who spoke to a man waiting for him on the ground.[24]

At the outset of war, much like in Britain, lights seen on the coast or on nearby hills were associated with the activities of spies.[25] Any German-Australians were treated with suspicion and interned.[26]

The Intelligence Branch of the RAN's War Staff and the Intelligence Section of the Directorate of Military Operations kept a keen interest in any sightings and if they seemed valid they investigated the case in further detail.

When several reports of a mystery flier came from Terrigal, Lieutenant Charles Kingsford Smith of the RFC, who was on convalescent leave, was sent to investigate the situation. He didn't find any evidence for its existence, except that, on the night of 8 May, he saw a small black object travelling swiftly inland. He was convinced it was a machine and not a meteor or a flock of birds.[27]

A more extensive two-week-long investigation into sightings in the area of Victoria was conducted by RFC officer Lieutenant A. Edwards and Detective Sickerdick of the Victoria police force. At the beginning of May, Detective Sickerdick regarded the sightings as being caused by pelicans or hawks rather than enemy aeroplanes 'over the Mallee'.[28] The Navy Office reporting to the Admiralty on 9 May 1918 came to a similar view, and thought the scare was created by '... news of initial reports in spreading caused people to anticipate aircraft thus stimulating imagination'.[29]

Imagination or not, sightings were still occasionally made and even a week after the Armistice HMAS *Coogee* was sent to investigate the sighting of two aeroplanes by witnesses on King Island.[30]

The prevailing view was that these aircraft were being operated from German vessels off the coast of Australia or secret bases hidden in remote areas. Yet, as historian Brett Holman points out, there were no German aircraft, spies or secret aerodromes. Brett concludes that:

> The aeroplanes seen in 1918 were for the most part delusions, an example of what Michael McKernan calls 'manufacturing the war'. They were the result of an emotional need on the part of Australian civilians to share in the struggle of their soldiers fighting overseas.[31]

One of the most intriguing aspects of this scare is that it helped bring about the creation of the Royal Australian Air Force (RAAF). On 29 April 1918, when the aeroplane scare was at its height, Major-General J.G. Legge put forward a document to the Australian Cabinet that asked for the creation of a civilian air force. He suggested it should comprise 200 aeroplanes and 12 balloons with 300 officers and 3,000 other ranks. Brett Holman notes:

> Baseless or not, the scare had cruelly exposed Australia's inability to defend its own shores from raiders and aeroplanes and hence the need for Australian air ... Senator Pearce approved Legge's request almost immediately, though in the event the RAAF did not come into being until 1921.[32]

References

1. Document in the archives of the Ministry of Defence, France, at: ovniparanormal. over-blog.com/article-ovni-region-de-versailles-et-de-corbeil-essonnes-au-sud-de-paris-les-12-et-13-aout-1914-112384114.html.

2. Holman, Brett, 'Dreaming war: Airmindedness and the Australian mystery aeroplane scare of 1918', *History Australia*, Vol. 10, No. 2, August 2013, at: journals. publishing.monash.edu/ojs/index.php/ha/article/view/918.

3. National Archives of Australia (NAA): MP1049/1, 1918/066, memo, Piesse, 16 May 1917; *Northern Star* (Lismore, NSW), 10 October 1914.

4. *Herald* (Melbourne), 18 March 1918, p.6.

5. NAA: MP1049/1, 1918/066, report, Constable J. Wright, 22 March 1918 and Directorate of Military Intelligence, General Staff, HB56, 'Aircraft, lights and objects reported seen in the air – summary and appreciation no. 3', 4 May 1918, p.12; *Ouyen Mail*, 10 April 1918, p.1.

6. NAA: MP1049/1, 1918/066, report, Detective F. W. Sickerdick, 1 May 1918; Intelligence Section, General Staff, 'Summary of war intelligence no. T.4', 30 March 1918; Statement, Harry A. McDonald, 30 April 1918.

7. NAA: MP1049/1, 1918/066, telegram, District Naval Officer Fremantle, 22 April 1918; ibid., Directorate of Military Intelligence, General Staff, HB64, 'Aircraft, lights and objects reported seen in the air – summary and appreciation no. 4', 11 May 1918, 11; ibid., report, Constable A E Duvanel, 8 May 1918.

8. Ibid., statement, Captain T. J. Wilson, 31 May 1918.

9. Ibid., memo, Captain W. S. Hinton, 30 April 1918.

10. Ibid., report, Constable Ramsay, 20 April 1918.

11. Guilliatt, Richard and Hohnen, Peter, *The Wolf: How One German Raider Terrorised Australia and the Southern Oceans in the First World War* (North Sydney, Australia: William Heinemann, 2009); Jose, Arthur W., *The Royal Australian Navy, 1914–1918* (Sydney: Angus and Robertson 1941), pp.343–352; *Sydney Morning Herald*, 16 March 1918, p.13.

12. *Sydney Morning Herald*, 14 March 1918, p.7.

13. NAA: MP1049/1, 1918/066, report, T. W. C. Deeby [Deeley?], 3 June 1918.

14. NAA: MP1049/1, 1918/066, letter, James French, 24 April 1918 and 'J. M. Maclachlan, M.L.C.' his real name was J. W. McLachlan, MLA, who regularly wrote to the government about suspicious signals.

15. Scott, Ernest, *Australia During the War* (Sydney, Australia: Angus and Robertson, 1941), p.198; Jose Royal Australian Navy, 373–374.

16. NAA: MP367/1, 437/1/115, Part 1, 'Press Censorship Conference', 16–19 April 1918, p.221.

17. Wilson, David Joseph, *The Eagle and the Albatross: Australian Aerial Maritime Operations 1921–1971* (PhD thesis, Australian Defence Force Academy, 2003), pp.6–7; NAA: MP1049/1, 1918/066, order, Major A. J. Boase (for Chief of the General Staff), 20 April 1918; Ibid., memo, Major E. L. Piesse, 30 April 1918; Ibid., letter, Petty Officer G. Benson, 24 April 1918; Ibid, telegram, Navy Office, 9 May 1918.

18. NAA: MP1049/1, 1918/066, telegram, Hastings police, 20 April 1918 and telegram, Navy Office, 9 May 1918.

19. NAA: MP1049/1, 1918/066, memo, Captain Finlayson, 23 April 1918; McCallum, Kerry and Putnis, Peter, 'Media management in wartime: the impact of censorship on press–government relations in World War I Australia', *Media History* 14, 2008, pp. 17–33.

20. NAA: MP1049/1, 1918/066, telegram, Navy Office, 27 April 1918.

21. Ibid, Directorate of Military Intelligence, General Staff, HB53, 'Aircraft, lights and objects reported seen in the air', 28 April 1918, 12.

22. *Sydney Morning Herald*, 20 July 1917, p.7.

23. *Cairns Post*, 6 April 1918, p.7.

24. NAA: MP1049/1, 1918/066, report, Constable G.T. Moyle, 19 April 1918.

25. Scott, pp. 106–108; Fischer, *Enemy Aliens*, 124–136; John McQuilton, *Rural Australia and the Great War: From Tarrawingee to Tangambalanga*, (Carlton South: Melbourne University Press 2001), pp. 161–165.

26. NAA: MP1049/1, 1918/066, anonymous letter, 25 March 1918.

27. NAA: MP1049/1, 1918/066, report, Lieutenant C. Kingsford Smith, 10 May 1918.

28. Ibid., report, Sickerdick, 1 May 1918.

29. NAA: MP1049/1, 1918/066, telegram, Hastings police, 20 April 1918 and telegram, Navy Office, 9 May 1918.

30. Op cit., report, Lieutenant Commander George D. Warren, 18 November 1918.

31. Holman, Brett, 'Dreaming war: Airmindedness and the Australian mystery aeroplane scare of 1918', *History Australia*, Vol. 10, No. 2, August 2013, p. 186, at: journals.publishing.monash.edu/ojs/index.php/ha/article/view/918.

32. Op cit.; Hyslop, Robert, 'War scares in Australia in the 19th century', *Victorian Historical Journal*, No. 47, 1976, pp. 23–44.

SIXTEEN

ANGELS AND VISIONS

On 23 August 1914 the British Expeditionary Force (BEF) had its first brutal encounter with the German Army at the Battle of Mons. This exhausting battle slowed down the German advance by just one day at the cost of 1,600 men, and forced the BEF to make a fighting retreat.

After the conflict many British solders reported that they had seen St George on a white horse in a cloud of light. Others described St Joan, St Michael, strange clouds, angels, lights, clouds of celestial horsemen, rows of shining beings or bowmen that came at times of crisis in the conflict that saved them from harm or even inevitable death.

In early 1915 the 'Angel' stories appeared in parish magazines and became the subject of sermons and intense debate in newspaper and magazine columns. Poems and paintings quickly followed. It was said that the stories 'proved' that some Christian or spiritual force was supporting the British against the evil enemy. As poet Dugald MacEhern put it:

They saw and heard the angels pass
Any misty squadrons glide,
They know that holy angels
Were fighting on their side!

DUBLIN SEES ANGELS IN THE SKY.

All The Population Staring At The Night Heavens.

WHAT WAS IT?

From Our Own Correspondent.

DUBLIN, Thursday.

The story that apparitions have been seen in the sky has been responsible for some remarkable scenes in Dublin for the past few nights after dark.

From about 10 o'clock until after midnight crowds assemble in the streets in various parts of the city watching the night sky for a return of the phenomenon.

Rumours of the apparitions first began to be circulated in the city on Monday.

So far there are only three points in the city where the claim is made that the apparitions were seen on successive nights by scores of people. One of these is in the vicinity of Christchurchplace, on the south side of the Liffey, where some of the residents are said to have seen the figure of an angel hovering in the sky.

The Policeman Fainted.

In the Ringsend district there is also a story of a similar visitation. The story goes that a policeman on his beat was one of the first to see the vision, and his six feet of too solid flesh was not equal to the strain. He fainted—so the local residents declare.

On the north side of the city, in the vicinity of Broadstone railway station and in the Dominickstreet area, it is also emphatically declared that the vision was seen on Tuesday night between halfpast ten and half-past eleven.

Stories differ as to the actual form of the apparitions; in some cases, it is stated, the appearance was that of the Blessed Virgin and an angel; in others that it was an angel only. Whatever the origin of the story, it has made an extraordinary impression.

The majority of the people are inclined to scoff at the whole thing, but in the popular mind it is treated with a great deal of solemnity.

Sober minded citizens are suggesting that an air ship or aeroplane has flown at a great height over the city, thus giving rise to the whole story by aid of the fervid imagination of a few people.

Crowds of people saw a vision of an angel and the Blessed Virgin in Ireland during 1916. (*Daily Sketch*, 28 July 1916)

915.

THE LEGEND OF MONS.

STORY OF MIRACULOUS INTERVENTION.

GHOSTLY FOES.

CALL TO THE SPIRIT OF AGINCOURT BOWMEN.

Dr. R. F. Horton's reference in a sermon to the story of a miraculous intervention on behalf of the British during the retreat from Mons has led Mr. Arthur Machen to describe in the "London Evening News" what he believes to be the origin of the story. The following is a condensed version of Mr. Machen's article:—

Some time in last September I was thinking of the terrible and heroic moment from Mons. It is many years since I have told a tale, but somehow there was a fire in that history that burned in me and made me wish that I could celebrate it in some poor fashion. And so the tale of "The Bowmen" came into my head. It is a story of the British troops at a point of agony and despair, hopelessly outnumbered in men and guns. One of our soldiers invokes the help of the champion of England, St. George. St. George brings up the spirits of the Agincourt bowmen in array, and the German host is annihilated by the ghostly arrows. That is all. It was quite a simple, ordinary little legend of the battlefield, and I wrote it and dismissed it, and wished I could have made it better.

HEARD NO RUMOUR.

I may say, once for all, that I had heard no kind of sort of rumour of any spiritual intervention during the retreat from Mons, nor any faintest echo of such rumour: "The Bowmen," as printed in the "Evening News," was invention as much as any story can be invention.

Then was the first telling of the tale. The second telling was done by the editorial department of this paper. It told the odd sequel to my little, harmless story. Everybody would have it that the tale was true. The clergy said so. The Army said so. All sorts of vague authorities—"an officer," "a soldier," "a correspondent"—were quoted to show that the incident of spiritual intervention, or something very like it, had actually happened. The names of these witnesses were not given.

All this is an affair of some weeks ago; and I thought that the matter had blown over. But last Sunday that distinguished Nonconformist pastor Dr. R. F. Horton, preaching at Manchester, said:—

There is a story repeated by so many witnesses that if anything can be established by contemporary evidence it is established—the retreat from Mons. A section of the line was in imminent peril, and it seemed as if it must inevitably be borne down and cut off.

Our men saw a company of angels interposed between them and the German cavalry, and the horses of the Germans stampeded. Evidently the animals beheld what our men beheld. The German soldiers endeavoured to bring the horses back to the line, but they fled. It was the salvation of our men.

So I went to see Dr. Horton and told him the story, and the story of the story, and he was incredulous that there might be something in my theory of derivation. His information was not at first so, I think, even at second hand, and as it is content to suspend his judgment pending further evidence.

But passing from the unimportant particular to the important general I was extremely interested to find that Dr. Horton held that such a case of spiritual intervention was eminently credible. Such phenomena, he said—and we may call them phenomena—are a constant fact in history; we have many attestes of supernatural beings appearing and exerting an influence on human life. And I was more particularly disposed to believe in the story of the angelic apparition during the retreat from Mons from what I hoped myself from an army reader. He told me that all the men who were in that retreat were changed men. They had prayed, and they had all felt a sense of spiritual uplifting, and so the tale seemed to me congruous with their experiences.

CONTINUED ...

LATEST ...

LONDON ...

LIVERPOOL ...

THE BOWMEN

~AND OTHER LEGENDS OF THE WAR

BY ARTHUR MACHEN

Sightings and stories of angels and other visions seen during the Battle of Mons and other conflicts took the nation by storm in 1915. Arthur Machen declares himself to be the originator of the 'little, harmless story' that got out of hand: 'Everybody would have it that the tale was true. The clergy said so. The Army said so. The occultists said so.' (*Liverpool Echo*, 18 June 1915)

Several highly influential books collected these reports and became best sellers. Harold Begbie's *On the Side of the Angels* notes an anonymous Lance-Corporal who testified that during the retreat on 28 August 1914:

> I could see quite plainly in mid-air a strange light which seemed to be quite distinctly outlined and was not a reflection of the moon, nor were there any clouds in the neighbourhood. The light became brighter and I could see quite distinctly three shapes, one in the centre having what looked like outspread wings, the other two were not so large, but were quite plainly distinct from the centre one. They appeared to have a long loose-hanging garment of a golden tint they were above the German line facing us.[1]

Another story from a wounded soldier who was at Mons, told of seeing an angel with outstretched wings at a critical moment in the retreat. It was like a luminous cloud that came between the two opposing armies, and at that moment the fury of the German attack abated.

A letter from the front, from an unnamed correspondent, tells of being trapped in a trench with thirty other men. Their officer said they had to either attack or be killed like rats in a trap.

The men decided to fight for their lives and charged forwards shouting 'St George for England'. As they made their charge they became aware of a company of men with bows and arrows charging alongside them. With their help they overran the enemy, and a German prisoner asked them who the officer was who rode the white horse that led them in the attack. Despite being a very conspicuous figure the Germans had been unable to hit him with their gunfire. The letter writer said he didn't see St George on his horse but he did see the archers. Another strange aspect of this incident is that the German dead did not seem to have any wounds on them. In other stories the German dead were discovered to have arrow wounds in them.

Begbie also tells of Joan of Arc or the Virgin Mary seen by French troops, and visions of St Michael the Archangel seen by soldiers during battles in Russia.

Explanations

The popular author, Arthur Machen claimed that this legend was created by his fictional 'The Bowmen' story published in the *Evening News* on 29 September 1914. This tells of how British soldiers at their lowest ebb call upon St George to help them. In response, deadly archers, the spirits of the archers who won victory for Britain at the Battle of Agincourt in 1415, come to their rescue and with their arrows decimate the enemy forces.

He was highly sceptical of the angel and other visions reportedly seen at Mons and elsewhere during the war. When the story was put into book form he admitted that although '... it is nothing, it has yet had ... odd and unforeseen consequences and adventures ...'. He notes the snowball of rumour began in April 1915 and that he was accused of having a 'foolish pride in boasting' about creating this wartime legend. His conclusion was, '... I cannot conceive of anyone being foolish enough to take pride in the begetting of some of the silliest tales that have ever disgraced the English tongue.'[2]

After a detailed study of this subject UFO and folklore expert David Clarke regards 'The Bowmen' as a potent story that 'believers' used as a framework to circulate 'true' stories of angelic or ghostly intervention on behalf of Britain and her allies.[3]

It has been difficult actually to find any account written before Machen's story was published, and many of the accounts are from second- or third-hand anonymous sources. One investigator who tried to track down supporting stories or eyewitnesses found it like a 'journey into fog'.

The only letter that pre-dated Machen's story was written by Brigadier-General John Charteris. He wrote:

> ... then there is the story of the 'Angels of Mons' going strong through the 2nd Corps, of how the angel of the Lord on the traditional white horse, and clad all in white with flaming sword, faced the advancing Germans at Mons and forbade their further progress.

The only problem is that Chartis worked for British Intelligence and could well have helped promote the legend of the Angel of Mons to help maintain morale at home and amongst the troops, and his letter was revealed after the visions had become well known.

Other theories

Even today the legend is surrounded by controversy. Theories about it include it being a myth based on Machen's story, the product of hallucinations due to stress and exhaustion, real angelic visitations, ghosts, swamp gas, airships or alien UFOs projecting or shaping themselves to the expectations of the witnesses.

Philip Mantle, the author of several UFO books, is sceptical:

> The so-called Angels of Mons are nothing more than a 20th cen-
> tury folktale. There is no objective reality to them and no real eye
> witnesses. It could be argued that battle weary soldiers may well
> have misidentified some form of rare natural phenomenon such
> as ice crystals in the atmosphere but it is only a remote possibility.

Paranormal researcher Nigel Wright considers what might have caused the sightings and their mythic predecessors:

1) The area was marshy, could this lead to a release of 'swamp gas' rising into the air over the battlefield?
2) The Germans were using an airship, that night, to observe the battlefield, using a searchlight. Mistaken identity?
3) There is a long history of phantom riders of horses, seen over battlefields … dating back to the 17th century or earlier. Even back to the Valkyries of Viking legends, seen collecting the dead to take to Valhalla.

He adds that he 'would just love it to be a genuine UFO event of course!' Albert S. Rosales, UFO researcher and compiler of humanoid encounters and other strange events, based in South Florida, also wonders about the mythic or folkloric aspects of such stories:

> Was supernatural entities seen specifically at Mons? Perhaps, in every war there are such stories which remain between the realm of folklore and truth, and perhaps was later exaggerated by religious authorities and maybe even the Government possibly to boost moral among the troops.
>
> There has been other so-called Angel encounters before and after this 'incident', but they are not necessarily 'true Angels in the Bible sense'.

There are several similarities between modern-day UFOs and the Mons stories according to UFO expert Robert Moore:

> The Angel of Mons was predominantly a work of fiction that was seemingly confirmed by various claimed observations of entities interpreted in a religious context, reported after Machen's story was published. Battlefield hallucinations are likely in the high stress, mechanised warfare environment of World War One.
>
> Some of these independent accounts may have been hoaxed and perpetuated by spiritualist magazines.
>
> There are some general comparisons between the Angels and modern UFOs.
>
> The first is that claimed sightings of both were spread by mass media.
>
> The second is that they relate to reputed otherworldly forces. Heavier than air-flight was a recent invention and, as such, concepts such as 'spaceships' had not developed by that time.
>
> Hence, those other worldly forces took forms consistent with the religious beliefs of the time.
>
> Also, both the Angels of Mons visionary rumours and UFOs occurred during a time of massive social change and insecurity.

UFO expert Kevin Goodman, agrees that:

The phenomenon has taken many guises throughout history. In times of stress, fear and possible imminent death one finds solace in something that we can relate to. As the UFO enigma was unknown during the First World War conflict, the troops would relate to an event such as this in the only way they could, by thinking that they had a sign from god.

Cas Lake, ET contact expert and *Unexplained Show* radio presenter, reinforces the idea that they were of angelic origin:

My belief would be, if these angels did appear it was to protect and alter the future, and maybe also to help the belief in Angels. I certainly believe spiritual beings can intervene when needed.

Andrew Hennessey, a paranormal researcher with an archive of digital images and author of *Alien Encounters and the Paranormal*, agrees with Cas Lake's viewpoint:

Whether there is fiction regarding Mons or not – there is always a real possibility that it could be true. I have been assisted several times by Angels and suspect the soldiers saw real 'biblical' angels.

The process of seeing such visions is considered by UFO researcher and experiencer Paul Bennett to be created in this fashion:

The subjective world (our experiential domain, from the intellect to the countless altered states) is immensely malleable. Our relative natural, personal and cultural psychologies affect the morphology of our visionary encounters. This neither undermines nor invalidates anyone's experience – but when it lacks a cultural context, our own projections supplement the loss of mythic structure. This applies to the Angel of Mons visions and to UFO encounters. The source of the vision is the same, only the 'outer' vision is morphed to suit the witness or witnesses.

Whether 'real' or not, John Rimmer, the editor of the online *Magonia Review*, agrees that Machen and the soldiers were responding to a spiritual need:

> Amid the horrors of the First World War the desire for such spiritual intercession would be so strong in the minds of soldiers that, unable to find expression in any more 'rational' way, it was projected externally in the form of a memorable vision. Machen, more remote from the grim reality, and as a writer possessing an acceptable way of expressing these deep emotional responses, created an equally memorable 'fiction' from the same set of stimuli.[4]

Kevin McClure, who has studied this and other Angelic visions, makes the point that, 'If there really was some element of divine intervention, they had earned that, and more besides.'[5]

Fátima: Visions of the Virgin Mary

Whereas the Angel or Angels of Mons visions were short on specific sightings, this wasn't an issue with the Fátima visions that occurred from May to October 1917, on the 13th day of each month. Three shepherd children saw a 'radiant lady', who was quickly assumed to be the Virgin Mary, floating above an holm oak tree, at Cova da Iria, in the parish of Fátima, Portugal.

The children, Lucia dos Santos, and her cousins, Jucinta and Francisco Marto, were aged 10, 7 and 9 respectively. Their visions were associated with sightings of lights, strange clouds, lightening, thunder, the falling of 'angel hair', perfume smells and miraculous cures.

The story spread widely and on her last prophesied appearance thousands of people gathered to see a miracle. Journalist Avelino de Almeida, in a report for his newspaper *O Século* on 15 October 1917, wrote about the highly charged atmosphere at the location:

> Cars full of latecomers arrive on the road … There are people, many people, in a kind of ecstasy; people moved by emotion, on

whose dry lips prayer has become paralyzed; people in a trance, with their hands in the air and their eyes rolling; people who appear to feel, to touch the supernatural.

Avelino de Almeida reported seeing the sun looking 'like a plate of tarnished silver and it is possible to watch it without any discomfort.' After that the crowd near the tree saw the sun changing colour, spinning and dancing in the sky, then plunging earthwards. Some even claimed they saw the Virgin Mary and other religious figures next to or inside the sun.

The Roman Catholic Church confirmed it as an official miracle on 13 October 1930, but in the UFO era the events in Fátima have been regarded as encounters with UFOs and aliens.

After analysing all the reports, long-time Fátima researcher, Dr Joaquim Fernandes, concluded that, 'we can consider Fátima as the prototype of the UFO experience process. It is perhaps the most spectacular mass sighting of the 20th Century.'[6]

References

1. Begbie, Harold, On the Side of the Angels (London: Hodder and Stoughton, 1915).
2. Machen, Arthur, The Bowmen and other Legends of the War (London: Simpkin Marshall, 1915).
3. Clarke, David, The Angel of Mons: Phantom Soldiers and Ghostly Guardians (West Sussex: John Wiley and Sons Ltd, 2004).
4. Quotes from UFO experts obtained via email dated May and June 2014.
5. McClure, Kevin, 'Visions of Bowmen and Angels', Magonia website, at: magonia. haaan.com/2009/visions-of-bowmen-and-angels-kevin-mcclure/.
6. Fernandes, Joaquim and D'Armada, Fina, Heavenly Lights: The Apparitions of Fátima and the UFO Phenomenon (Victoria, B.C.: EcceNova, 2005).

SEVENTEEN

RECOLLECTIONS OF UFOS PAST

The Aldeburgh platform

Several UFO-like encounters were allegedly made during the First World War but many are recollections reported to ufologists in the 'flying saucer' era that began in June 1947. One such report surfaced in 1968, when Mr A.E. Whiteland, of Saxmundham, Suffolk, wrote this letter to the *Daily Mirror* newspaper:

> My mother has often told the following story over the years and, as she is eighty-four, I would like to find out for her who these mystery men were and what they were doing.
>
> This is the story. It was about the middle of World War One and on a weekday. Mother was living at Aldeburgh, Suffolk. She had gone upstairs just before dinner, opened the casement window and looked out to see who might be on the road.
>
> Having looked up and down and noticed there was no one in sight, she was about to step back when something urged her to look again.
>
> A little above the level of the house eight to twelve men appeared on what seemed to be a round platform with a handrail around it. This they were gripping tightly.

She could see them so clearly. They were wearing blue uniforms and little round hats, not unlike sailors'. She heard no sound
from the machine as it came off the marshes. It turned a bit and
went over the railway yard to disappear behind some houses.[1]

The first explanation for this was that she had seen an observation
carriage lowered from a Zeppelin. UFO researcher Carl Grove wrote
to aviation historian Charles H. Gibbs-Smith asking if this was possible, his reply emphatically stated that these observation gondolas

… were tiny streamlined things to take one man, and he was in
telephonic touch with the Commander up above. They were also
never suspended low down near the ground since they could be
easily attacked by rifle and machine gun fire. There is not the
remotest possibility that what Mrs Whiteland saw was anything
connected with Zeppelins.[2]

Even though Carl carried out a thorough investigation, he was
not able to come up with any plausible explanation. The only
possibility was that over years the witness had perhaps confused
this incident with an actual Zeppelin crash at nearby Holly Tree
Farm, Theberton on the night of 17 June 1917. Sixteen of the crew
were burnt to death and buried in the local churchyard. Indeed,
it is wondered if her UFO sighting was a screen memory of this
crash as a form of mental protection from a horrific incident.[3]
A more recent explanation is that this was a sighting of visitors using a time machine to come back to a significant time in
human history.[4]

Flaming onions

The story of 'flaming onions' has more credibility and is just as
intriguing. Denis Winter recounted in his book, *The First of the Few:
Fighter Pilots of the First World War*:

Then there were the feared 'flaming onions', fired from rocket guns to become green glowing balls which twisted about like live things and seemed to chase an aeroplane, turning over end on end in a leisurely way ...[5]

They were terrifying because they moved too fast for an aircraft to take evasive action, and nobody knew what they were. There was speculation that they were ranging mechanisms like tracer bullets, or phosphorescent Napoleonic-type cannon balls linked by wire or chain.

One explanation is that the flaming onions were fired by a German anti-aircraft gun called a 'Lichtspucker' (light splitter). This was like a Gatling gun that had five rotating barrels that could fire a string of flares a distance of 5,000 feet. Since they were fired so rapidly they gave the impression to pilots that they were connected by a wire.[6]

The Red Baron

The so-called Red Baron, Manfred Freiherr von Richthofen, is alleged to have shot a UFO out of the clear blue sky while on an early morning mission over Western Belgium in the spring of 1917.

German Air Force ace Peter Waitzrik was flying in an accompanying Fokker triplane when the object that carried undulating orange lights suddenly appeared. The craft looked like an upside-down, silver-coloured saucer about 136 feet in diameter, according to Waitzrik who recalled:

We were terrified because we'd never seen anything like it before. The U.S. had just entered the war, so we assumed it was something they'd sent up. The Baron immediately opened fire and the thing went down like a rock, shearing off tree limbs as it crashed in the woods.

Fighter ace Baron Manfred von Richthofen about to board his personal transport, the sole prototype Albatros C IX, presented to him after its failure to gain full operational acceptance. Not many pilots are given their own aircraft by a grateful nation, a pointer to the god-like status of the knights of the air.

It was incredible enough that the Baron had shot this down, even weirder was that two bruised and battered occupants climbed out of the crashed object and ran into some nearby woods.

Waitzrik said:

> The Baron and I gave a full report on the incident back at head-
> quarters and they told us not to ever mention it again. And except
> for my wife and grandkids, I never told a soul.

He continued to think it was a secret US aircraft until the late 1940s when flying saucer reports hit the headlines. The 105-year-old retired airline pilot felt that he had nothing to lose by making it public eighty years after the event, and Waitzrik concluded:

> So there's no doubt in my mind now that that was no U.S.
> reconnaissance plane the Baron shot down, that was some kind
> of spacecraft from another planet and those little guys who ran
> off into the woods weren't Americans, they were space aliens of
> some kind.

The main problem with this story is that it first appeared in the 31 August 1999 edition of the *Weekly World News* (p.4), known more for its sensational headlines than factual details. Another flaw with the story is that Fokker triplanes were not put into operational service until 22 August 1917. We should also wonder what happened to the crashed vehicle and the two crew members. They would have been conspicuous even in the heat of a battle zone!

On his UFO Related Entities Catalog (URECAT) website, Patrick Gross notes that this story is totally fictional. Besides the Fokker triplane error, the flying ace Peter Waitzrik is an invented character. A picture of him with his fellow flying officers used with the *Weekly World News* story is real, but the person circled as Peter Waitzrik was really Lieutenant Otto Brauneck.[7]

Lady Sopwith

This is an equally unlikely story that features a mystery aviatrix that haunted the skies over France. She was first spotted by Lieutenant Frederick Ardsley as he was flying from Amiens to Villers-Bocage, northern France, on an early morning patrol. On this Wednesday, 9 January 1918, he was flying at a height of 10,000 feet when he suddenly saw an identical S.E. 5 (Scout Experimental 5) biplane flying next to him. The odd thing about the aircraft was that its engine made a buzzing sound like something out of a toy shop, and it had a golden symbol for Venus on the fuselage rather than the normal red, white and blue RFC roundels and identification numbers.

Even stranger, the pilot removed their goggles with a loud laugh, revealing a cascade of golden hair. The female pilot with 'cornflower blue eyes' waved and kissed at Ardsley before conducting a Can Can dance on the edge of her cockpit. Returning to the cockpit the woman sharply banked left and Ardsley went in hot pursuit of her. Yet he struggled to keep up with her as her aircraft darted, rolled and dipped or suddenly accelerated out of range of his guns.

Her aircraft easily climbed to a bank of clouds at an altitude of 20,000 feet. He tried shooting her down with his fuselage machine guns, but they jammed after four seconds, and his Lewis gun also jammed. Ardsley's aircraft struggled as it tried following the other S.E. 5, and it inevitably stalled, forcing him to make a controlled dive.

This encounter was supposedly viewed by observers on the ground who were surprised to see a dogfight between two S.E. 5s. On landing, Ardsley was debriefed by his squadron leader, who on hearing the full story said he couldn't forward that report as they would 'think I've gone starling raving mad'.

This apparently was the start of the legend of Lady Sopwith. At the end of January, a German pilot, Albert Roehl, was shot down behind Allied lines. When he was interrogated he said he was shot down by a female pilot, 'Die Walkure' (The Valkyrie) as he called her.

From then on many German aviators encountered a red-nosed S.E. 5 or a red Sopwith triplane piloted by a woman who shot them down. Her aircraft outflew every other aircraft in the sky and dozens of Allied pilots saw her shooting the tails off enemy aircraft, as easily as shooting fish in a barrel.

Lady Sopwith was also seen by civilians, including 6-year-old Robert Tuchel who was just about to get spanked by his mother when a S.E.5 zoomed overhead making a loud roar. The distraction enabled Robert to run free and wave his thanks to the blonde pilot.

A variant of Lady Sopwith was the sighting of a German *fräulein* with long yellow braids who flew a black and white Fokker biplane. She was seen whenever things looked bad for the Allies.

Theories about her ranged from her being the sister of the Red Baron seeking her revenge for his death on 21 April 1918, which would not account for earlier sightings, to her being the tomboy sister of British RFC ace Captain Albert Ball who was killed on 7 May 1917. Rather than personal revenge, Americans tended to think there was a secret squadron of lady pilots, or the legend was just a publicity or propaganda stunt.[8]

The novelist Arch Whitehouse thought he had the answer to this mystery:

> I think I know the actual basis for this flossy legend that began innocently enough on a field near Chipilly near the Somme. We had a squadron of S.E.5 pilots on the same field with us, and these young scout pilots were always up to some healthy devilment. Around Christmas of 1917 … they decided to enliven the dreary days by organising a squadron party complete with a theatrical performance.[9]

The legend was born when some mechanics saw a pilot in drag climb into the cockpit of a S.E.5 after the performance. Certainly it sounds like the stuff of legend and myth with a good dollop of wish fulfilment thrown into the mix. The Lady was a protector and saviour to the Allies and yet there was also the German *fräulein* pilot who seemed to be her polar opposite.

A few things shoot down the reality of the first encounter experienced by Lieutenant Frederick Ardsley. First of all Ardsley doesn't appear in the list of RFC pilots for that period, and secondly it was claimed he was in the 49th Squadron, which did not use S.E.5 aircraft.[10]

If Ardsley was a real person, the aviatrix could have been a trick of his imagination caused by him blacking out after flying too high. More likely, this was a work of fiction dressed as fact that satisfied the needs of the time. In our own day it is all too easy to suggest that she was an alien or part of a squadron of aliens who flew high-tech flying saucers disguised as biplanes, which relates to our own psychological, sociological and culturally specific need to read everything in terms of UFOs.

References

1. *Daily Mirror*, 8 August 1968.
2. *Daily Mirror*, 17 August 1968; Anon, 'The Aldeburgh Platform,' *Flying Saucer Review*, Vol.15, No.1 Jan–Feb 1969; The Aldeburgh Platform, at: aldeburghplatform.blogspot.co.uk/.
3. The Aldeburgh Platform, at: aldeburghplatform.blogspot.co.uk/p/aldeburgh-03.html.
4. Hassall, Peter, 'Aeronauts from the Future', *Fortean Times*, September 2009, No. 240, at: www.forteantimes.com/features/articles/2176/aeronauts_from_the_future.html
5. Winter, Denis, *The First of the Few: Fighter Pilots of the First World War* (London: Allen Lane, 1982).
6. The Aerodrome Forum, at: www.theaerodrome.com/forum/2000/9836-flaming-onions.html.
7. Gross, Patrick, 'Spring 1917, Western Belgium, Belgique, Manfred von Richtofen and Peter Waitzrik', URECAT – UFO Related Entities Catalog website, at: ufologie.patrickgross.org/ce3/1917-belgium-westernbelgium.htm.
8. Trainor, Joseph, '1918: Lady Sopwith', *UFO ROUNDUP*, Vol. 9 No. 18, 5 May 2004, at: Editor: Joseph Trainor www.ufoinfo.com/roundup/v09/rnd0918.shtml Reynolds, Quentin, *They Fought for the Sky* (New York: Holt, Rinehart & Winston, 1957), pp.168–169.
9. Whitehouse, Arch, *Heroes and Legends of World War I* (Garden City, New York: Doubleday & Co., 1964), pp.328–331.
10. 'Aircraft', 49 Squadron Association website, at: www.49squadron.co.uk/aircraft.

EIGHTEEN

THE DISAPPEARING SOLDIERS

The killing fields of the disastrous Gallipoli Campaign is the location of one of the most famous mass alien abduction cases, which claims that the Royal Norfolk Regiment was swiftly taken away in a giant UFO. The main evidence for the UFO aspect to the disappearance is given by three New Zealand soldiers who witnessed the event, along with eighteen other men of their field company.

They wrote a statement about the sighting in April 1965, on the 50th Jubilee of the ANZAC (Australia and New Zealand Army Corps) landing. In it they said that, on 21 August 1915, they saw six or eight light grey coloured clouds over Hill 60, Suvla Bay. A more solid looking cloud, 800 feet long, 220 feet high and 200 feet wide rested on the top of the hill. Their statement continues:

A British regiment, the First-Fourth Norfolk, of several hundred men, was then noticed marching ... towards Hill 60. However, when they arrived at this cloud, they marched straight into it, with no hesitation, but no one ever came out to deploy and fight at Hill 60. About an hour later, after the last of the file had disappeared into it, this cloud very unobtrusively lifted off the ground and, like any cloud or fog would, rose slowly until it joined the other similar clouds … (then) they all moved away northwards, i.e. towards Thrace. In a matter of about three-quarters of an hour they had disappeared from view.[1]

They concluded that the regiment consisted of between 800 and 4,000 men, and that when Turkey surrendered in 1918 the first thing the British did was to demand the return of the regiment. The Turkish declared that they had no knowledge of the regiment.[2]

When Paul Begg looked into this report he found several discrepancies that indicated it was a hoax. His main points being:

1. The First-Fourth Norfolk was not a regiment, but a battalion of the Royal Norfolk Regiment.
2. The First-Fourth Norfolk actively served throughout the campaign, so they did not suddenly disappear.
3. The First-Fifth Battalion did disappear when they attacked Hill 60 but this was on the 12 August, not 21 August.
4. If the ANZAC's got the dates mixed up, they were at best four and a half miles (7 kilometres) from Hill 60. Their eyesight must have been exceptional to have viewed what they reported.
5. Hill 60 was three miles (5 kilometres) south of the position the Norfolk's attacked on 12 August.
6. Why did it take them until their 50th anniversary, in 1965, to report this strange circumstance?[3]

To be charitable, some of these errors can be put down to the lapse of time since the event, but without any documentary evidence prior to 1965 their story unravels like a cheap cardigan. Before we dismiss it as a hoax there is support for their story in The Final Report of the Dardanelles Commission (1917):

By some freak of nature Suvla Bay and Plain were wrapped in a strange mist on the afternoon of 21 August. This was sheer bad luck as we had reckoned on the enemy's gunners being blinded by the declining sun and upon the Turks' trenches being shown up by the evening sun with singular clearness. Actually, we could hardly see the enemy lines this afternoon, whereas to the westward targets stood out in strong relief against the luminous light.

This paragraph faces the page that refers to the disappearance of the First-Fifth Battalion. This could explain how a 'strange mist' got connected with their disappearance, and it is significant that the declassified version of this report was issued in 1965.

The disappearance of 267 men of the First-Fifth Battalion occurred on the afternoon of 12 August when as part of the 163rd Brigade they made their first attack on the enemy. The advance turned into a disaster when they came under heavy machine-gun fire. On the right flank, the First-Fifths met less resistance and were able to press forward under the command of Sir Horace Proctor-Beauchamp. The British Commander-in-Chief at Gallipoli, General Sir Ian Hamilton admitted that it was at this moment '… there happened a very mysterious thing …'. In the same dispatch to Lord Kitchener, he went on to note:

The fighting grew hotter, and the ground became more wooded and broken … But the Colonel, with 16 officers and 250 men, still kept pushing forward, driving the enemy before him … Nothing more was seen or heard of any of them. They charged into the forest and were lost to sight or sound. Not one of them ever came back.

Given the circumstances, it was not difficult for these men to 'disappear'. The vagueness of their location was convenient as this body of soldiers consisted of E Company of the 5th Territorial Battalion of the Royal Norfolk Regiment. The company consisted of the staff of King Edward VII's Sandringham country estate. At his own behest, they were set up in 1908 with his land-agent Frank Beck as their captain. When they were sent to war 54-year-old Beck insisted on going with his one hundred part-time territorials or 'buddies' as they were known.

Relatives of the men only got a telegram to say they were simply missing. They put messages in the papers and made enquiries with the Red Cross but there was no news of the men.

Even Queen Alexandra drew a blank when she contacted the American ambassador in Constantinople to find out if the men were in prisoner-of-war camps. All George V was told was that the men had fought with 'ardour and dash'.

After the war the Graves Registration unit discovered the bodies of 180 of these soldiers. A Turkish farmer had dumped them in a small ravine, and 122 of them were of the First-Fifth Norfolk. Most of the bodies had been found in and around the ruins of a small farm where they had made their last stand. The Rev. Charles Pierre-Point Edwards, MC, who was probably sent to look for the men by Queen Alexandra, confirmed that they were the missing Norfolks. Any hope that Beck was still alive disappeared when his gold fob watch was found in Turkey a few years later – it had apparently been looted from his body. It was only when the BBC made a documentary on the subject in 1991 that it came to light that all the 180 bodies had been shot in the head. It is probable that they had surrendered to the stronger Turkish force and then been executed. What happened to the other men? They probably died in action either here or in other First World War theatres.[4]

A TV film was made about the story called *All The King's Men*, which focuses on the men of E Company. This highlights the reluctance by the authorities to let the Royals know for certain the fate of their estate workers. So 'a very mysterious thing' hid the brutality of this conflict and suited everyone concerned.

Just when you would think nothing more could be wrung out of this story, the disappearing Norfolks turned up again in 'Annex C' of the Majestic-12 Project – 1st Annual Report. This was part of a set of fifteen Majestic-12 documents publicised by Dr Robert Wood and his son Ryan in 1998. These were meant to confirm the existence of a secret government group called Majestic-12 who retrieved alien spaceships and dealt with alien encounters.

In his criticism of the Annual Report's version of the incident, UFO historian Barry Greenwood notes it is flawed for two reasons: Firstly, it wrongly gives the date of the disappearance as 28 August 1915; Secondly, it relies on details from the ANZAC affidavit. The latter point is the most damning, because if it was a document of

1952 vintage how could it include information that did not come to light until 1965? As Greenwood puts it:

> The MJ-12 document recounts a flawed version of a story, which was unknown before 1965 ... The MJ-12 version is based more upon 1960s UFO pulp and newsletter accounts than it is on historical record.[5]

References

1. Hinfelaar, Henk, 'Incident at Gallipoli', *Spaceview*, September–October 1965.
2. Hinfelaar, Henk, 'Research on "Incident at Gallipoli"', *Spaceview*, February–March 1966.
3. Begg, Paul, 'The Day the Norfolks Disappeared', *Out of this World. Mysteries of Mind, Space and Time* (London: Black Cat, Macdonald & Co, 1989), pp.60–63; Begg, Paul, *Into Thin Air* (Newton Abbot: David & Charles, 1979).
4. 'The Vanished Battalion of the King's Own Sandringhams', at: www.historic-uk.com/HistoryUK/England-History/LostSandringhams.htm (accessed August 6, 2005).
5. Barry Greenwood, 'Majestic 12 Follies Returns', *UFO Historical Revue*, No. 3, January 1999, www.ufoevidence.org/documents/doc842.htm

ADDITIONAL REFERENCES

Introduction

Aan de Wiel, Jérôme, 'German Invasion and Spy Scares in Ireland, 1890s–1914: Between Fiction and Fact', Etudes Irelandaises at: etudesirlandaises.revues. org/2936.

Baker, Simon, 'Early Spy Films: Intrigue and Paranoia in pre-WWI Britain', BFI screen online, at: www.screenonline.org.uk/film/id/1114408/.

Bartholemew, Robert E. and Howard, George S., *UFOs and Alien Contact* (New York: Prometheus Books, 1998).

Bartholemew, Robert E. and Goode, Erich, 'Mass Delusions and Hysterias: Highlights from the Past Millennium', *Skeptical Inquirer*, Vol. 24, No. 3, May/June 2000, at: www.csicop.org/si/show/mass_delusions_and_hysterias_highlights_ from_the_past_millennium/.

Clarke, I.F., 'Future-War Fiction: The First Main Phase, 1871–1900', *Science Fiction Studies*, November 1997, at: www.depauw.edu/sfs/clarkeess.htm.

'Collaborative Bibliography: Aviation', International Society for First World War Studies website at: www.firstworldwarstudies.org/bibliography-detail. php?cID=4K32I3FS&t=Aviation.

Fernandez, Gilles, 'Cracking the 1896/97 Airships Mystery? Toward a Psycho-SocioCultural Explanation', Sceptics v. les Soucoupes Volentes blog at: skepticversustheflyingsaucers.blogspot.co.uk/2014/01/cracking-189697-airships-mystery-toward_11.html.

Maloney, Mack, *UFOs in Wartime – What They Didn't Want You To Know* (New York: Berkley, 2011).

Playne, Caroline E., *The Pre-War Mind in Britain* (London: Allen & Unwin, 1928).

Sandell, Roger, 'The Airship and Other Panics', *Magonia*, New series 12, Autumn 1978. At: magonia.haaan.com/2009/panic/.

Vallee, Jacques and Aubeck, Chris, *Wonders in the Sky: Unexplained Aerial Objects from Antiquity to Modern Times* (New York: J.P. Tarcher, 2010).

Wood, Harry, 'Island Mentalities, Edwardian invasion-scare fiction' blog at: invasionscares.wordpress.com/about/.

Chapter Two

Gollin, Alfred, *No Longer an Island: Britain and the Wright Brothers, 1902–1909* (London: Heinemann, 1984).

Clarke, Dr & David Dr, 'Scareships over Britain. The Airship Wave of 1909', at: www. ufo.se/english/articles/wave.html.

Grove, Carl, 'The Airship Wave of 1909', *Flying Saucer Review*, Vol. 16, No. 6, 1970, pp.9–11 and Vol. 17, No. 1, 1971, pp.17–19.

Lowe, Charles, 'About German Spies', *Contemporary Review*, January 1910.

Screeton, Paul, 'Newspaper Looks At The Airship', *MUFOB*, new series, No. 11, 1978, at: magonia.haaan.com/2009/screeton/.

Watson, Nigel, 'Men in Black, Phantom Airships and UFOs', *Darklore*, No. 4, 2009.

Chapter Three

Auchettl, John, 'An Old Australian Phenomenon', *The Australian Annual Flying Saucer Review*, 1983, pp.18–22.

Brunt, Tony, 'The New Zealand UFO Wave of 1909', *Xenolog*, No. 100 and No. 101, November/December 1975. Available on the UFO Focus New Zealand Research Network (UFOCUS NZ) website at:

www.ufocusnz.org.nz/content/THE-NEW-ZEALAND-UFO-WAVE-OF-1909/53.aspx

Bullard, Thomas, *The Airship File* (Bloomington, Indiana: privately published, 1982), p.269.

Chalker, Bill, 'The Search for Historical UFO Reports in Australia', The Oz Files blog, 03 March 2012, at: theozfiles.blogspot.co.uk/2012/03/search-for-historical-ufo-reports-in.html.

Chalker, Bill, *Preliminary Listing of Australian Historical UFO Events: Pre-History to 1949*, unpublished manuscript, 1981.

Clark, Jerome and Farish, Lucius, 'The New Zealand "Airship" Wave of 1909', *Saga's UFO Report*, Vol. 2 No. 2, Winter 1974.

Dyke, Mervyn, *Strangers in Our Skies* (Lower Hutt, New Zealand: INL Print Ltd. 1981).

Hassall, Peter, 'The Great "Scareship" Wave of 1909', *Fortean Times*, No. 260, March 2010, at: www.forteantimes.com/features/articles/3178/germans_secret_inventors_or_hot_air.html.

Hinfelaar, Mrs, 'The New Zealand "Flap" of 1909', *Flying Saucer Review*, Vol. 10, No. 6.

Knapman, Harold, 'Historical New Zealand UFO Reports', *UFORA Newsletter*, Vol. 4, No. 3.

Mackrell, Brian, 'The Great UFO Scare of 1909!', *Parade*, August 1980.

Norman, Paul, 'Items from the Australian Flap, 1909–1910', *Flying Saucer Review*, Vol. 22, No. 6, 1976 (published April 1977).

Stott, Murray, *Aliens Over Antipodes* (Sydney: Space Time Press, 1984).

Chapter Four

Bartholomew, Robert E., and Whalen, Steven. 'The Great New England Airship Hoax of 1909', *The New England Quarterly*, Vol. 75, No. 3, September 2002, pp. 466–476.

Bartholomew, Robert E., 'Two Mass Delusions in New England', The New England Skeptical Society website, at: www.theness.com/index.php/two-mass-delusions-in-new-england/.

Bullard, Thomas, *The Airship File* (Bloomington, Indiana: Privately published, 1982), pp.269–291 and p.384.

Gross, Loren, Charles Fort: *The Fortean Society & Unidentified Flying Objects* (Freemont, California: privately published, 1976).

Johnson, Donald, '60 years Ago in New England Skies', *Flying Saucer Observer*, No. 15, October 1969.

'The Worcester Aeroplane Hoax, 1909', The Museum of Hoaxes website, at: www.museumofhoaxes.com/hoax/archive/permalink/the_worcester_aeroplane_hoax/.

Chapter Five

Gollin, Alfred, *The Impact of Air Power on the British People and their Government, 1909–14* (Stanford: Stanford University Press, 1989), pp.223–7.

Holman Brett, 'The Sheerness Incident', Airminded website, 14 October 2007, at: airminded.org/2007/10/14/the-sheerness-incident/

Oldroyd, Granville and Watson, Nigel, 'The Sheerness Incident: Did a German Airship Fly Over Kent in 1912?', *Fortean Studies*, Vol. 4, 1998, pp.151–159.

Chapter Six

Bullard, Thomas, *The Airship File* (Bloomington, Indiana: Privately published, 1982), pp.293–306.

Dangerfield, George, *The Strange Death of Liberal England* (St Albans, Herts: Paladin, 1983), pp.115–119.

Fort, Charles, *The Complete Books of Charles Fort* (New York: Dover, 1974), pp.512–516.

Playne, Caroline E., *The Pre-War Mind in Britain* (London: Allen and Unwin, 1928), pp.102–103.

Watson, Nigel,; Oldroyd, Granville and Clarke, David, *The 1912–1913 British Phantom Airship Scare* (Mount Rainier: Fund for UFO Research Inc., 1988).

Watson, Nigel, The 1912–1913 British Phantom Airship Scare Catalog (Mount Rainier: Fund for UFO Research Inc., 1988).

Chapter Eight

Public Record Office (PRO) file number AIR 1/565 16/15/89; GHQ Home Forces General Correspondents File: *Movements and Rumoured Movements of Hostile Aircraft Etc., 3/8/14-2/1/15*.

Chapter Nine

Bartholomew, Robert E., 'The South African Monoplane Hysteria: An Evaluation of Smelser's Theory of Hysterical Beliefs', *Sociological Inquiry*, Vol. 59 No. 3, 1989, pp287–300.

Bullard, Thomas, *The Airship File* (Bloomington, Indiana: Privately published, 1982), pp.306–313 and p.373.

Chapter Ten

Aan de Wiel, Jérôme, 'German Invasion and Spy Scares in Ireland, 1890s–1914: Between Fiction and Fact', Etudes Irlandaises, at: etudesirlandaises.revues. org/2936#ftn59.

Watson, Nigel and Oldroyd, Granville, 'Snow on Their Boots', *Fortean Studies*, Vol. 2, 1995, pp.186–197.

Chapter Twelve

Bullard, Thomas, *The Airship File* (Privately published: Bloomington, Indiana, 1982), pp.314-315.

Bullard, Thomas, *The Airship File. Supplement One* (Privately published: Bloomington, Indiana, 1983), pp.36-41.

Evans, Hilary and Bartholomew, Robert E., 'Phantom German Air Raids On Eastern Canada: 1914–1917' in *Outbreak! The Encyclopedia of Extraordinary Social Behavior* (Anomalist Books, 2009), pp.489-494.

Holman, Brett, 'The air raid that didn't', Airminded blog, at: airminded org/2014/02/13/the-air-raid-that-didnt/.

Shoemaker, Michael T., 'UFO Saboteurs', *Fate*, December 1985.

Whalen, Dwight, 'What Were Those Strange Airborne Noises?', *The Standard*, 13 November 1982.

Mr. X, 'The Spying Aviators', in *The Scareship Mystery* (Corby: DOMRA, 2000), pp. 111–128.

Chapter Thirteen

Public Record Office (PRO) file number AIR 1/565 16/15/89; *GHQ Home Forces General Correspondents File: Movements and Rumoured Movements of Hostile Aircraft Etc.*, 3/8/14-2/1/15.

Redfern, Nick, 'UFOs and the Military, 1915: Pt.1', Mysterious Universe website, 7 May 2014, at: mysteriousuniverse.org/2014/05/ufos-and-the-military-1915-pt-1/

Redfern, Nick, 'UFOs and the Military, 1915: Pt.2', Mysterious Universe website, 8 May 2014, at: mysteriousuniverse.org/2014/05/ufos-and-the-military-1915-pt-2/.

Chapter Fourteen

Bullard, Thomas, *The Airship File: Supplement 1* (Privately published: Bloomington, Indiana, 1983), pp. 36–42.

Brænne, Ole Jonny, 'Pre-1947 UFO-Type Incidents in Norway', UFO Norge website, at: webcache.googleusercontent.com/search?q=cache:http://www.ufo.no/english/articles/afu.html.

'Historical UFO Quotes', UFO Evidence website, at: www.ufoevidence.org/documents/doc1742.html.

Chapter Fifteen

Holman, Brett, 'List of Australian mystery aircraft sightings', Airminded website, 12 January 2012, at: airminded.org/2012/01/12/anxious-nation-v/.

Holman, Brett, 'Dreaming war, seeing aeroplanes', Airminded website, 9 June 2011. A series of articles about the WWI Australian and New Zealand aircraft sightings, at: airminded.org/2011/06/09/dreaming-war-seeing-aeroplanes-i/.

Chapter Sixteen

Dunning, B, 'The Angel of Mons', Skeptoid Podcast, Skeptoid Media, Inc., 20 January 2009. Website, 15 July 2014, at: skeptoid.com/episodes/4137.

Fernandes, Joaquim and D'Armada, Fina, *Celestial Secrets: The Hidden History of the Fátima Incident* (Victoria, B.C.: EcceNova, 2006).

McClure, Kevin, *The Evidence for Visions of the Virgin Mary* (Wellingborough: The Aquarian Press, 1983).

The Fatima Network – Our Lady of Fatima Online, at: www.fatima.org/.

Chapter Seventeen

'WWI Mystery Sightings?', The Aerodrome Forum website, at: www.theaerodrome.com/forum/other-wwi-aviation/18896-ww1-mystery-sightings.html.

The Great War Forum website, at: 1914-1918.invisionzone.com/forums/index.php?showtopic=99663&hl=flaming+onions.

Watson, Eric, '"Flaming Onions" – The Great Enigma', at: www.ww1aero.org.au/pdfs/Sample%20Journal%20Articles/Onions1969.pdf.

Chapter Eighteen

McCrery, Nigel, *The Vanished Battalion* (London: Simon & Schuster 1992).

McCrery, Nigel, *All The King's Men* (London: Simon & Schuster 1992).

Petre, F. Loraine, The History of the Norfolk Regiment, at: user.online.be/~snelders/sand.htm

'The Vanishing Norfolks', Imperial War Museum Information Sheet No. 6, (undated).

Websites

Dr David Clarke. Folklore and Journalism, at: drdavidclarke.co.uk/.

Robert Bartholomew. The Sociologist, at: robertebartholomew.com/.

The Fortean website of Mr. X, at: www.resologist.net/.

Barry Greenwood UFO Archive, at: www.greenwoodufoarchive.com/.

Brett, Holman, Airminded, at: airminded.org/.

Island Mentalities, Edwardian invasion-scare fiction blog at: invasionscares.wordpress.com/about/.

The Magonia Blog, at: pelicanist.blogspot.co.uk/.

Magonia Exchange, private group for exchanging pre-1947 data, at: groups.yahoo.com/neo/groups/magonia_exchange/info.

INDEX